THE FOUNDING FATHERS AND THE
POLITICS OF CHARACTER

The Founding Fathers and the Politics of Character

Andrew S. Trees

PRINCETON UNIVERSITY PRESS

PRINCETON AND OXFORD

COPYRIGHT © 2004 BY PRINCETON UNIVERSITY PRESS

PUBLISHED BY PRINCETON UNIVERSITY PRESS, 41 WILLIAM STREET,

PRINCETON, NEW JERSEY 08540

IN THE UNITED KINGDOM: PRINCETON UNIVERSITY PRESS, 3 MARKET PLACE,

WOODSTOCK, OXFORDSHIRE OX20 1SY

LIBRARY OF CONGRESS CATALOGING-IN-PUBLICATION DATA

TREES, ANDREW S., 1968–

THE FOUNDING FATHERS AND THE POLITICS OF CHARACTER / ANDREW S. TREES.

P. CM.

INCLUDES BIBLIOGRAPHICAL REFERENCES AND INDEX.

ISBN 0-691-11552-4 (ALK. PAPER)

1. STATESMEN—UNITED STATES—HISTORY—18TH CENTURY. 2. UNITED STATES—POLITICS
AND GOVERNMENT—1783–1809. 3. CHARACTER—POLITICAL ASPECTS—UNITED
STATES—HISTORY—18TH CENTURY. 4. NATIONAL CHARACTERISTICS, AMERICAN.
5. UNITED STATES—HISTORY—REVOLUTION, 1775–1783—INFLUENCE. 6. SOCIAL VALUES—
UNITED STATES—HISTORY—18TH CENTURY. 7. POLITICAL CULTURE—UNITED
STATES—HISTORY—18TH CENTURY. 8. RHETORIC—POLITICAL ASPECTS—
UNITED STATES—HISTORY—18TH CENTURY. I. TITLE.

E302.1.T74 2004

973.4—DC21   2003043329

BRITISH LIBRARY CATALOGING-IN-PUBLICATION DATA IS AVAILABLE

THIS BOOK HAS BEEN COMPOSED IN SABON

PRINTED ON ACID-FREE PAPER. ∞

WWW.PUPRESS.PRINCETON.EDU

PRINTED IN THE UNITED STATES OF AMERICA

1   3   5   7   9   10   8   6   4   2

For My Family

CONTENTS

ILLUSTRATIONS

PREFACE

The American war is over; but this is far from being the case
with the American Revolution. Nothing but the first act of
the drama is closed.
—BENJAMIN RUSH, January 1787

The American Revolution had swept away the old world of British rule,
but the work of creating a new political world remained. How to create
that world was no simple task. The founders distrusted both politicians
and politics. They viewed themselves as disinterested guardians of the
public good, even as they found themselves in an increasingly democratic
political world. Although largely of their own making, this world seemed
to demand the kind of political activities that they disdained. They faced
a dilemma: how to act in the political sphere without being politicians.
George Washington succinctly articulated the task both for his peers and
for the nation, writing, "We are a young Nation and have a character to
establish. It behooves us therefore to set out right for first impressions
will be lasting, indeed are all in all."[1] The founders' attempts to establish
character would be their answer. If they could not allow themselves to be
politicians, they would create other political identities for themselves.
And if they could not accept a political world of competing interests, they
would reimagine that world along similar lines, a character for the nation
to match their own.

Washington's use of the word "character" is instructive on a number of
levels. It reveals the close connection between personal and national
character. The founders spoke of the two projects in largely identical
terms, and their personal characters became the models according to
which they attempted to reshape the nation's. That is where the similar-
ity among the founders ends, though. They came to very different conclusions about what the proper character was. *The Founding Fathers and
the Politics of Character* focuses on four of the most significant efforts:
Thomas Jefferson created a political character based on his conception of
friendship and imagined the nation in similar terms; Alexander Hamilton

relied on honor; John Adams drew upon his ideas about virtue; and James Madison employed justice. Although all four drew upon their under-standing of the Revolu-tion as the basis for their characters, all came to strikingly different conclusions.

The word "character" is instructive on another level—its use as a term of the stage is a valuable reminder that the founders were engaged in a process of invention. Implicit in the word is the unstable, slippery, protean nature of the identities they were trying to create. In one of his frequent moments of pique, John Adams suggested that George Washington's char-acter rested on a cleverly engineered facade. Mockingly enumerating Washington's qualities, he wrote:

> Talents! you will say, what talents? I answer. 1. An handsome face. That this is a talent, I can prove by the authority of a thousand instances in all ages. . . . 2. A tall stature, like the Hebrew sovereign chosen because he was taller by the head than the other Jews. 3. An elegant form. 4. Graceful attitudes and movements. 5. A large, imposing fortune. . . . There is nothing, except bloody battles and splendid victories, to which mankind bow down with more rever-ence than to great fortune. . . . 6. Washington was a Virginian! This is equivalent to five talents. Virginian geese are all swans. . . . 7. Washington was preceded by favorable anecdotes. . . . 8. He pos-sessed the gift of silence. This I esteem as one of the most precious talents. 9. He had great self-command. . . . 10. Whenever he lost his temper as he did sometimes, either love or fear in those about him induced them to conceal his weakness from the world.[2]

Adams's remarks suggest the gnawing awareness among even the founders of the brittleness of their characters. That is not to say that their characters were not heartfelt representations of their beliefs, only that those charac-ters were more fragile than they themselves wanted to believe.

Perhaps most important, the use of the word "character" uncovers one of the crucial fault lines running through early American politics. The word uneasily straddled the fluid and ill-defined boundary between pub-lic and private life, a boundary that played a central role in shaping the politics of the new nation. In struggling to create their characters, all the founders also struggled to define the proper line between the personal and the political and between inclusion and exclusion in the political life of the nation.

Their chief tool in this act of invention was writing. The nation's founding documents provide ongoing evidence of the founders' mastery of literary self-invention, their ability to create something where nothing had existed before. The Constitution begins with a simple assertion of national identity, "We, the people," creating a rhetorical "people" when the nation's actual citizens had not even decided to accept the identity promoted in the new Constitution. This fictional collectivity echoed that other moment of national beginning, the Declaration of Independence, a document whose opening relies on the same assertion of a collective "we" when that "we" was actually deeply divided. Both beginnings revealed the rhetorical underpinnings at the heart of the creation of national character.

Rather than a literary analysis of the founders, though, *The Founding Fathers and the Politics of Character* situates writing within a political culture where a primary task was the construction of character. These chapters are not biographical; instead, they focus on the rhetorical acts of creation in which each of the founders was engaged. Relying on close textual analysis to understand what could be called the poetics of politics, this study moves beyond the usual political concerns to consider stylistic components of political action, such as rhetoric, genre, and narrative structure. This focus on political style matches the founders' own. Far from irrelevant, matters of style, including rhetorical style, not only influenced matters of substance—they *were* matters of substance, a crucial means by which the founders attempted to translate their visions for themselves and the nation into reality.

This approach sheds light on a number of aspects of early American political culture. It offers a fresh perspective on the founders themselves and places them in relation to one another as well as revealing the range of political identities available in the new nation. The study of their characters also provides a new context in which to see the founders' politics, moving beyond policy prescriptions to a more elusive and symbolic level of action, which frequently reveals their entanglement in a host of issues usually seen as far removed from the political sphere. Finally, their characters set the parameters for political behavior and continue to influence politics today. The founders' very concern with character is one of the most obvious signs of their continued relevance to us—public and private remain contested terms in our own time, and the issue of character remains central to our politics. Although muted and transformed, the characters that they created still underlie much of the rhetoric of today's politicians. The politics of character is still very much with us.

ACKNOWLEDGMENTS

A book, like character, is supposed to appear as a self-conscious act of individual creation. Like character, though, it is the product of countless influences and individuals. My own book is no exception. Most important, I want to thank Peter Onuf, who has been far more than my dissertation adviser. His inimitable style always made me feel that I was engaged in a grand adventure.

I also want to thank my family. They were among my first and most generous readers and never failed to encourage me. And I want to thank Heesun Chei for her unfailing support.

A number of friends have provided invaluable assistance over the years. Peter Kastor sharpened my thinking and my prose. Jenry Morsman devoted many hours to helping me revise the manuscript. Joanne Freeman assisted me in defining the central issues of the project. Brian Balogh provided sustenance in a variety of forms. And Peter Sheehy played too many roles to enumerate. I am grateful to all of them and thankful to be able to count them as my friends.

I am indebted to many people at the University of Virginia. In particular, Sophia Rosenfeld provided generous assistance. I would also like to thank Stephen Innes, John Stagg, Edward Ayers, J. E. Lendon, Joseph Kett, Alon Confino, Richard Rorty, Stephen Cushman, Michael Levenson, Marion Rust, and my colleagues in the Early American Seminar.

Numerous friends and colleagues helped sustain me throughout the research and writing of the book. My fellow members of the dissertation dinner group, Amy Murrell, Andy Morris, Josh Rothman, and Stephen Norris, helped me enormously. In addition, I would like to thank Barry Bienstock, Caroline Bartels, Doug Wilson, James Horn, Andy Lewis, and Amy Feely. Jan Lewis's insightful comments improved the book in countless ways, and I owe a great debt of gratitude to her. I want to extend a special thanks to John McPhee for teaching me lessons that I still try to apply every time I sit down to write.

My editors at Princeton University Press deserve the highest praise for their efforts, particularly Thomas LeBien and Brigitta van Rheinberg. I also want to thank my production editor, Dale Cotton, and my copy editor, Will Hively.

Earlier versions of chapters 1 and 4 were published in *The Virginia Magazine of History and Biography* and *The Journal of the Early Republic* respectively, and I thank the editors of those publications for permission to reprint those chapters and for their editorial efforts.

A number of institutions provided financial support. The International Center for Jefferson Studies in conjunction with the Thomas Jefferson Memorial Foundation provided generous support on more than one occasion. The Intercollegiate Studies Institute also offered generous financial assistance. Additionally, the Gilder Lehrman Society, the Society of the Cincinnati, and The Horace Mann School helped fund my efforts.

THE FOUNDING FATHERS AND THE
POLITICS OF CHARACTER

Figure 1. *Congress Voting on Independence*, engraved by Edward Savage (1906 strike from an early nineteenth-century plate). Courtesy of the National Portrait Gallery, Smithsonian Institution.

Introduction

THOUGH POLITICAL INDEPENDENCE had been won by 1783, Americans, individually and collectively, still needed to establish their identity or, as they would have said in the eighteenth century, their "character." Indeed, neither an end to war nor the ratification of the Constitution represented a final revolutionary settlement. As Washington warned in 1783,

> [T]his is the moment to establish or ruin . . . national Character forever. . . . It is yet to be decided, whether the Revolution must ultimately be considered as a blessing or a curse: a blessing or a curse, not to the present age alone, for with our fate will the destiny of unborn Millions be involved.[1]

The meaning of the Revolution, according to Washington, would only be established once the newly independent people agreed upon a character that would draw them together as a purposeful union.[2] That would prove a most difficult task, as briefly discussed in the preface and more fully elaborated here.

Americans were far more prepared to say who they were not. They knew, for example, that they were not English.[3] Winning the Revolution brought to an abrupt close the many years of striving to be British. They knew, too, that they did not want to be politicians. The Revolution had been an effort, in many ways, to cleanse America from the taint of British corruption, but Americans saw the republican governments created to replace imperial rule as fragile creations, easily susceptible to corruption themselves. The politician, a man of self-interest rather than the common good, embodied the corruption that so many Americans feared. Alexander Hamilton could write sneeringly in *Federalist #11* of "the little arts of little politicians," confident that such a feeling would meet widespread support.[4] According to Samuel Johnson's *Dictionary*, the very word meant something unsavory. The great lexicographer defined the politician as a "man of artifice, of deep contrivance." If politicians were dangerous individually, their combination in a party or a faction compounded the threat, creating a profound hostility in most Americans to political parties.[5] Political circumstances reinforced these attitudes. In colonial and revolutionary times, legislative battles with royal governors and later military battles with Britain had demanded unity, not division.[6]

The newly established national government provided no established institutions or rules to fill this void. The fluid postrevolutionary environment offered only broad and vague guidelines, and even the most mundane

issues, such as the manner of dress or the president's title, were bitterly contested.[7] The hostility to politicians and parties meant that politics in the
early republic would have to be practiced in a somewhat oblique manner.
Continuing to contest the meaning of the Revolution, American leaders
struggled to impose their own different understandings of the Revolution
and to use that to form political characters for themselves and the nation
that would allow them to act politically, while not acting as politicians.[8]

Engaging in a highly personalized form of politics that could aptly be
termed the politics of character, they wrestled with this problem on two
levels: their own individual political characters and the nation's character. They considered the two projects as interrelated and viewed their
own characters as templates that could shape that of the country.[9] To understand their struggles, we must first begin to understand what character
meant to them. In the eighteenth century, the word meant something far
different than it does today. It possessed a largely public meaning that was
virtually synonymous with reputation, rather than an intrinsic quality. It
was almost a tangible possession, something one fashioned, held, and
protected, so that one would speak of "acquiring" a character.[10] By the
end of the century, though, the meaning of character was undergoing a
process of redefinition. The larger trajectory of its meaning is readily apparent. Publicly weighted conceptions in the early part of the eighteenth
century would give way to nineteenth-century notions of character that
relied predominantly on private life. But that shift was not preordained
or readily apparent to the founders. The relative importance of the public and private sides of one's character during this period was a subject of
constant debate.[11]

The distinction between public and private life has received considerable scholarly attention, particularly from those studying gender, who
have persuasively argued for the interdependence of the two terms.[12]
Political historians have generally paid less attention to the issue.[13] But in
the political world of the early republic, the ambiguity between public
and private life was both pronounced and central to defining the nature
of the emerging polity. Authority and legitimacy were under negotiation
not only with one's peers but with the nation's citizens, and choices about
how to distinguish public from private life had direct implications not
just for the elite political world but for the nation as a whole.

Embroiled in this redefinition by the personalized nature of political
life, the founders articulated a broad spectrum of possibilities in their
struggles to give shape to this undefined world. In a famous example of one
of the narrowest constructions of public life, Thomas Paine in "Common
Sense" called government "the badge of lost innocence." He noted that
"even in its best state [it] is but a necessary evil."[14] In Paine's rendering,
government was an affliction, and public life needed to be circumscribed

as narrowly as possible. A few years later, Benjamin Rush claimed that a citizen was "public property. His time and talents—his youth—his manhood—his old age—nay more, life, all belong to his country."[15] In this view, citizens did not have private lives, only public ones to be devoted to the nation. One of the most vexing problems facing the revolutionaries was how to navigate the territory staked out between these two extremes. Focusing on four of the most significant efforts, this study explores the attempts of Thomas Jefferson, Alexander Hamilton, John Adams, and James Madison to shape the new republic according to their conceptions of character.[16]

All four, not surprisingly, undertook this task largely through writing, a choice dictated simply by the size of the new nation. Indeed, writing became one of the crucial arenas for the politics of character in revolutionary America.[17] In his contemporary history of the American Revolution, David Ramsay made his own claim for the centrality of writing. "In establishing American independence," he wrote, "the pen and the press had merit equal to that of the sword."[18] Although the war was the means for gaining independence, the meaning of that independence was largely determined through writing, first with the Declaration of Independence and later with the multitude of efforts at constitution writing throughout this period.[19] Washington Irving fittingly called the new nation a "LOGOCRACY," a "*government of words.*"[20] The founders recognized the power of the written word, crafting thousands of letters, pamphlets, and essays in an attempt to shape the new nation. The centrality of writing to them remains largely underappreciated during our own day—literary critics usually focus on the few poems and novels from this period, and historians often overlook issues of rhetoric and style.

The Founding Fathers and the Politics of Character explores the founders' attempts to construct character through particular forms of writing, the rhetorical "how" of the creation of identity. More specifically, it considers each founder in tandem with a genre that was particularly well suited to represent his "character."[21] These pairings are not programmatic; letter writing, for instance, was central to all of the founders. But they do provide a useful tool for better understanding the founders' attempts to construct character. The documents used are not always the typical ones for studying the politics of the early republic. Instead of exploring the usual sources—constitutions, official correspondence, legislative debates—this book focuses on more personal texts that reveal both individual and national dimensions of character building. Although employing an historical framework, this work is shaped by that most fundamental of literary questions: how does a text accomplish its purposes? Crossing some of the usual boundaries between history and literary studies, it sees literary and rhetorical choices as profoundly intertwined with politics.

Each chapter is structured around one particularly revealing textual performance. Episodic in structure, the chapters first consider the generic resources available to that founder. Then, they examine the character that each of the founders attempted to create, concentrating in turn on its personal, political, and national implications. Finally, each chapter explores the problems that the founder encountered as a result of his character. Throughout, this study focuses on the rhetorical attempts to navigate and shape the complicated terrain of character in the early republic and on the centrality of that terrain to the emerging national political realm.

The chapters also outline a larger trajectory in the politics of character. Instead of following a chronological order, they trace the differing distinctions that the founders made between the public and private sides of character. Moving from Jefferson's convoluted intermingling of public and private life to increasingly well articulated ideas about how to distinguish between the two, the clearer distinctions correspond to a decreasing reliance on personal character by the founders. To make use of the metaphor suggested by one meaning of character, Jefferson remained backstage because of fears about the believability of his character. Hamilton confidently walked the stage only to find that the audience judged him harshly. Convinced of his own character, Adams placed himself in the audience, judged the performances of others, and proposed new roles for them to play. Seeing character itself as the problem, Madison attempted to leave behind the stage altogether. The conclusion explores the tentative and incomplete resolution of these issues through the character of George Washington as it was fashioned by Mason Locke Weems in his famous biography. Weems recast Washington's distinctly eighteenth-century concerns about character into a form more in tune with nineteenth-century conceptions, as character came to be associated with private life, rather than public, a shift that also marked the end of the sharply personalized politics of character at the heart of this study.[22]

Four Revolutions

While serving as the model for the characters of the founders, the American Revolution revealed different lessons to each one—four contrasting understandings of what the Revolution meant that led to four contrasting visions of how to secure the Revolution not just on the battlefield but, as John Adams once phrased it, in the hearts and minds of American citizens. For Thomas Jefferson, Alexander Hamilton, John Adams, and James Madison, the urgency of the Revolution crystallized various inchoate beliefs based on an array of biographical, psychological, social, economic, political, and cultural considerations into distinct ideas about character.

For Thomas Jefferson, those lessons were learned largely from the land that he called his country, Virginia. Jefferson spent most of the war years in the Virginia government, rather than in the Continental Congress, and he attributed the success of the war effort to what he viewed as the spontaneous outpouring of the voluntary efforts of citizens and states on behalf of the nation, direct proof that a strong national government was not only unnecessary but counterproductive. Near the end of his 1786 letter to Maria Cosway, Thomas Jefferson's thoughts turned to his great touchstone, the Revolution:

> If our country when pressed with wrongs at the point of the bayonet, had been governed by it's heads instead of it's hearts, where should we have been now? Hanging on a gallows as high as Haman's. You began to calculate & to compare wealth and numbers: we threw up a few pulsations of our warmest blood; we supplied enthusiasm against wealth and numbers; we put our existence to the hazard when the hazard seemed against us, and we saved our country.[23]

For Jefferson, the Revolution and even politics were matters of the heart, of pulsations of warm blood rather than rational calculation. The same understanding of the Revolution can be found in the Declaration of Independence, in which Jefferson claimed that the British were deaf to the voice of "consanguinity," which should have united the British with the Americans in affective bonds.[24] In language cut from his draft by the Continental Congress, he denounced England's lack of feeling in even stronger terms, writing, "These facts have given the last stab to agonizing affection, and manly spirit bids us to renounce forever these unfeeling brethren."[25] The heart alone spoke for some larger sense of public good, of a sentimental journey in which no man's misfortune would go unnoticed and in which the people, bound together by affection, would triumph.

Affective bonds, the pulsations of warmest blood, would always be what Jefferson sought in his own relationships, in his politics, and in his imaginative vision for the country. He cast these relationships as friendships, uncoerced ties of mutual affection among equals. This conception provided the means for Jefferson to act in the political sphere without running afoul of his cherished beliefs about the natural unanimity of the country and the illegitimacy of political disagreement.

To explore this Jeffersonian vision of character, the first chapter focuses on a 26 January 1799 letter from Jefferson to Elbridge Gerry, a vexatious and unpredictable Massachusetts leader who became Jefferson's only significant non-Republican, New England correspondent during the late 1790s. The genre of the familiar letter cast Jefferson in his most comfortable persona, a friend renewing ties with another friend, even as he attempted to use the letter for more instrumental, political purposes. His reliance on the letter illustrated his problematic combination of public and private life in his attempt to refashion the political world in the image of his domestic society, and his "character" only exacerbated the ambiguity between public and private in the early republic. On the personal level, his attempt to use bonds of emotion to cement political alliances undermined his sincerity. On the national level, his solution allowed no legitimacy for political differences and threatened to create not union but disunion.

Unlike Jefferson, who was born into the Virginia gentry, Alexander Hamilton struggled to overcome his humble origins, an experience that prepared him to see the Revolution in a different light. In his earliest surviving letter, written at the age of twelve when he was stranded on the periphery of the British empire, Alexander Hamilton complained of "the groveling and condition of a clerk." Wanting to "exalt my station," Hamilton hoped for the chance to prove himself, writing simply, "I wish there was a war."[26] He would get his wish only a few years later, serving in the Continental Army during the American Revolution. Like many other committed nationalists of the early republic, Alexander Hamilton formed his understanding of the Revolution from the frustrations and humiliations of serving in a national army that was hampered by fears of centralized power. He turned to honor as a code of behavior that would assure not just his own glory but the glory of the nation.

Hamilton had little faith in the American people and in Jefferson's so-called bonds of affection. The behavior that Hamilton witnessed as an officer left him with a sour view of his countrymen's character. Merchants profiteered at the expense of the army, a practice so widespread that Hamilton called it an *"epidemical sprit of extortion."*[27] Gangs roamed the countryside, stealing private property while claiming to combat traitors. Much of the South degenerated into complete lawlessness. Perhaps worst of all, Americans seemed unable to rouse themselves to the task of securing their liberty. Hamilton complained to a friend, "Our countrymen have all the folly of the ass and all the passiveness of the sheep in their compositions. They are determined not to be free and they can neither be frightened, discouraged nor persuaded to change their resolution."[28] Even Congress failed to exhibit the character Hamilton expected. Although he thought that its first members "would do honor to any age or nation," he watched them be drawn off by "local attachment, falsely operating," replaced by members he considered second-rate men. In contrast to Jefferson, Hamilton saw the individual states as obstacles to national glory. Blinded by local loyalties, political leaders failed to see that their true duty and the crucial work of the country was at the national level.[29] His faith in the Continental Congress eroded and led him to lament Congress's "folly, caprice [and] a want of foresight" and to accuse it of "ductility and inconstancy" as well as "feeble indecisive and improvident" treatment of the army.[30] His feelings of disgust for the situation overwhelmed him, and he wrote despairingly in 1780, "I hate Congress—I hate the army—I hate the world—I hate myself. The whole is a mass of fools and knaves."[31]

Revealing the link between personal and national character, Hamilton felt the shortcomings of his country personally. "These things wound my feelings as a republican more than I can express," he wrote.[32] When the country seemed unable to win the Revolution through its own efforts, he complained, "I have the most pigmy-feelings at the idea."[33] Even the failures of Congress, "the great council of America," Hamilton took as a reflection on himself, claiming that their actions "in some degree make me contemptible in my own eyes."[34]

Hamilton would work to rectify those humiliations for the rest of his life. His early desire for personal glory would be transmuted through the experience of the Revolution into a broader desire to achieve personal and national glory. At the close of the war, he made a special request to Washington. "I build a hope that I may be permitted to preserve my rank," he wrote, "as an honorary reward for the time I have devoted to the public. As I may hereafter travel, I may find it an agreeable circumstance to appear in the character I have supported in the revolution."[35] Although his request was denied, Hamilton carried the self-understanding shaped by the "character" he had "supported in the revolution." Distrusting the mass of men, he attempted to fashion a political elite to lead the nation to glory. Seeing loyalty to individual states rather than to the nation as a defect in the national character, he hoped to create a national government powerful enough to command respect. Throughout, he shaped his conduct and his country according to the dictates of honor.

To understand the Hamiltonian vision, the second chapter focuses on his infamous "Reynolds pamphlet," in which he defended his conduct as secretary of the treasury by admitting to adultery. The personal-defense pamphlet fit neatly with Hamilton's character. It was the genre most suited to a written defense of honor for a public audience. In the pamphlet, he also attempted to construct his own distinction between public and private life. He argued that the private lives of elite men had little, if anything, to do with their fitness for office. His reliance on honor, however, undermined the very character that it was intended to secure. On the personal level, his use of honor subverted his effort to construct a wall between public and private life, because dishonor in one realm meant dishonor in the other. On the national level, the elitist code of honor, never the only guidebook to political behavior even during colonial times, was overwhelmed by a rapidly democratizing and increasingly partisan public who cared little for the elaborate etiquette that was supposed to guide the behavior of gentlemen.

John Adams's experience in the Continental Congress and as a diplomat gave him a nationalist perspective, but he did not share Hamilton's confidence in the nation's elite. He embraced at different times both Jefferson's optimism and Hamilton's pessimism regarding his fellow countrymen, an ambivalence that remained at the core of his thinking. In contrast to both men, John Adams feared that the real Revolution would never be understood by his fellow countrymen. Eyewitness to the complicated backroom maneuvering of the Continental Congress as well as to the insincerity and cloaked messages of diplomatic life, he wrote to one correspondent, "I consider the true history of the American revolution & of the establishment of our present Constitutions as lost forever."[36] He asked Jefferson, "Who shall write the history of the American revolution? Who can write it? Who will ever be able to write it?"[37]

From his earliest days working for American independence when he attacked the "dark intrigues and wicked machinations" of British officials, Adams saw the nation as beset by plots and conspiracies.[38] To unmask the lies and deceptions that he saw all around him, he clung to an austere sense of virtue, which he thought would allow him to probe beneath the facades that all men presented (a stance that left him equally distrustful of what he viewed as the deceitful face of friendship and the blinding self-importance of honor).

With virtue as his beacon, he set himself the task of unmasking the deceptions that befuddled the American people, a Sisyphean effort when he considered how often they were misled by appearances. "I admire Bonaparte's expression 'The Scenery of the Business.' The scenery has often if not commonly in all the business of human life, at least of public life, more effect than the characters of the dramatis personae or the ingenuity of the plot," he wrote after retiring from public life. "Recollect within our own times. What but the scenery did this? or that? or the other? Was there ever a *coup de theatre* that had so great an effect as Jefferson's penmanship of the Declaration of Independence?"[39] Adams worried that the entire history of the Revolution would come to be seen through the distorted lens of one vast coup de théâtre. He joked in a letter to Benjamin Rush that the "History of the Revolution will be one continued lie. . . . The essence of the whole will be *that Dr. Franklin's electrical Rod smote the Earth and out spring George Washington. That Franklin electrized him with his Rod—and henceforth these two conducted all the Policy, Negotiations, Legislatures and War.*"[40]

For Adams, though, the dangers of deceit and dissimulation were not simply a product of the instability of the Revolution or even of politics but were part of the fabric of human nature. In an essay written as a young man, Adams claimed that self-deceit was "the source of far the greatest and worst part of the vices and calamities among mankind."[41] And no one was exempt. "Even the few favorites of nature, who have received from her clearer understandings and more happy tempers than other men," he noted, "are often snared by this unhappy disposition in their minds, to their own destruction, and the injury, nay, often to the utter desolation of millions of their fellow-men. . . . the greatest genius, united to the best disposition, will find it hard to hearken to the voice of reason, or even to be certain of the purity of his own intentions."[42] In a world where appearances often misled and where one's own motives were cloudy, virtue was his guide, serving as both his own stringent code of conduct and as the lens through which he judged the behavior of others. Only strict attention to the dictates of virtue, according to Adams, could ensure that the nation would remain true to its revolutionary heritage.

To understand Adams's struggle to keep himself and his nation virtuous, the third chapter focuses on his diary. Removed from the lure of public approval that so often tempted men away from the path of virtue, the diary provided a forum for the kind of searing self-examination on which Adams relied to determine the motives behind his own action and the actions of others. Assailed by self-doubt about even his own virtue, though, Adams struggled to find some way to distinguish true from false virtue, a struggle that the diary, with its lack of any outside standards to confirm or deny his own judgments, only exacerbated. His reliance on virtue also undermined any clear distinction between public and private life because it straddled both. His corrosive examination of the demands of virtue eventually convinced him that the nation's character would have to be built on a different foundation.

As one of the youngest founders, most of James Madison's formative revolutionary experiences occurred in the 1780s, a period when Jefferson serenely surveyed the new nation from Virginia and talked of his retirement, when Hamilton finished his military service and began his legal training, and when Adams served as a diplomat in Europe. During this time, Madison struggled to work under the unwieldy Articles of Confederation and watched state legislatures break into unruly factions bent on pursuing private interests rather than the public good. He realized that the politics of character was itself part of the problem. For himself, he created a personal character so circumspect that most who first met him usually felt nothing but an overwhelming disappointment. He fashioned a character based on justice, in which the personal would be cleaved from the political, and personal predilection would give way to unbiased reflection.

On the eve of the Constitutional Convention in Philadelphia, Madison wrote "Vices of the Political System of the United States," an attempt to address the various problems that were afflicting the nation and to offer his own blueprint for a just government.[43] The American Revolution had ignited an intense and prolonged bout of constitution writing in the nation, as states were forced not simply to replace the royal charters that had governed them but to attempt to apply the lessons of the Revolution.[44] If these constitutions can be read as commentaries on the meaning of the American Revolution, Madison's own thoughts were a commentary on those commentaries, not simply assessing the failure of state legislatures to act according to a just standard but also reconsidering the meaning of the Revolution itself.

In his extended analysis, attempting to recover lessons that had been neglected in the intervening years, Madison offered a précis of his own ideas on the difficulty of postrevolutionary governance in America. At the end of his composition, he focused on problems within the state governments, which revealed where the ideals of the Revolution had not been met. He complained of the "multiplicity of laws in the several states" and the "mutability of the laws of the states." Such instability could never be the foundation for proper government, because laws were "repealed or superseded, before any trial can have been made of their merits, and even before a knowledge of them can have reached the remoter districts within which they were to operate." He complained of the "luxuriancy of legislation" that state legislatures seemed to produce on a yearly basis. In a nation in which laws were supposed to provide the foundation for a just and prosperous order, the state governments had failed miserably, not even supplying a readily interpretable legal framework. Worst of all, according to Madison, was the "injustice of the laws of the states," a failure to protect the central value of government, justice.

Madison was criticizing a fundamental premise of revolutionary thought—that government should express the will of the majority. Madison's critique did not represent a rejection of the Revolution. One of the vices he identified, the "want of ratification by the people of the Articles of Confederation," recognized the importance of a central lesson of the Revolution: the political legitimacy of a republican government rested on the people themselves. Popular sovereignty was only one of many political lessons, though. State politics in the 1780s had given ample evidence that majority rule was, at best, an insecure foundation for the public good. Madison himself recognized the profundity of this challenge. He noted that the injustice of state laws "brings more into question the fundamental principle of republican Government, that the majority who rule in such governments are the safest Guardians both of public Good and private rights." Even "respect for character," according to Madison, would not restrain men from injustice.[45]

Arguing that these problems had to be overcome if America was to secure the benefits of the Revolution, Madison's answer was to create a government that stood above partisan self-interest, one that was sufficiently neutral to protect the interests of all its citizens. He wrote, "The great desideratum in Government is such a modification of the sovereignty as will render it sufficiently neutral between the different interests and factions, to controul one part of the society from invading the rights of another, and at the same time sufficiently controuled itself, from setting up an interest adverse to that of the whole Society." If government could be a sufficiently neutral judge, a just government would surely be the result.

To understand Madison's personal and national vision of justice, the fourth chapter explores *Federalist #37*. The essay provided the perfect generic medium for Madison's politics of justice. The anonymity of the essay mirrored Madison's own desire to escape the politics of character. Its persuasive power rested not on the character of its author but on the strength of its arguments. Even as personal character was shorn from national character, though, Madison still found himself facing an intractable foe, the ambiguity inherent in language itself, "that cloudy medium," as he called it.

As the Earl of Shaftesbury warned, "Of all the artificial Relations, formed between Mankind, the most capricious and variable is that of *Author* and *Reader*."[46] Shaftesbury's remark is a useful reminder as this study begins examining the founders' written efforts to craft their characters—a tale rich in irony as they all too often found that the responses to their efforts were as capricious and variable as Shaftesbury promised.[47] In the process of articulating the relationship between author and reader, these men attempted to define the polity in ways no less profound than their comments on more familiar political subjects. That they struggled in their efforts to give shape to the emerging nation proves not just the truth of Shaftesbury's words but the vexing elusiveness of character in the fluid postrevolutionary political world.

Figure 2.   *Thomas Jefferson*, painted by Gilbert Stuart, 1805. Courtesy of the National Portrait Gallery, Smithsonian Institution.

ONE

Friendship

In late January 1799, Thomas Jefferson wrote a letter to Massachusetts native Elbridge Gerry, his longtime friend. Jefferson feared that the revolutionary promise of the nation, a union held together by the "pulsations of warmest blood," was on the verge of complete ruination. From his vantage point, everything seemed to be working against the true friends of America. Stirred by the XYZ affair and exacerbated as France and America engaged in a partial and undeclared naval war with one another, anti-French feeling threatened to push America into war with France and an alliance with Britain that Jefferson feared would contaminate, if not destroy, the young republic. Jeffersonian Republicans also found themselves not just contending against popular sentiment but facing a substantial Federalist majority in Congress, which pushed through measures to increase the size of the navy, legalize the arming of merchant vessels, and expand the standing army, a proliferation of patronage that Jefferson feared would only further entrench the Federalists in power. Perhaps worst of all, the Alien and Sedition Acts threatened to silence Republican newspapers and trim Republican voting rolls. Jefferson's once optimistic hopes for his country lay in tatters.

His hopes were reawakened by a letter from Gerry. After spending more than a year in Paris attempting to negotiate a treaty with France to prevent war, Gerry returned to the United States and found himself the victim of almost universal vilification. Shortly after returning home, Gerry wrote to Jefferson "for such political information, as may be interesting to myself, in regard to the embassy. During my absence I find that I have been abused alternately by both parties: but for what, I am yet to learn."[1]

Gerry's request presented Jefferson with an opportunity to turn the political tide. Attempting to draw Gerry into the Republican camp, Jefferson hoped to persuade him to offer the "proper" Republican interpretation of the negotiations with France, one that would blame Gerry's Federalist co-commissioners for undermining the negotiations from the start and help counter the anti-French feelings created by the public airing of the XYZ affair. In addition, Jefferson wanted Gerry to provide crucial Republican leadership in the Federalist stronghold of New England during the upcoming elections.

Achieving or even pursuing these political goals was hardly a simple task in the undeveloped world of early American politics. Both vice president and de facto head of the Republicans, Jefferson had to balance his place in the government with his deeply held political opposition, a delicate task given a political context that still offered no legitimacy for political parties, let alone precedents for determining what was allowable as an opposition leader in the new nation. The recently passed Sedition Act made such political maneuvering even more difficult. Although watered down from its harshest version, the Sedition Act promised to give Federalists a powerful tool to silence the Republican opposition. Anticipating a sedition law months before an actual one was passed, Jefferson predicted that it would be used against Republican newspapers and Republican congressmen, a political weapon to silence any critics of the government.[2] Added to that, Gerry was one of the most unpredictable politicians of the day, a man distrusted by both parties. He was also close to John Adams, who was scarcely speaking to Jefferson by the end of the 1790s. Jefferson could not be sure that Gerry would not report everything to Adams or possibly even provide the Federalists with fodder for political abuse. Finally, Jefferson was deeply uncomfortable with the type of politicking that he needed to practice with Gerry, and he generally avoided it by delegating it to others. His letter to Gerry represented one of the only occasions during the late 1790s when he personally appealed to a politician whose political loyalties were unclear.[3]

Forced to bridge the gap between his philosophical ideas of affective union and the vitriolic political world of the 1790s, Jefferson attempted to enact in microcosm his hope that the nation could be united by the same effusion of spontaneous emotion that he saw as America's great revolutionary legacy. To do this, he relied on an expansive notion of friendship that allowed him to deny any untoward political maneuvering by collapsing his practical appeal to Gerry into the supposedly nonpolitical arena of friendship.[4] Claiming to value sincere bonds of emotion over public or political bonds, Jefferson relied primarily on his (still carefully constructed) "private" self to cement his political relationship with Gerry. By using the letter to fashion his political character as that of a friend, Jefferson was able to satisfy his practical political needs while remaining true to his revolutionary ideals, because friendship, like his conception of the Revolution, relied on ties of emotion among freely consenting and equal citizens. Ultimately, he hoped to impose similar values on the political sphere and the nation by remaking both in the image of his harmonious domestic society of friends and family.[5]

But Jefferson's reliance on friendship as a political relationship threatened to undermine the emotional bonds that he was trying to construct. As he attempted to reach out to an ever wider group of "friends" to create a Republican majority in the late 1790s, Jefferson's use of private emotions for political purposes increasingly called into question his sincerity and threatened to undermine the character based on friendship that he was trying to create for himself.[6] By making politics dependent on private emotions, Jefferson's character confounded, rather than separated, public and private life. His use of friendship also created problems for his vision of national character. Imagining true Americans linked in harmonious ties of affection, Jefferson offered an expansive view of the people and their role in the new nation, a view that found the reality of political disagreement impossible to accept. Ironically, although he envisioned a homogeneous brotherhood of like-minded Americans, out of which individual rights and freedoms would emerge, Jefferson's construction of the national character undercut the grounds for legitimate political differences, creating the framework not for harmony but for disunion.

"It is a charming thing to be loved by every body"

Jeffersonian Friendship

The first pages of Jefferson's letter to Gerry framed their epistolary exchange not as political correspondence but as a familiar letter between friends. Jefferson wrote Gerry that he had received the 12 November 1798 letter with "great satisfaction." He recalled to Gerry "our very long intimacy as fellow-laborers in the same cause." Jefferson was at his ambiguous best, leaving it unclear whether he was referring to laboring together in the Revolutionary War or in recent party battles. He effectively made the two the same cause, as they were in his mind, so that a failure to side with the Republicans was no less than a betrayal of the American Revolution. Jefferson then reminded him of. "the recent expressions of mutual confidence which had preceded your mission."[7] Finally, Jefferson obliquely addressed Gerry's potentially crucial role as a provider of a pro-French interpretation of the diplomatic mission: "The interesting course which that [the mission] had taken, and particularly and personally as it regarded yourself, made me anxious to hear from you on your return." His sentence carefully sidestepped his own practical needs. Jefferson also offered himself as a fellow sufferer from gossip, complaining that he had been a "constant butt for every shaft of calumny which malice and falsehood could form, and the presses, public speakers, or private letters disseminate."[8] Throughout his early remarks, Jefferson repeatedly emphasized his private and personal friendship with Gerry and omitted all mention of Gerry's potential usefulness as a political ally.

His avowals of friendship found a congenial home in the genre of the familiar letter, a genre that provides additional insight into Jefferson's efforts to court Gerry as well as highlighting aspects of Jefferson's political vision. Personal predilection dictated his reliance on the letter.[9] Although he needed to reach out to his fellow citizens to achieve his political vision of union based on bonds of emotion and affection, he almost never wrote for a public, undifferentiated audience, relying on friends to shoulder that burden.[10] His careful avoidance of public appeals allowed him to avoid any obvious politicking, and in a personal letter, Jefferson could tailor his missive to the individual, offering more solid ground to establish the emotional connection that he sought.

The genre reinforced Jefferson's efforts to renew his friendship with Gerry. Eighteenth-century belletrists were in wide agreement: the familiar letter was most intimately concerned with friendship.[11] Samuel Johnson called such letters "a pure voice of nature and of friendship," and William Cowper spoke of them as "the natural fruit of friendship."[12] Familiar letter writing, according to the wisdom of the day, was friendship exemplified. Further generic reinforcement for Jefferson's emotion-laden appeal came from the increasing emphasis that familiar letters, aspiring to emotional transparency between correspondents, display one's "authentic" private self. Abandoning classical models, the best letters, Johnson thought, exhibited a "strict conformity to nature . . . an artless Arrangement of obvious sentiments."[13] As Scottish rhetorician Hugh Blair, in his extensively reprinted lectures, said, "The style of letters should not be too highly polished; it ought to be neat and correct, but no more. . . . What the heart or the imagination dictates, always flows readily."[14] Familiar letters were supposed to offer an unshuttered window into the writer's heart, providing, many commentators believed, "the best pictures of their personal characters."[15]

Even as the familiar letter offered the means for Jefferson's appeal to Gerry, the genre contained within it an unresolved ambiguity that complicated Jefferson's sharing of his private, "sincere" self. Despite his earlier remarks, Blair recognized that letters were not without their complexities. He noted, "It is childish indeed to expect, that in letters we are to find the whole heart of the author unveiled. Concealment and disguise take place, more or less, in all human intercourse."[16] The intimacy of a familiar letter was the result of a particular type of performance. As Johnson wrote, "There is indeed no transaction which offers stronger temptation to fallacy and sophistication than epistolary intercourse. A friendly letter is a calm and deliberate performance in the cool of leisure, in the stillness of solitude, and surely no man sits down to depreciate by design his own character."[17] In other words, the achievement of spontaneous intimacy occurred on the problematic grounds of strenuous self-fashioning, in which learned behavior was supposed to appear natural.[18] Although the genre was supposed to embody the sharing of sincere and private emotions between friends, readers and writers also understood that the supposedly heartfelt was an artfully constructed performance. So, even as Jefferson attempted to renew his friendship with Gerry, he did so in a genre that carried within it ambiguities that mirrored his own difficulties.

The genre and Jefferson's appeal shared a final ambiguity. Jefferson's letter blurred the distinction between private and public life by pursuing political goals through private friendship. Familiar letters frequently blurred the distinction as well.[19] In the republic of letters, readers valued the free and public exchange of letters. Letters originally intended to be private frequently found much larger (and even international) circulation, as recipients read letters aloud to others or gave away copies.[20] Circulation of supposedly "private" letters was especially common in the early republic, as a means of sharing political information.[21] In addition, a number of famous men in the eighteenth century arranged for their private letters to be printed, further blurring the boundary.[22]

Jefferson himself repeatedly worried that his private letters would find their way into the public world of print. Warning one correspondent in 1799 not to let his letters fall into the wrong hands, he wrote that "a very short text will for a long time furnish matter for newspaper stricture."[23] As the election of 1800 drew near, he often said that he was going to stop writing letters because he was worried about newspaper slander.[24] At one point, as he waited for the election of 1800 to be resolved in the House of Representatives, he even claimed that he had decided "never to write another sentence of politics in a letter."[25]

Jefferson had reason to worry. In a letter he wrote to Philip Mazzei in April 1796, Jefferson made some strong remarks, including what many viewed as a thinly veiled attack on George Washington. Mazzei translated the letter into Italian and indiscreetly gave it to a Florentine paper. A Parisian newspaper then translated it into French and printed it. And finally, over a year after Jefferson had written the letter, it was retranslated into English and printed in a New York paper. The letter created a storm of controversy, furthering Federalist suspicions that Jefferson's sympathy for France made his patriotism suspect. Jefferson never acknowledged authorship of the letter and refused to enter the public debate over it. He also remained forever guarded about his private correspondence.[26]

Added to these problems, the most difficult challenge for any letter writer was the unpredictable nature of the reader, a difficulty especially relevant in the case of Elbridge Gerry.[27] Despite his confident words about their friendship, Jefferson clearly remained uneasy about his correspondent. He betrayed his anxiety with his mention of some news "of a nature to touch yourself," a rumor that Jefferson had authorized Dr. George Logan to go to Paris for private negotiations with France.[28] Jefferson dismissed this imputation, proposing as preposterous the notion that he lacked confidence

THE PROVIDENTIAL DETECTION

Figure 3. Political cartoon of Thomas Jefferson. Courtesy of the American Antiquarian Society. This political cartoon, probably published during the presidential election of 1800, reveals why Jefferson was so hesitant to include political information in his letters. Jefferson kneels at the "Altar to Gallic Despotism." The fire on the altar is fueled by a variety of controversial works. An American eagle appears to seize the U.S. Constitution from Jefferson before he can burn it. Jefferson's 1796 letter to Philip Mazzei, which Mazzei indiscreetly allowed to be published, falls from his right hand. The letter included what many viewed as an attack on Washington. Even years later, this private letter continued to be used against Jefferson as proof of his apostasy.

in Gerry or would usurp powers committed to him.[29] But Jefferson was clearly worried that Gerry would not find this preposterous at all and felt obliged to spend a considerable part of the letter explaining his relation to Logan and the true nature of Logan's trip.[30] Jefferson's avowals of friendship could not banish the political realities of the late 1790s or the precariousness of his own appeal.

An overview of Gerry's public career reveals the reason behind Jefferson's unease. Nearly everyone agreed that Elbridge Gerry was a man of unquestionable rectitude and principle; yet he invariably managed to bring on himself strident denunciations. Perhaps Abigail Adams explained Gerry as well as anyone when she wrote, "Poor Gerry always had a wrong kink in his head."[31] A brief look at his accomplishments belies any sense of his peculiarity: signer of the Declaration of Independence, member of the Federal Constitutional Convention, minister to France, governor of Massachusetts, and vice president of the United States. An actor in every major drama of the early republic, Gerry would seem to be the epitome of a respectable founder. So why did he arouse such angry feelings among his contemporaries, and why did Jefferson betray so much unease in his letter? The simple explanation is that no one could predict what side he would take on an issue. Even when he did choose a side, Gerry frequently changed his mind.[32] He played an important role in the Continental Congress during the Revolutionary War, but he allowed a minor question of parliamentary privilege to interrupt his service for three critical years (1780–83). Four years later, after calling for a stronger national government, Gerry spent his time at the Constitutional Convention of 1787 objecting to everything that he did not propose.[33] He was the only member to stay for the entire convention but not to sign the Constitution. Once elected to the new Congress, Gerry again changed his tack from Antifederalist to a strong supporter of Hamilton's financial plan and a large stockholder of the United States Bank.[34] Jefferson knew about this. In a "list of paper-men" Jefferson possessed, Gerry was listed as a stockholder who had "avowed it in the presence of Thomas Jefferson."[35] But Gerry's antiratification stance and his refusal to quit his antiparty position for an explicitly Federalist one made him suspect in Federalist circles and prompted Federalist leaders to oppose Gerry's appointment as an envoy to France.[36] Confirming Federalists' worst fears, Gerry eventually split from his fellow envoys and remained in France after they departed, ensuring the lasting enmity of most Federalists. On his return to Boston on 1 October 1798, he was ostracized. As one observer wrote, "The Federalists, by agreement took not the least notice of him as he walked up State Street; not a hat was moved."[37] Jefferson knew how the Federalists were treating Gerry. When Gerry wrote Jefferson asking for political information, Jefferson chose to take a calculated risk to reach out to him. This contrary,

Figure 4. *Elbridge Gerry*, painted by James Barton Longacre, c. 1820. Courtesy of the National Portrait Gallery, Smithsonian Institution.

irascible, inscrutable, antiparty republican became Jefferson's only signifi-cant non-Republican, New England correspondent during the late 1790s—a severe test for Jefferson's hope of revitalizing a union based on affection.

Even as he reached out to Gerry, Jefferson found himself negotiating the shifting grounds of friendship, a relationship undergoing a transformation similar to that of its generic embodiment, the familiar letter.[38] This shift found literal expression in Samuel Johnson's *Dictionary*, first published in 1755. Johnson's definitions of friendship embraced both affective union and practical considerations. The first two definitions emphasized the affective: "state of minds united by mutual benevolence; amity," "highest degree of intimacy." The third neatly balanced between practicality and affection: "favour; personal kindness." And the final two were concerned with practical effects: "assistance; help . . . aptness to unite."[39] In short, Johnson's dictionary staked out two poles of friendship, which embraced everything from disinterested affection to practical aid, and revealed the tension between public and private within the term itself. Friendship as an instrumental relationship looked back to colonial times, when the relationship often played a crucial role in public life. Friendship as an affectionate relationship looked forward to the nineteenth century, when the relationship was primarily conceived of as a private one.

The Revolution had ushered in a new politics that hastened this transformation to a world in which equal access to power was theoretically shared by all. In this world, instrumental friendship was becoming increasingly suspect.[40] At least in theory, friendship was being divested of its instrumental dimension.[41] Or perhaps it would be more accurate to write that friendship was in the process of undergoing that transformation, carrying traces of both the instrumental and the affectionate conceptions. Men were praised for having risen through their own efforts alone, and success in securing patronage from high places, though pursued with as much avidity as ever, became something of an embarrassment.[42]

Throughout his life, Jefferson professed his attachment to the new conception of friendship based not on utility but on affection. As a youth selecting passages for his commonplace book, he found in Hippolytus the central dilemma between affectionate and instrumental friendship expressed: "Man needs should have some certain test set up to try his friends, some touchstone of their hearts, to know each friend whether he be true or false; all men should have two voices, one the voice of honesty, expediency's the other, so would honest confute its knavish opposite, and then we could not be deceived."[43] Jefferson's solution to this was to reveal his own heart. Jefferson selected a pointed passage from Euripides' *Medea*: "May he perish and find no favour, whoso hath not in him honour for his friends, freely unlocking his heart to them. Never shall he be friend of mine."[44] The heart served as both medium and proof of true friendship.

Jefferson's 1786 letter to Maria Cosway in which his heart does battle with his head became, in many ways, a debate about instrumental versus affective friendship. In the role of the heart, he extolled affective friendship in which the heart took preeminent place. Rejecting the idea of instrumental friendships, he wrote, "Wealth, title, office, are no recommendations to my friendship. On the contrary great good qualities are requisite to make amends for their having wealth, title, & office." The head offered a practical case of friendship based on a calculation of gains and costs: "Everything in this world is a matter of calculation. Advance then with caution, the balance in your hand." From this perspective, the head argued that friendship entailed unacceptable risks:

> Friendship is but another name for an alliance with the follies & the misfortune of others. Our own share of miseries is sufficient: why enter then as volunteers into those of another? Is there so little gall poured into our cup that we must needs help to drink that of our neighbor?

But Jefferson's heart spoke for the innate sociability of man: "In a life where we are perpetually exposed to want & accident, yours is a wonderful proposition, to insulate ourselves, to retire from all aid, & to wrap ourselves in the mantle of self-sufficiency! For assuredly nobody will care for him who cares for nobody. But friendship is precious. . . . Let the gloomy monk, sequestered from the world, seek unsocial pleasures in the bottom of his cell." Such monkish behavior, from Jefferson's perspective, was unnatural. The heart established a clear division of labor: "To you [the head] she allotted the field of science; to me that of morals." The heart claimed that the head had no understanding "of sympathy, of benevolence, of gratitude, of justice, of love, of friendship." In contrast, the heart followed the superior wisdom of sentiment: "Morals were too essential to the happiness of man to be risked on the uncertain combinations of the head. She laid their foundation therefore in sentiment, not in science."[45] Although the heart had the last word in the letter, the answer was not so clear in Jefferson's political life.

As part of his commitment to affective friendship, Jefferson attempted to shed that frequent encumbrance of affective friendship, patronage. For example, when asked by Catherine Church Cruger in 1808 to secure a post for her husband, he wrote her, "However gratifying it might be to our private feelings to indulge these by dispensations in particular cases, yet for the mass of society the doctrine of an equal measure to all is of unquestionable value, & I am sure will be approved by our good understanding & disinterested justice."[46] In this conception, friendship had no place in the public world. It was strictly a private affair. Despite these beliefs, when the need arose, Jefferson took full advantage of the powers of patronage, for example, hiring Philip Freneau as a translator at the State Department to induce him to move to Philadelphia and establish a Republican newspaper.[47]

Madison and Jefferson's friendship became so intertwined with political matters that Jefferson felt compelled to write a circular letter as his presidency was ending in March 1809, addressing the issue of patronage: "The friendship which has long subsisted between the [incoming] President of the United States and myself gave me reason to expect, on my retirement from office, that I might often receive applications to interpose with him on behalf of persons desiring appointments. . . . It therefore became necessary for me to lay down as a law for my future conduct never to interpose in any case, either with him or the heads of departments (from whom it must go to him) in any application whatever for office." Jefferson claimed that the major impulse behind this pronouncement was the friendship itself: "Such an abuse of his dispositions towards me would necessarily lead to the loss of them, and to the transforming me from the character of a friend to that of an unreasonable and troublesome solicitor."[48]

Because of his belief in affective and private, rather than instrumental and public, friendship, he argued vehemently that his friendships were too important to be turned to political purposes. In the fall of 1792, when Washington delicately raised the subject of Jefferson's battle with Hamilton, including the emerging political alliances, Jefferson could scarcely contain his anger. His contempt for Hamilton was matched only by his outrage that his "friendships" could be seen as political relationships, arguing that the kind of intrigues under discussion were unimaginable among friends: "As I never had the desire to influence the members, so neither had I any other means than my friendships, which I valued too highly to risk by usurpations on their freedom of judgment, & the conscientious pursuit of their own sense of duty." True friends chose each other freely and acted independently. Any sense of dependency in friendship had to be rejected out of hand. All Jefferson would admit to was an occasional friendly conversation, "the mere enunciations of my sentiments in conversation, and chiefly among those who, expressing the same sentiments, drew mine from me."[49] Even in this, Jefferson made it clear that he was a passive participant, since others "drew" his opinion from him only after they had expressed the same sentiments.

To attempt to form any sort of party would negate the very basis of the relationship for Jefferson, and he disdained any association with political parties. In the wake of the Revolution, most men still saw parties as antithetical to a republican government based on considerations of the public good. When asked which party he supported during the constitutional ratification process, he denied being either a Federalist or an Antifederalist, claiming, "Such an addiction is the last degradation of a free and moral agent. If I could not go to heaven but with a party, I would not go there at all."[50] To throw his lot with either party would corrupt the independence of mind and spirit that he cherished. To confine one's self in such a way threatened to undo the fruits of the Revolution, forcing men once again to kneel to a higher power, even if one of their own making. Party affiliation was simply unimaginable for Jefferson, and he rejected any suggestion of countering the Federalists by building his own political party (even though that is exactly what he would do), refusing to call Republicans a party because "the term is false and degrading."[51]

Jefferson also repeatedly complained that politics was intruding on the private realm of friendship. Writing to Edward Rutledge in June 1797, Jefferson noted, "You and I have formerly seen warm debates and high political passions. But gentleman of different politics would then speak to each other, and separate the business of the Senate from that of society. It is not so now. Men who have been intimate all their lives, cross the street to avoid meeting, and turn their heads another way, lest they should be obliged to touch their hats."[52] Jefferson abhorred disputatious behavior, and he warned his grandchildren against it. He wrote to his grandson to "never [enter] into dispute or argument with another." For Jefferson, nothing good could come of arguing. Only distance from conflict allowed reason to hold sway: "Conviction is the effect of our own dispassionate reasoning, either in solitude, or weighing within ourselves dispassionately what we hear from others standing uncommitted in argument ourselves." It was best to stay away from those who insisted on arguing, "as you would from the infected subjects of yellow fever or pestilence. Consider yourself, when with them, as among the patients of Bedlam needing medical more than moral counsel."[53] Offering similar advice to other grandchildren, Jefferson wrote, "It is a charming thing to be loved by every body: and the way to obtain it is, never quarrel or be angry with any body."[54]

In his letter to Rutledge, Jefferson rejected the idea that politics could intrude on his friendships. He claimed that he "never considered a difference of opinion in politics, in religion, in philosophy, as cause for withdrawing from a friend."[55] Jefferson's tolerance, though, was based on a distinction between opinion and principle. And in the 1790s, every difference of opinion seemed to be a difference of principle.[56] Despite his protestations to Rutledge, Jefferson would turn to his friends for political help, leading to a complex intermingling of the private world of friendship and the public world of politics. Although he claimed to want to separate the business of politics from that of society, his reliance on friendship would make that impossible.[57]

"Profession of my political faith"
Friendship and Politics

Jefferson's letter to Gerry contained a passage that revealed the complicated intermingling of the personal and the political at the heart of both the character that he created for himself and the political sphere that he imagined. Although warm and spontaneous effusions of the heart were supposed to be the mark of the familiar letter and friendship, Jefferson opened the body of his letter with a curiously stiff and formal pronouncement. To confound all future "calumnies," Jefferson proposed to make to Gerry a "profession of my political faith."[58] Jefferson typically made such professions at times of great stress when he felt compelled to reach out to potential allies to solidify a political friendship.[59] His professions revealed the central problem in his use of a private relationship for public purposes: achieving a viable concept of political friendship without corrupting friendship's basis in sincere affection. Breaking the rules of the familiar letter, Jefferson's pronouncement called attention to his difficulties in reconciling his desired affective union with the dictates of political party building. It even ran afoul of his beloved Laurence Sterne, who complained about letter writers who "surprize me with an Essay . . . to me inconsiderate Soul that I am, who never yet knew what it was to speak or write one premeditated word, such an intercourse would be an abomination; & I would as soon go and commit fornication with the Moabites, as have a hand in any thing of this kind unless written in that careless irregularity of a good and an easy heart."[60] His "profession" threatened to reveal that his appeal was not based on affection and that he was not a disinterested public servant—that he was, in fact, a party intriguer.[61] Worst of all, his profession seemed to refute his claims of friendship with Gerry, for close friends would have no need to catalogue their principles to each other.[62]

Demonstrating the seriousness, in his mind, of what he was doing, Jefferson began his profession with a formal invocation: "I do then, with sincere zeal, wish an inviolable preservation of our present federal constitution, according to the true sense in which it was adopted by the States, that in which it was advocated by it's friends." Even as he pronounced his loyalty to the Constitution, he was shaping his profession so that Gerry would concur. Jefferson's assertion that he supported the Constitution as it was adopted by the states, not the people, was technically correct, since the Constitution had to be ratified by individual states. By emphasizing the primacy of the states, though, Jefferson was implicitly rejecting the Federalist calls for a stronger national government. Jefferson claimed that his interpretation was based on the "true sense" of the Constitution "advocated by it's friends." He then chose a curious locution—"and not that which it's enemies apprehended, who therefore became it's enemies." The original supporters of ratification were largely the same men who now supported a strong national government. Jefferson's awkward phrasing reflected the fact that these "enemies" were originally considered the Constitution's strongest friends. Jefferson announced that he was against the "monarchising" of these enemies who hoped gradually to "worm out the elective principle" and to concentrate all power in the executive branch. His profession continued with the standard litany of republican values: condemnation of an increased public debt, of the multiplication of offices, of a standing army or a larger navy, and of entanglements with Europe. He was for free commerce, freedom of religion, and the progress

of science. He obliquely criticized the Alien and Sedition Acts by de-
nouncing "all violations of the constitution to silence by force and not by
reason the complaints or criticisms, just or unjust, of our citizens against the
conduct of their agents."[63]

To this point, Jefferson's profession, half diatribe and half republican
catechism, was incendiary only in tone. Men of either party would have
avowed most of its principles. Jefferson saved the most difficult issue for
the end of his profession. While Jefferson admitted that he was "a sincere
well-wisher to the success of the French revolution," he had "not been
insensible under the atrocious depredations they have committed on our
commerce." "The first object of my heart," Jefferson solemnly intoned,
"is my own country," addressing indirectly the many attacks accusing
him of rampant Francophilia by referring back to his heart, the symbolic
incarnation of his private, sincere self. Jefferson disclaimed even "one
farthing of interest . . . one fibre of attachment" to any other nation,
except "in proportion as they are more or less friendly to us." After denying any undue attachment to France, Jefferson stated that, "though
deeply feeling the injuries of France, I did not think war the surest means
of redressing them. I did believe, that a mission sincerely disposed to preserve peace, would obtain for us a peaceable and honorable settlement and
retribution." Jefferson then made the crucial turn in this long list of political principles by calling on Gerry to corroborate his version of events:
"I appeal to you to say, whether this might not have been obtained, if
either of your colleagues had been of the same sentiment with yourself,"
a subtle attempt to turn a defense of himself into an appeal for Gerry to
privately corroborate his account (Jefferson's call for a public corroboration
would come later).[64]

Jefferson's reliance on statements of principle as the catalyst for potential alliances revealed his conception of political friendship, a relationship
charged with tensions between practical political considerations and ide-
alistic notions of affective union. For Jefferson, despite his many claims to
the contrary, friendship based on shared political principles necessarily
linked friendship and politics. When Jefferson declared his principles in
letters, the declaration functioned rhetorically as Jefferson's expression of
his true, "private" self and an invitation of political friendship, in which
he paradoxically offered an affective union based on that most rational
and public of grounds, a list of political principles. In fact, Jefferson far
more often expressed strong sentiments and feelings in letters to potential
political allies than in letters to close friends. In his letter to Gerry, Jefferson
"unbosomed" himself and apologized for his "strong feelings"—his words
contrasted sharply with his long correspondence with Madison, which
rarely made an explicit reference to their friendship.[65] In Jefferson's attempts to build political alliances, though, feeling and principle became

virtually identical, and friendship incorporated both. Indeed, friendship served as the threshold of legitimate political activity.[66]

This connection of friendship to principle allowed Jefferson to have an expansive conception of the relationship that included all who held similar principles. In other words, all citizens who held the proper republican (i.e., Republican) principles were, imaginatively, Jefferson's friends, creating a union based on the affective bonds that Jefferson valued so highly—as long as all believed in the proper principles. He could tolerate no deviance from "the principles of '75." As Jefferson wrote ominously in 1798 as political tensions began to run high, "Those who are conscious of no change in themselves have nothing to fear in the long run."[67]

As partisan differences grew in the spring of 1797, Jefferson was willing to recognize that political differences were "inseparable from the different constitutions of the human mind, and that degree of freedom which permits unrestrained expression." He was even willing to countenance these differences to an extent, remarking that "political dissension is doubtless a less evil than the lethargy of despotism." Jefferson tolerated this dissension only grudgingly, though. Calling these divisions "artificial lines," he wrote, "Still [political dissension] is a great evil, and it would be as worthy the efforts of the patriot as of the philosopher, to exclude it's influence, if possible, from social life."[68] Though Jefferson claimed to want to eliminate dissension from social life, his conflation of friendship, principle, and politics made such a goal impossible.[69]

Jefferson's combination of friendship and politics also created problems for his own character. Relying on supposedly affective relationships for instrumental purposes, Jefferson constantly risked undermining the character that he constructed for himself by his problematic use of private emotions for public purposes.[70] The difficulties inherent in Jefferson's mixture of friendship and politics were never more apparent than in his letter to John Adams in the waning days of 1796. Adams's victory in the recent presidential election seemed assured, and Jefferson decided to write a letter to his old friend in order to smooth away any potential ill will from their political opposition in recent years. Jefferson wrote to Adams motivated by an almost inescapable combination of friendship and politics. With the retirement of Washington, the Federalists had lost their greatest weapon in the battle over the nation's future, and the political calculus had changed. Although Jefferson had increasingly come to suspect Adams of holding unrepublican views, he still had some hope that the president-elect could be persuaded to recommit himself to the proper principles. Revealing the fluid nature of politics in the 1790s, Jefferson wrote, "There is reason to believe that he is detached from Hamilton and there is a possibility he may swerve from his politics."[71] Any influence that Jefferson hoped to have within Adams's administration depended on his continuing friendship with Adams. Political events had pitted them against one another on other occasions. Jefferson now faced the delicate task of reassuring Adams that Jefferson's feelings of friendship had not changed, in the hope that Adams would feel similarly.

Refusing to acknowledge any grounds of potential difficulty in his friendship with Adams (a tactic he would later employ in the letter to Gerry), he placed the blame for any problems between them on outsiders. In other words, the public was intruding on the private realm of friendship. "The public and the papers have been much occupied lately in placing us in a point of opposition to each other," he wrote. "I trust with confidence that less of it has been felt by ourselves personally." From the disavowal of personal enmity, Jefferson moved to a larger disavowal of the political world in general. He noted his own distance from political infighting: "In the retired canton where I am, I learn little of what is passing: pamphlets I see never: papers but a few; and the fewer the happier." And he stressed his attachment to his rustic life at Monticello. He claimed that domestic society contained all he needed. "My neighbors . . . see my occupations and my attachment to them," he wrote. "I leave to others the sublime delights of riding in the storm, better pleased with sound sleep and a warm berth below, with the society of neighbors, friends and fellow-laborers of the earth, than of spies and sycophants. No one then will congratulate you with purer disinterestedness than myself." He ended the letter with a call to look beyond temporary differences and to remember the deeper basis of their affection and esteem for one another forged during the Revolution (also similar to his letter to Gerry). In short, Jefferson professed his own continued friendship and hoped for similar feelings from Adams.

Much as Jefferson's profession of political faith threatened to undermine the rhetoric of friendship that he employed with Gerry, his letter to Adams contained statements that unhinged his neat rhetorical opposition between his domestic retirement and the outside political world, an eruption of politics into his letter that undermined his claims about himself, his "pure disinterestedness" in wishing for Adams's success. After claiming to see few newspapers, Jefferson offered a succinct and savvy analysis of electoral politics to show that he never doubted that Adams would triumph (not because of any inherent superiority in Adams as a candidate but because of the regional logic of the electoral vote). In doing so, he revealed himself as a man thoroughly conversant with the latest political intelligence. Later, alongside his professed attachment to his secluded society, politics once again forced its way onto the page. Alluding to Hamilton's plot to place Charles Cotesworth Pinckney in the presidency over Adams, Jefferson wrote, "You may be cheated of your succession by a trick worthy of your arch-friend of New York who has been able to make of your real friends tools to defeat their and your just wishes."

His remark revealed how thoroughly entangled friendship was with the political world of the 1790s. Finally, in disdaining any desire to exercise political power, Jefferson still managed to insert his own wishes, if obliquely, for how the president-elect should act. Jefferson wrote, "I devoutly wish you may be able to shun for us this war by which our agriculture, commerce and credit will be destroyed." Despite his encomium to private life, Jefferson repeatedly revealed himself as thoroughly enmeshed in the public world of politics.

In the letter, he unwittingly revealed the difficulties that his instrumental use of private emotions created when discussing his feelings about his loss of the presidency. "I have never one single moment expected a different issue [than Adams's victory]," he wrote, " and though I know I shall not be believed, yet it is not the less true that I have never wished for it."[72] His lament that he would not be believed highlighted the problem that bedeviled him repeatedly: an overarching problem of sincerity that Jefferson faced in his attempt to combine politics with friendship. Friendship provided emotional sustenance precisely because of its separation from concerns of utility. To combine it with politics threatened to undermine this emotional attachment in favor of an instrumental one. On the other hand, given Jefferson's intense dislike of parties, friendship offered a chance to organize politically along legitimate lines based on affection and benevolence. The crux of the problem was how to use friendship and, at the same time, keep it uncorrupted from its association with politics.

The fate of the letter revealed the difficulty of Jefferson's task. Despite his "sincere" avowals of friendship, Jefferson did not send this letter to Adams. He sent it to James Madison, not simply a friend but a political ally, "for your [Madison's] perusal, not only that you may possess the actual dispositions between us, but that if anything should render the delivery ineligible in your opinion, you may return it to me." He wrote that he had not sent the letter to Adams immediately "under the discouragement of a despair of making him believe I could be sincere in it," a statement that again highlighted Jefferson's difficulties. In effect, Jefferson asked Madison to determine if Jefferson's avowals of friendship seemed sincere.

He stated this concern even more forcefully in a letter a few months later to Elbridge Gerry. "I cannot help fearing, that it is impossible for Mr. Adams to believe that the state of my mind is what it really is; that he thinks I view him as an obstacle in my way," he fretted. Jefferson continued in the same letter: "I have no supernatural power to impress truth on the mind of another, nor he any to discover that the estimate he may form, on a just view of the human mind as generally constituted, may not be just in its application to a special constitution. This may be a source of private uneasiness to us; I honestly confess that it is to me at this time."[73]

Leaving aside the difficulty of assessing "special constitutions" such as Jefferson's, his sincerity remained very much at issue.

Madison's reply revealed the delicate nature of Jefferson's letter. Madison offered six arguments against sending the letter, reasons that increasingly moved from concerns of friendship to concerns of politics, from a simple desire to maintain the relationship to far more instrumental purposes that called attention to the problematic grounds of Jefferson's appeal. Madison himself noted the strained nature of Jefferson's performance: "There is perhaps a general air on the letter which betrays the difficulty of your situation in writing it, and it is uncertain what the impression might be resulting from this appearance." He also pointed out the claims of the band of "friends" who had worked for Jefferson: "The tenderness due to the zealous & active promoters of your election, makes it doubtful whether, their anxieties & exertions ought to be depreciated by any thing implying the unreasonableness of them." Madison even went so far as to mention obliquely the party organization: "Considering the probability that Mr. A.s course of administration may force an opposition to it from the Republican quarter, & the general uncertainty of the posture which our affairs may take, there may be real embarrassments from giving written possession to him, of the degree of compliment & confidence which your personal delicacy & friendship have suggested." In other words, concerns of "friendship" were to be sacrificed to those of politics, a rejection of the alleged purpose of the letter. With this final argument, he revealed the deeply problematic combination of friendship and politics. In a final sentence that revealed the somewhat deceptive nature of the entire enterprise, Madison told Jefferson that if he did send the letter, "it may not be amiss to alter the date of it."[74]

The intricacies of this exchange went to the heart of the problem for Jefferson in a politically divided world. He thought of his friendships as private, but in the absence of party legitimacy, he also relied on his friendships to achieve political goals. To do this, he crafted a character for himself that attempted to deny his participation in political life, a character that collapsed questions of political utility into the affectionate union of friendship, where disagreement and insincerity were unknown. This unstable compound, political friendship, placed increasingly difficult demands on Jefferson. The private world of personal relationships was supposed to represent his true self. To make larger political appeals based on that private self threatened to undermine it, though, by calling into question its sincerity. And when he attempted to prove his sincerity, as in the letter to Adams, the effort frequently backfired. Adams himself later complained of Jefferson's "want of sincerity."[75]

In the end, Jefferson followed Madison's advice, never sending the letter to Adams. Instead, Madison handled the entire matter in a different manner, which took advantage of the generic conventions of the familiar letter in which the author was thought to reveal his true self. Rather than any direct communication with Adams, Madison showed Benjamin Rush a letter Jefferson had written him on 17 December 1796, in which Jefferson wrote that in the event of a tie vote between Adams and himself, Adams should be given preference over himself. As expected, Rush relayed this information to Adams, who, greatly pleased, wrote to his wife, Abigail, "Mr. Jefferson's Letter to Mr. Madison was yesterday in the mouth of everyone."[76] Madison thus avoided attempting to communicate Jefferson's sentiments directly to Adams, instead relying on a supposedly "private" letter to carry the message indirectly, a method that offered greater proof of sincerity precisely because the letter was not intended for public display.[77] Madison's solution revealed the labyrinthine complexity of navigating between public and private life in the early republic.[78] With Gerry, though, Jefferson was forced to make the appeal himself, a task that once again put his sincerity to the test.

"As members of the same family"
Affective Union

Jefferson's letter to Gerry also revealed the central place that friendship held in Jefferson's vision for the nation. The letter provides a window into his hopes for reshaping the national polity based on ties of affection, hopes that he would try to persuade Gerry to foster. As always in the letter, Jefferson's first goal was to reaffirm his friendship. In responding to Gerry's request for political information, Jefferson again seized the opportunity to promote an alliance. "As a proof of my entire confidence in you," Jefferson wrote, "I shall give it [political information] fully and candidly."[79] Given the undeveloped nature of national politics, sharing political information played a crucial role in building and maintaining political relationships in the early republic. Jefferson's offer of information implicitly placed Gerry within the Republican circle of friends, a position Jefferson hoped he would accept.[80]

Jefferson then gave a reasonably accurate, if predictably Republican, account of the impact on American relations with France after President Adams revealed the XYZ affair (which involved an attempt by the French foreign minister, Charles Maurice de Talleyrand-Périgord, to extract a bribe for himself as well as a loan for his nation before he would open negotiations with the American diplomatic mission to resolve the rising hostilities between the two nations).[81] He described a rising tide of popular concern over the government's overly aggressive position toward France. Meetings on the subject had spread "like a wildfire." But the first dispatches from the American envoys undid everything. "The odiousness of corruption" stirred the people to indignation. Denying that X,Y, and Z were sanctioned by the French government, Jefferson regretted that the people "did not permit themselves even to suspect that the turpitude of private swindlers might mingle itself unobserved."[82]

Jefferson left unspoken his increasing desperation at the political turn of events. War with France seemed imminent, an event that he believed would push America irrevocably into the arms of the British and ruin the young nation's republican character.[83] He proposed his own desperate measures in response, including one suggestion that the president's discretionary authority be limited and his Kentucky Resolutions, which offered vague and menacing intimations of how far Jefferson would be willing to go to try to halt the Federalists, even as he attempted to hide all traces of his authorship in fear of the Sedition Act and his political enemies.[84]

Jefferson wrote the letter to Gerry in the wake of the Virginia and Kentucky Resolutions, but Jefferson presented a far more moderate front to his correspondent. He betrayed some disappointment that Gerry had not negotiated a treaty when he remained in France after the departure of his colleagues, even though Gerry was not empowered to negotiate without the other commissioners. "It was hoped by the lovers of peace," he wrote, "that a project of treaty would have been prepared, *ad referendum*, on principles which would have satisfied our citizens, and overawed any bias of our government towards a different policy."[85] Rather than blame him, however, Jefferson assured Gerry that his abrupt recall as well as "the suggestions of the person [Secretary of State Timothy Pickering] charged with your despatches, and his probable misrepresentations of the real wishes of the American people," had prevented these hopes. Despite Pickering's imputations, Jefferson optimistically predicted, Gerry's dispatches showed France's sincere wishes for peace and would help turn the tide against the Federalists. Combined with the effects of the Alien and Sedition Acts in the South and the tax gatherer in the East, "the unquestionable republicanism of the American mind will break through the mist under which it has been clouded."[86]

Jefferson also denied that the Republicans had abused Gerry. Then, he unfolded a possible area of criticism that served as an invitation to criticize the Federalists' anti-French position:

Unless we were so to construe their [Republicans] wishes that you had more boldly co-operated in a project of a treaty, and would more explicitly state, whether there was in your colleagues that flexibility, which persons earnest after peace would have practiced? Whether, on the contrary, their demeanor was not cold, reserved, and distant, at least, if not backward? And whether, if they had yielded to those informal conferences which Taleyrand [*sic*] seems to have courted, the liberal accommodation you suppose might not have been effected, even with their agency?[87]

He accused his opponents of failing to offer the kind of open and honest communication that he proffered and claimed that their "cold" and "distant" behavior accounted for the failure to reach a treaty agreement with France (an unsurprising analysis from someone who saw the great success of the Revolution in emotional terms). By speaking of Republican criticisms in the third person, Jefferson distanced himself from them, even as he invited Gerry to respond with an interpretation favorable to the Republican cause.

Additionally, by posing these "possible" criticisms as questions, Jefferson was seeking a politically useful response. Hewing to his avoidance of direct political appeals, he denied any political motivations behind his request for this information; instead, he called on Gerry to reply for "your fellow-citizens." "It may be in your power to save them . . . by full communications and unrestrained details," wrote Jefferson, "postponing motives of delicacy to those of duty." Asking Gerry to reply to his fellow citizens about hypothetical questions actually posed by Republicans, Jefferson, in effect, collapsed the distinction between Republicans and citizens. He couched his plea in a way that allowed him to prod Gerry to challenge the Federalist version of events for the sake of Gerry's fellow citizens, a plea that carefully screened Jefferson from looking like a party intriguer. In this guise, Jefferson suggested that Gerry's silence was not a high-minded refusal to engage in party maneuvering but a failure to do his duty. Jefferson implored Gerry "to come forward independently; to take your stand on the high ground of your own character; to disregard calumny, and to be borne above it on the shoulders of your grateful fellow citizens; or to sink into the humble oblivion, to which the Federalists . . . have secretly condemned you."[88] Jefferson cloaked his pragmatic political goals behind a high-minded call to Gerry to defend his own character, making it a duty to the people rather than a partisan appeal (and precisely the sort of appeal that would motivate an antiparty man such as Gerry). The Federalists, Jefferson wrote, were the ones who had "ulcerated against you." He claimed that they would still be attacking Gerry if they did not fear that he might be provoked into writing a self-justification that would undercut the Federalist campaign for war with France. The Federalists, Jefferson warned Gerry, will "crush you for ever" as soon as "they can do it without danger to themselves."[89]

Jefferson's analysis of the situation could not help but emphasize the divided political landscape, a landscape that seemed to offer no possibility for the heartfelt unity that he believed was America's revolutionary legacy.

His attempt to appeal to Gerry as a friend, rather than as a political ally, made perfect sense for a man who continually reminded all his correspondents of his vast preference for the comforts of domestic life, particularly during the late 1790s, when political tensions seemed to be spiraling out of control. "No other society gives me now any satisfaction," he wrote in 1800, "as no other is founded in sincere affection."[90] According to Jefferson, the domestic sphere was the one place that satisfied his craving for "natural feelings." In 1792, he wrote to his daughter Martha of "the desire of being at home once more, and of exchanging labour, envy, and malice for ease, domestic occupation, and domestic love and society."[91] In 1798, he wrote again to Martha about the felicity of her own situation: "For you to feel all the happiness of your quiet situation, you should know the rancorous passions which tear every breast here, even of the sex which should be a stranger to them. Politics and party hatreds destroy the happiness of every being here. They seem like salamanders, to consider fire as their element."[92] When Maria became engaged in 1797, Jefferson expressed to Martha delight about the family's future domestic circle: "I now see our fireside formed into a groupe, no one member of which has a fibre in their composition which can ever produce any jarring or jealousies among us. No irregular passions, no dangerous bias, which may render problematical the future fortunes and happiness of our descendants." But whenever he invoked the bliss of domestic life, it almost inevitably led to a discussion of the nastiness of political life. In the same letter, he immediately contrasted their domestic tranquillity with the political world: "When I look to the ineffable pleasures of my family society, I become more and more disgusted with the jealousies, the hatred, and the rancorous and malignant passions of this scene, and lament my having ever again been drawn into public view. Tranquillity is now my object. I have seen enough of political honors to know that they are but splendid torments."[93] Jefferson's vision of affective union threatened to unravel in that other, crueler world, where his private self could find no place.[94]

Just as friendship carried within it the seeds of political action, though, domestic life (in which friendship played an integral role) was more than a foil for the rancorous nature of politics—it carried within it the means to remake the nation. The familial, domestic world of Monticello was not just his source of happiness and peace but his model for the nation. Jefferson's solution to the rancorous world of politics was not to retreat into the harmonious domestic sphere of private life but to remake the political world in the image of his private world. His conception of friendship would be at the core of this transformative vision. The challenge for Jefferson as he sought to counter the political machinations of his enemies was to broaden his notion of friendship until it could literally subsume

politics, wrapping all Americans under the mantle of benevolent, sentimental, and affective union. It was a sleight of hand worthy of Machiavelli
and a political plan worthy of Sterne.

Following Scottish moral sense theorists, Jefferson and others saw affection not simply as a private emotion but as a social one that could bind
society together.[95] Family and state in the eighteenth century were seen as
part of the same continuum: the same relationships were appropriate for
each. Society was simply family writ large, and marriage, seen as a kind
of exalted friendship, became a model for the kind of political union
based on affection for which Jefferson hoped.[96] Rethinking political life
in terms of his idealized domestic society at the height of partisan conflict
in 1798, Jefferson wrote, "As to myself I sincerely wish that the whole
Union may accommodate their interests to each other, and play into their
hands mutually as members of the same family."[97] To Rush in 1803, he
criticized people who had an overly narrow conception of those who fall
"within the circle of benevolence." He claimed that the universality of
Christian charity extended "not only to kindred and friends, to neighbors
and countrymen . . . but to all mankind, gathering them into one family,
under the bonds of love, charity, peace, common wants and common
aims."[98] For him, society offered no higher pleasure than such concor-
dance, and he claimed in 1797 that "social harmony" was "the first of
human felicities," and one that he hoped to share with the Union, even as
political conflict seemed to threaten the nation itself.[99]

Jefferson's ideal was exacting, though. To achieve domestic harmony
on a national scale, Jefferson was willing to think in drastic terms. In a
letter to William Short discussing the French Revolution in 1793, he wrote,
"Rather than it should have failed, I would have seen half the earth des-
olated. Were there but an Adam & an Eve left in every country, & left free,
it would be better than as it now is."[100] In reimagining a new beginning,
Jefferson did not imagine a world without nations. Rather, he imagined
each nation beginning anew. In this prelapsarian view of innocence, the
boundaries of the family and the nation would become coterminous, at
last leading to the perfect harmony—national and familial—that Jefferson
envisioned for America.

Although Jefferson's conception of the nation would seem to offer some
opportunities for the participation of women, his imagined national political family had no role for them. Even in the domestic sphere, Jefferson
counseled submission to patriarchal authority and counted on his daughters to ensure the tranquillity of his private life. He advised his daughters
time and again to sacrifice their own needs and desires to those of their
husbands. When one of his daughters married, Jefferson told her, "You
new condition will call for an abundance of little sacrifices. . . . The happiness of your life depends now on continuing to please a single person."[101]

In the political sphere, women were supposed to have no presence at all. While in France, he complained of the politically active women there: "All the world is now politically mad. . . . Society is spoilt by it." In America, he argued, women understood their proper role, which was to promote harmony in the domestic sphere, not to foment disagreement in the political one: "But our good ladies, I trust, have been too wise to wrinkle their foreheads with politics. They are contented to soothe & calm the minds of their husbands returning ruffled from political debate. They have the good sense to value domestic happiness above all other." When women did become politically active, Jefferson saw it not only as a breach of the political order but of the natural one. In comparing French with American women, Jefferson called it "a comparison of Amazons and Angels," heaven apparently being associated with a life free from the taint of politics (an unsurprising view given Jefferson's expressions of distaste for political life).[102] Even from this point of view, though, women were effectively silenced by their elevation. Although Jefferson claimed to envision the nation as one family, his actual conception was closer to the notion of the political nation as a brotherhood, a view that relied on gender to construct equality among white men, although an equality built largely on the backs of the excluded. Paradoxically, Jefferson's expansive vision of the political participation of white males seemed to depend on a corresponding subordination of other groups, such as women.[103]

African Americans suffered a similar fate in Jefferson's familial imagination. He could envision no role in his nation for other races that did not place the different races in a state of war with one another.[104] As with women, he found reasons based in nature to exclude blacks. In *Notes on the State of Virginia*, he wrote of "a difference fixed in nature." Consider the "fine mixtures of red and white" in a white person's face. Is it not better suited for "the expression of every passion by greater or less suffusions of colour" than the "eternal monotony, which reigns in the countenances, that immovable veil of black which covers all the emotions of the other race?"[105] Jefferson's polity was predicated on the sharing of emotion. Black skin, that "eternal monotony" that "covers all the emotions," left blacks out of the affective union of his imagination.[106]

Jefferson used his first inaugural address to project the harmonious union of his imagination. His speech is instructive in both its similarities to and differences from the letter to Gerry. Speaking publicly at a time when his principles were triumphant, Jefferson identified his personal beliefs with the will of the nation, so that his own voice became the "voice of the nation . . . united in common efforts for the common good."[107] His private declarations allowed little room for such ventriloquism, because they occurred before outcomes were known and forced Jefferson into a more ambiguous and uncomfortable role. The easy confidence of the inaugural was in marked contrast to the strained nature of Jefferson's letter to Gerry, where similar claims smacked of partisan intrigue. In his inaugurals, Jefferson could legitimately project a vision of a nation at least symbolically united. The first inaugural also contained a statement of principles, the rational ground, as always, for Jefferson's affective union, except that those principles were, for Jefferson, no longer personal but "the essential principles of our Government." These principles were nothing less than the principles of 1776, forming "the creed of our political faith, the text of civic instruction, the touchstone by which to try the services of those we trust; and should we wander from them in moments of error or of alarm, let us hasten to retrace our steps and to regain the road which alone leads to peace, liberty, and safety."

In his second inaugural, as the Federalists continued to fade from power, Jefferson found himself presiding over precisely the kind of affective union that he had always imagined. He confidently predicted the return of all Americans to the "union of sentiment." He could not help but project forward to the moment when "truth, reason, and their own interests, will at length prevail, will gather them into the folds of their country, and will complete their entire union of opinion, which gives to a nation the blessing of harmony, and the benefit of all its strength."[108]

When Jefferson enumerated his basic principles for government in his first inaugural, he gave friendship a prominent place, both implicitly and explicitly. Implicitly, he revealed the expansive conception of friendship that he had developed in his remark, "We are all republicans, we are all federalists," inviting Federalists to join with the Republicans in a union based on "harmony and affection," to admit their ties of consanguinity to the all-embracing Jeffersonian family. Calling the political differences between the two parties differences of opinion, not principle, he wrote, "We have called by different names brethren of the same principle." Jefferson blamed the recent political differences not on differences among Americans but on disturbances from abroad, noting that "it was not wonderful that the agitation of the billows should reach even this distant and peaceful shore." His election would allow a return to the type of affective unity that had been the supposed hallmark of the American Revolution, and he called on his fellow citizens to "unite with one heart and one mind. Let us restore to social intercourse that harmony and affection without which liberty and even life itself are but dreary things." As with the revolutionary uprising, the union would be all the stronger because it was not coerced. He noted with satisfaction, "I believe this . . . the strongest Government on earth. I believe it the only one where every man, at the call of the law, would fly to the standard of the law, and would meet invasions of the public order as his own personal concern."[109] According to this vision, affection had triumphed over discord.

Jefferson's public world was at last coming into conformity with his private one.

Jefferson's first inaugural had dark undertones, though. The political battles of the 1790s were too important and too close for him to be able to forget them. The threat of political discord always loomed over the horizon, and his words were not as conciliatory as they seemed. Although virtually all Americans could subscribe to the principles of federalism and republicanism, any discussion of the specific meanings of those words quickly revealed the vastly different meanings that they could hold for people. Jefferson's first inaugural made it clear what his beliefs were. His comments were a rejection of the political actions and beliefs of the Federalists, and his offer of political reconciliation was as much a gesture to cast off the principles of the Federalists as it was to embrace the American people. He wrote revealingly in one letter, "If we can hit on the true line . . . which may conciliate the honest part of those who were called Federalists, . . . I shall hope to . . . obliterate, or rather to unite the names of federalists & republicans."[110] Although quickly retreating from the idea of obliteration, the word made clear that his intention was not conciliation. As he wrote on another occasion, "Where the principle of difference is as substantial, and as strongly pronounced as between the republicans and monocrats of our country, I hold it as honorable to take a firm and decided part, and as immoral to pursue a middle line, as between the parties of honest men and rogues, into which every country is divided."[111]

Jefferson was prepared to cast out those who failed to meet his criteria. His vision of political union based on bonds of affection had no place for political disagreement. Only one party represented the nation. On the eve of the War of 1812, with the Federalists threatening to rise from the ashes once again, Jefferson wrote: "For the republicans are the *nation*. . . . The last hope of human liberty in this world rests on us."[112] For him, New England's attachment to the Federalists simply was not "natural," and he repeatedly referred to it as a kind of sickness, likening it to "an epidemic," "taint," and "gangrene."[113] He maintained a strict distinction between the New England people and their leaders, who fostered "the delusion of the people."[114] Lapsing into the language of dogma when discussing his foes, he talked of "apostacy" and "heresies," recasting Federalists as foreigners and contrasting them with his ideal of "pure Americanism."[115] As he waited anxiously for a resolution to the deadlocked election of 1800, he wrote his daughter in January 1801, "There is such a mixture of the bad passions of the heart that one feels themselves in an enemy's country."[116] At times, he even considered other American states as foreign.[117] Writing in 1797, he complained that the Federalists were largely a "faction composed of English subjects residing among us."[118] Less than a month later, Jefferson wrote that he wanted a "divorce" from both England and France and wished for "an ocean of fire between us and the old world," revealing a familial conception not just of the nation but of the relationship among nations.[119] The dark side of Jefferson's reliance on friendship was a refusal to recognize the legitimacy of any political opposition. His belief in affective union served only to heighten the political differences that it was supposed to heal.

"The slipperiness of human reason"

Jeffersonian Sincerity

At the end of the letter to Gerry, Jefferson stumbled again on the problem of sincerity that shadowed his conception of political friendship. He apologized for his "passionate" feelings: "Pardon me, my dear Sir, if my expressions are strong. My feelings are so much more so, that it is with difficulty I reduce them even to the tone I use." In this most carefully crafted and controlled letter, Jefferson made a final attempt to prove his friendship through a supposed inability to control the warm feelings of his heart. He then went on to explain to Gerry that two courses had presented themselves when he sat down to write this letter, "either to say nothing or everything; for half confidences are not in my character," emphasizing yet again that there was no calculation in his address. "I could not hesitate that which was due to you," he wrote, driving the point home one final time, "I have unbosomed myself fully; and it will certainly be highly gratifying if I receive like confidence from you."[120] Claiming to have bared himself before Gerry, Jefferson asked Gerry to reciprocate.

Even as Jefferson made these final efforts to achieve political friendship, though, he attempted to destroy the record of it. He repeatedly asked Gerry at the end of the letter "to burn the 2d and 3d leaves . . . which, though sacredly conformable to my firm belief, yet would be galling to some, and expose me to illiberal attacks." And he ended this most personal of letters with the line, "I need not add my signature." Even as Jefferson attempted to share his private "character," an act that was crucial to his republican ideals of affective union, he anxiously retreated from his brief moment of self-display. At the end, he wrote, "And did we ever expect to see the day, when, breathing nothing but sentiments of love to our country and it's freedom and happiness, our correspondence must be as secret as if we were hatching it's destruction!"[121]

With his final lines, Jefferson raised the previously unmentioned possibility that the two men might differ, a potentially devastating blow to his political goals. He wrote, "I know too well the texture of the human mind, and the slipperiness of human reason, to consider differences of opinion otherwise than differences of form and feature. Integrity of views more than their soundness, is the basis of esteem."[122] Coming on the heels of Jefferson's "unbosoming," his remarks threw into stark relief the complications at the core of Jefferson's ideas about political friendship, with its intermingling of public and private. He claimed that political differences were the inevitable result of the "slipperiness" of reason, the opaqueness inherent in all transactions. Differences, Jefferson opined, were not of principle but merely of form or feature. What provided the grounds for determining this? The decisive factor was "integrity of views more than their soundness"—in other words, sincerity provided a basis for resolving these differences. As previously noted, though, sincerity was as much problem as solution when used for political purposes. Jefferson embraced the new ideal of friendship as an affective, noninstrumental, private relationship; however, he used friendships in an instrumental, public way that undermined his affective conception. When triumphant, Jefferson could paper over such political conundrums, but Jefferson's appeal to Gerry offered no such refuge. In that situation, the "integrity" of his views would always be at question.

"The Revolution of Sentiment"

Postscript

Jefferson succeeded in his larger task. His election as president in what he called the "Revolution of 1800" confirmed his faith in the American people and his hopes for the nation. And Gerry? Did Jefferson's efforts succeed with him, or did they reveal problems in Jefferson's political vision? Gerry did become a Republican, although not because of Jefferson's entreaties. In the crucial election of 1800, even as Gerry ran on the Republican ticket for governor of Massachusetts, he voted for Adams for president. Perhaps most tellingly, he waited more than two years before responding to Jefferson's letter.[123]

In victory, Jefferson was inclined to consider Gerry's conduct generously. When Gerry finally did write to Jefferson in 1801, giving a long account of his version of the XYZ affair (which no longer mattered), Jefferson replied that his original suggestions to Gerry were based on his understanding of "the southern pulse. I suspect that of the north was different and decided your conduct; and perhaps it has been as well. If the

Figure 5. Newspaper tally of the 1800 electoral ballot. Courtesy of The Library of Virginia. This tally of the electoral college votes in the presidential election of 1800 reveals the political circumstances that prompted Jefferson to reach out to Gerry. Jefferson was elected by the narrowest of margins—without a single electoral vote from New England.

RETURN OF THE VOTES
Of the STATES, as far as received, for
PRESIDENT
AND
VICE-PRESIDENT.

STATES.	Adams	Jefferſon	Pinckney	Burr	Scattering
N. Hampſhire	6		6		
Maſſachuſetts	16		16		
Rhode Iſland	4		2		2
Connecticut	9		9		
Vermont	4		4		
New York		12		12	
New Jerſey	7		7		
Pennſnylvania	7	8	7	8	
Delaware	3		3		
Maryland	5	5	5	5	
Virginia		21		21	
N. Carolina	4	8	4	8	
S. Carolina		8		8	
Georgia		4		4	
Kentucky					
Tenneſſee					
	65	66	6	66	

revolution of sentiment has been later, it has perhaps been not less sure."[124] Although calling the New England leadership "incurable," he claimed that "your people will rise again." And he still courted Gerry as a leader on whom he could depend: "You, my friend, are destined to rally them again under their former banner, and when called to the post, exercise it with firmness and with inflexible adherence to your own principles."[125]

Through the years Gerry did move more firmly into the Republican camp. He served as the Republican governor of Massachusetts for two years and eventually became the Republican vice president under James Madison. In one of his last letters to Gerry, written in 1812, Jefferson recalled their lifetime acquaintance, beginning in 1764 when they happened to take lodgings in the same house in New York.[126] Through it all, Jefferson saw a "harmony of principle." "Et idem velle, atque idem nolle, ea demum amicitia est," Jefferson wrote, enigmatically suggesting the complicated grounds of Jeffersonian friendship.[127] He still worried about "the Anglomen" and their machinations, but even if they raised an army, Jefferson claimed that it would be "an army of officers without soldiers."

Jefferson's thoughts eventually turned to future generations. In a remarkable passage, he moved from his children to a future Massachusetts-Virginia alliance, bringing together family and politics once again:

> How many children have you? You beat me, I expect, in that count, but I you in that of our grand-children. We have not timed these things well together, or we might have begun a re-alliance between Massachusetts and the Old Dominion, faithful companions in the war of Independence, peculiarly tallied in interests, by wanting exactly what the other has to spare; and estranged to each other in latter times, only by the practices of a third nation, the common enemy of both. Let us live only to see this re-union, and I will say with old Simeon, 'Lord, now lettest thy servant depart in peace, for mine eyes have seen thy salvation.' In that peace may we long remain, my friend, and depart only in the fulness of years, all passed in health and prosperity.[128]

Jefferson imagined an affective familial union between the two states, a world without corrupting foreign influence or political dissension. The voices of the generations—of children and grandchildren—would echo in union through the ages. In his imagination, Jefferson overcame the problems that had troubled him during his lifetime.

Jefferson's optimistic vision failed to take account of the unavoidable nature of political differences, though. By refusing to offer a legitimate place to politics or even a firm separation between public and private life, Jefferson's belief in affective union opened him to the charge of hypocrisy, even as he claimed to be "unbosoming" himself fully. Worse, Jefferson's conception of union provided the script not for the harmonious union of his imagination but for the political conflicts of the nineteenth and twentieth centuries. Disagreements almost inevitably became signs that some Americans were falling away from their "true" republican natures, that some opponents were no longer fellow countrymen, and that some disagreements could only be solved by disunion.

Figure 6. *Alexander Hamilton*, painted by John Trumbull, c. 1792. Courtesy of the National Gallery of Art.

TWO

Honor

ON 25 AUGUST 1797, Alexander Hamilton published a defense pamphlet with the innocuous and lengthy title *Observations on Certain Documents Contained in No. V & No. VI of "The History of the United States for the Year 1796," In Which the Charge of Speculation Against Alexander Hamilton, Late Secretary of the Treasury, is Fully Refuted. Written by Himself.* A reply to a July 1797 pamphlet written by James Callender accusing Hamilton of speculating while secretary of the treasury, Hamilton's pamphlet ruthlessly sacrificed the privacy of his family to protect his public reputation. He refuted the charge of speculating in Treasury securities while secretary by admitting to an adulterous affair.

Hamilton's sense of honor dictated his decision to write a defense pamphlet publicizing such an embarrassing fact from his personal life.[1] Unlike friendship, on which Jefferson relied at least in part because of its private nature, honor had to be publicly enacted and recognized.[2] Callender's attack threatened Hamilton's honor and, thus, his claim to leadership within a political sphere he conceived of in terms of honor. Adding urgency to Hamilton's defense of himself, America's increasing difficulties with the revolutionary regime in France appeared likely to lead to war, and Hamilton desperately wanted to be able to serve his country in a military capacity. Even his previous successes as secretary of the treasury were at risk. If his honor was tarnished, he feared that his carefully constructed financial system, already despised by the Republican party, would be undermined as well. In the world of early American politics, government measures and individual characters were inextricably intertwined (particularly in the case of Hamilton and the nation's financial system), so that an attack on one was an attack on the other. To salvage his public character, he would sacrifice the domestic tranquillity that Jefferson so cherished.

In his defense pamphlet, Hamilton attempted to build a wall of separation between his actions in private life and his public character. Similar to Jefferson's reliance on friendship, though, Hamilton's use of honor confounded the distinction between private and public life, because the code of honor applied to both. Although honor freed leaders from the charge that they were mere politicians, it contributed to the highly personalized nature of politics in the early republic with its promiscuous intermingling of the personal and the political.

Jefferson, Madison, and Adams were all critical of honor as a code of behavior. Jefferson warned against the kind of argumentative behavior that so often led to affairs of honor. He told his grandson never to enter into a dispute, writing a letter that was, as one historian has written, "a primer on how to avoid the duel."[3] His advice was unsurprising, because friendship as a mode of relationship was quite different from honor. For example, whereas friendship overlooked slights, honor seized on them. Whereas friendship depended, at least rhetorically, on a natural sincerity, honor relied on a rigid formality. Madison suggested that too much concern about one's honor was suspect; in his commonplace book, he wrote, "People who are too tender of their Reputation, and too deeply piqued by Slander, are conscious to themselves of some inward Infirmity."[4] (Offering confirmation of this epigram, Hamilton's own sensitivity probably stemmed, in part, from his humble and impoverished childhood.) Madison's comment revealed how different his outlook was from Hamilton's, for whom nothing was more precious than reputation. Disparaging the numerous controversies surrounding rank in the army during the Revolution, John Adams offered the most pungent commentary. In 1777 he wrote General Nathaniel Greene, "This delicate Point of Honour, which is really one of the most putrid Corruptions of absolute Monarchy, I mean the Honour of maintaining a Rank Superior to abler Men, I mean the Honour of preferring a single Step of Promotion to the Service of the Public, must be bridled." He argued that such punctiliousness was "incompatible with republican Principles," by placing individual glory above "the Rank, the Dignity, and the Rights of whole States."[5] Decades later, Adams also found much to criticize about Hamilton's sense of honor, calling it "such as one of those Irish duelists, who love fighting better than feasting."[6]

In contrast to Jefferson's expansive conception of the nation, Hamilton envisioned a polity carefully circumscribed by the elitist demands of honor, which would bar most citizens from active participation in political life. In the emerging political regime, though, even the foremost leaders had misgivings about honor. And politics was quickly expanding beyond the domain of elite men, so that Hamilton's attempts to fashion himself as a man of honor took place before a diverse and often unsympathetic audience. What Hamilton failed to account for was that although the code of honor remained fairly consistent throughout this time, the society in which it was embedded was rapidly changing.[7] Men would continue to follow honor's precepts long into the nineteenth and even twentieth centuries, but honor's usefulness for negotiating the emergent democratic political culture was problematic at best. As the press and the electorate expanded, a wide array of people from outside the tight-knit world of honorable gentlemen began to judge the political elite by other standards.[8] This politicized electorate would contest Hamilton's conception of a politics based on honor and his distinction between private actions and public character. As a result, Hamilton's attempts to fashion an honorable character for himself foundered in the increasingly democratic polity.

"No character . . . is a match for constantly reiterated attacks, however false"
Defending Honor in the Public Realm

In 1792, James Reynolds, husband to the woman with whom Hamilton had the affair, and a friend of Reynolds had attempted to defraud the government and had been imprisoned. In an attempt to free themselves, they concocted a story that they possessed information that proved Hamilton had been deeply involved in illegal speculations while secretary of the treasury. Eventually, the story reached Pennsylvania representative Frederick Muhlenberg, who relayed the information to Virginia representative Abraham Venable and Virginia senator James Monroe. The three men decided to confront Hamilton directly—a decision to handle the matter among gentlemen and to leave the public out of it, in recognition of the danger of allowing elite reputations to become subject to the whims of unsubstantiated gossip. Satisfied with Hamilton's explanation, the three men let the matter rest.

One factor undid their discretion: the national polity was not confined to elite men who considered themselves bound by the code of honor. Other men, unconstrained by honor's strictures, could not resist the political opportunity that Hamilton's alleged speculation offered, and five years later the charge appeared in a pamphlet written by Callender, an impecunious Republican journalist who later turned on Jefferson and published the first allegations of Jefferson's affair with Sally Hemings.

Hamilton's decision to write a defense pamphlet to counter Callender's accusations revealed the shifting ground on which political character was established in the early republic. The Revolution had spurred both democratization and the growth of an active print culture.[9] As the political tensions of the 1790s mounted, Americans, already politicized by the Revolution, became increasingly active participants in national politics as both Republicans and Federalists attempted to win adherents to their cause.[10] Even Federalists who believed in elite rule were forced to appeal to the people to ratify that rule. Honor, a code of conduct more conducive to settling conflicts among a small group of peers, faced a far different landscape with the politics of the 1790s.[11]

Despite these new political realities, Hamilton's friends attempted to dissuade him from responding to Callender's pamphlet; a public response, they argued, would give new life to something that had been satisfactorily settled in the past. "You will judge for yourself, but in my opinion it will be best to write nothing at least for the present," one friend wrote. "I think you may be certain that your character is not affected, in point of integrity & official conduct. The indignation against those who have basely published this scandal, is I believe universal."[12] Another friend assured him that his "friends and every impartial Man are convinced of your purity as a public Officer" and warned that his defense would "furnish the Presbyterian pulpits with subject matter of declamation."[13] Both men rested their arguments on the belief that Hamilton's public character remained untarnished and left aside how the revelation of adultery affected his private reputation. They implicitly accepted a distinction between public and private conduct that Hamilton would make explicit in his pamphlet. Hamilton himself apologized in the pamphlet to his friends "for condescending to give a public explanation." In justification, he noted that the charges seemed "to derive a sanction from the names of three men of some weight and consequence in the society: a circumstance, which I trust will excuse me for paying attention to a slander that without this prop, would defeat itself by intrinsic circumstances of absurdity and malice."[14] Because his political peers were involved, his "public" as he defined it, Hamilton felt that he had to defend himself publicly or risk losing his honor and his political influence.[15]

Hamilton also recognized that the makeup and role of the public was changing in ways that made him uneasy. Honor was inherently elitist. Its ability to establish a man's character depended upon the acceptance of common standards of behavior by a fairly circumscribed, self-selecting group. If believed, accusations by men he thought were beneath him, such as James Reynolds, threatened this world, and he complained in his pamphlet: "For frail indeed will be the tenure by which the most blameless man will hold his reputation, if the afflictions of three of the most abandoned characters in the community . . . are sufficient to blast it" (250). Hamilton envisioned a polity that excluded such men from an active role in political life. Jefferson's optimism allowed him to imagine a nation in which all free men, regardless of class, were given equal place as friends. Hamilton's reliance on honor contributed to a far different vision in which only a select group would play an important role. He believed that this was the only way that a gentleman's honor could be safely protected. If citizens were indiscriminately allowed to participate in national politics, Hamilton argued, a man's reputation would slip entirely out of his own possession and would rise and fall, like a commodity, in relation to popular demand. He wrote, "The business of accusation would soon become in such a case, a regular trade, and men's reputations would be bought and sold like any marketable commodity," a situation, in other words, like the increasingly democratic political realm (250). To defend his honor in the emerging court of public opinion, Hamilton turned to the defense pamphlet.[16] As with Jefferson and the familiar letter, Hamilton's chosen genre provided advantages in his effort to fashion himself as an honorable man; however, the genre also crystallized problems with the political use of honor.

Defense pamphlets made explicit the centrality of honor to much of the political writing in this period. Elite politicians recognized this, frequently discussing political writing as a form of honorable combat. "There is nobody who can & will enter the lists against [Hamilton]," Jefferson wrote Madison at one point, and William Maclay wrote of "gladiators of the quill."[17] The defense pamphlet served as a means to defend one's honor publicly, particularly when allegations had seeped into the press. Even if the allegations were untrue, these tales "still continue in corroding whispers to wear away the reputations which they could not directly subvert," according to Hamilton (238).[18] The only response was to force those whispers into the public realm where they could be disputed, hence the defense pamphlet. It was the strongest form of written defense available, and it followed an established formula. First, a defense pamphlet was signed. Much of its power rested on the politician's willingness to include his name, placing his authority and reputation before the public for judgment.[19] Second, the pamphlet included an attack on the motives of the author's opponents and the author's own explanation of the truth. Third, it concluded with documentary evidence to substantiate the author's case. In Hamilton's pamphlet, the narrative comprised thirty-five pages, while the documentary evidence continued for another fifty-eight pages. Although Hamilton's narrative framed the evidence, the space accorded to the documents revealed their centrality to the genre. The documentary evidence at the end highlighted the pamphlet's appeal to reason and its author's belief that the evidence, if carefully read, would persuade educated readers.[20]

In this evolving political arena, where the "marketplace" of honor began to grow beyond the confines of elite politicians, defense pamphlets offered the means to maintain an individual's honor according to the demands of the developing political culture and the enlarged public. Authors such as Hamilton were attempting to reconstitute an elite prerogative in a democratic idiom, but the pamphlets themselves were unwieldy instruments. Instead of solidifying one's claim to honor, a defense pamphlet frequently heightened the sense that one's honor was a subject for debate. The crucial and unpredictable aspect of a defense pamphlet was the response. For one to have honor, the community itself had to recognize one's claim, and the defense pamphlet explicitly called on that community for such recognition.[21] Ambivalent responses to Hamilton's attempts to articulate his honorable character revealed the difficult task he faced in defending his honor through print in an increasingly democratic polity. He tried to limit his audience to fellow men of honor, but he found his work reaching an ever expanding audience of readers, many of whom were unsympathetic to claims to rule based on the elite's notion of honor. Defense pamphlets were printed in limited quantities and intended for an educated audience. Jefferson wrote that pamphlets were for "the thinking part of the nation" who could "set the people to rights."[22] But they were usually reprinted more widely in newspapers. Just as private letters often found their way into the public realm, pamphlets intended for a limited audience frequently found their way to a larger public, exhibiting not so much an instability in the genre as an instability in the audience. Ironically, despite his elitism, Hamilton chose a genre that left him dependent on public opinion—and not just the narrowly constructed public of his intentions but a much broader public. Although frequently expressing contempt for "the people," he unwittingly invited them to judge him.

The manner in which the accusations against Hamilton found their way into print revealed the intrusion of a larger public into the elite political world of honor that he hoped to construct. Although Hamilton thought that he had settled the issue five years earlier. The ubiquitous John Beckley, a key political operative for the Jeffersonian Republicans who performed numerous tasks that elite leaders would have disdained as beneath them, likely played a role in publicizing the whole affair.[23] Given the constraints that bound them, elite leaders often relied on men such as Beckley to take care of certain kinds of unsavory political activities. Beckley's clerk had copied the papers that Hamilton had used to prove to Monroe, Muhlenberg, and Venable that his connection with Reynolds had nothing to do with speculation. Instead, it involved Reynolds's wife. According to Monroe, when Hamilton told Beckley that he considered him bound not to disclose the affair, "B. replied . . . that he considered himself under no injunction whatever."[24] Not of a high enough class to consider himself bound by the laws of honor, Beckley freely used the documents about the affair to his party's political advantage in a way that Monroe and others leaders would not. His actions confirmed Hamilton's fears about the frailty of character in a political world not confined to elite gentlemen. The marketplace of public opinion was indeed undermining Hamilton's attempt to fashion both his personal character and the national polity based on honor.

"All characters in public life . . . should be indubitably and decidedly fixed"

Fashioning an Honorable Self

Early in his pamphlet, Hamilton described his 1792 encounter with Muhlenberg, Venable, and Monroe. The description revealed the qualities necessary to fashion an honorable character in the early republic. When Muhlenberg broached the subject of Reynolds's accusation, according to the pamphlet, Hamilton immediately took offense at their manner of inquiry: "I arrested the progress of the discourse by giving way to very strong expressions of indignation." Muhlenberg then retreated, "telling me in substance that I had misapprehended them—that they did not take the fact for established" (257). At a later meeting, when Hamilton began to explain that the connection was of an amorous rather than a pecuniary nature, "they delicately urged me to discontinue it as unnecessary. . . . They also expressed regret at the trouble and embarrassment which had been occasioned to me." The three men also asked Hamilton about their own conduct. Hamilton noted, "One of the gentlemen . . . expressed a hope that I also was satisfied with their conduct in conducting the inquiry—I answered, that they knew I had been hurt at the opening of the affair—that this excepted, I was satisfied with their conduct and considered myself as having been treated with candor or with fairness and liberality" (258). By understanding the nuances of Hamilton's description, we can better comprehend the code of honor and what it demanded from gentlemen.

To do this, it is useful to compare the episode with the practice of dueling. Like many American gentleman of his generation, Hamilton received his introduction to the code duello while in the army, which was a breeding ground for a culture of honor among officers.[25] Hamilton first stepped onto the field of honor as the second of Lieutenant Colonel John Laurens in 1778, and he later wrote a short account of Laurens's duel with Major General Charles Lee, a seemingly strange response given that dueling was generally frowned upon and even illegal in some states.[26] Written accounts of duels were actually quite common, though, and their existence exposed a central truth about duels: they were not really private acts. They were performances for a larger community and acted as proof of a man's honor, shown both by his willingness to sacrifice his life for it and by his ability to show the proper qualities under the strain of having another man shoot a pistol at him.[27] Written accounts publicized this performance and showed the world at large the successful or unsuccessful attempt of a man to vindicate his honor, which existed or failed to exist depending on a community's willingness to recognize it.[28] In this sense, the function of a duel was similar to that of Hamilton's defense pamphlet, which also asked for an endorsement from the community. As one officer wrote to Hamilton in 1779, "It is of the highest importance that, at this period, all characters in public life especially, should be indubitably and decidedly fixed."[29] The code of honor provided a context to evaluate a man's character, to "indubitably and decidedly" fix it.

Written accounts of duels focused on the qualities seen as most essential to honorable conduct. In his account, Hamilton provided the standards by which to judge the honorable performance being represented. He closed his account of the duel by noting, "Upon the whole we think it a piece of justice to the two Gentlemen to declare, that after they met their conduct was strongly marked with all the politeness generosity coolness and firmness, that ought to characterize a transaction of this nature," a list of characteristics intended to offer both the standard for and the confirmation of the honorable character of the duelists. Confirming Hamilton's judgment, Lee's second also signed the account. Similarly, Hamilton's description in his 1797 pamphlet of his encounter with his three interlocutors included the grounds by which to judge their behavior. He noted that he had been "treated with candor or with fairness and liberality." In both cases, the written accounts offered a brief overview of the major attributes of honorable conduct. Affairs of honor were supposed to resolve ambiguity about a man's character.

Honor relied on one final, crucial quality: sensibility. A man of honor was, by necessity, also a man of feeling and sentiment. Far from weakness, a man's sensibility allowed him to be aware of the smallest slight. A refined sensibility bespoke the necessary delicacy to feel one's honor appropriately, to understand at what point "wounded" honor needed to be defended. Making that determination was not an idle question. Honor was an all-or-nothing proposition. A man could not lose a little honor, which accounts for the willingness of men to risk death in a duel to defend their honor. Slowness to take offense could itself be interpreted as dishonorable, which explains Hamilton's immediate response (his "strong expressions of indignation") to having his honor questioned by the three men. Because many saw honor as a necessary prerequisite to leadership, political leaders were particularly sensitive to guard against any possible dishonor.[30]

Honor's reliance on sensibility helps clarify the most puzzling aspect of the 1792 encounter—the concern Hamilton's interrogators felt about their own behavior during the encounter (when they asked Hamilton if he was "satisfied with their conduct in conducting the inquiry" [258]).[31] Although the three men were questioning Hamilton, the situation demanded that they comport themselves according to the etiquette of honor as well. In any dispute touching on a man's honor, all the parties involved were held to the same standard of conduct. All were involved in a performance that demanded the strictest adherence to certain rules, and a man's sensibility was what enabled him to adhere to those rules and to protect his own honor. In evaluating their conduct, Hamilton focused on their sensibility, noting, "Mr. Muhlenberg and Mr. Venable, in particular, manifested a degree of sensibility on the occasion" (258). Hamilton was praising their honor by confirming their possession of honor's most important attribute. Because sensibility was based on delicately calibrated personal feelings, though, it was a volatile standard for determining if one's reputation needed to be defended.

Hamilton's interaction with Monroe during the affair demonstrated the volatile nature of sensibility (and explained why Hamilton did not credit Monroe with sensibility). Although the code of honor offered fairly rigid prescriptions for how to behave, applying these prescriptions to any but the most blatant offenses was complicated. Honor was not without its complexities, even among gentlemen. Not so much a settled script, honor was yoked to a whole range of social and political considerations and was under constant and intense negotiation with one's social and political peers—a man could not have honor unless society was willing to recognize his claim to such. Because of this, honor was highly volatile, as men constantly jockeyed to claim and assert their own honor, a situation that contributed to an unstable political atmosphere, even among the elite.[32]

Initially, though, Hamilton's defense promised to be a relatively simple matter. When Reynolds's claims found their way into print in 1797, Hamilton's first response was to ask the three gentlemen who had questioned him for a declaration that "they were perfectly satisfied with the explanation I had given and . . . there was nothing in the transaction which ought to affect my character as a public Officer or lessen the public confidence in my Integrity."[33] He did so in terms that made it clear that it was an affair of honor.

With such a cue, everyone immediately became sensitive to the slightest nuances of tone and manner, as befitted men of sensibility. Venable complained to Hamilton that Hamilton endeavored "to impute to party motives, the part which I have had in this business. . . . I appeal to your candour, and ask you if any part of my conduct in this whole business has justified such an imputation."[34] Muhlenberg and Monroe also found themselves bristling at Hamilton's comments, writing him a joint letter, similar to Venable's. Considering themselves gentlemen guided by considerations of honor, all three men were troubled by the accusation of having acted from party spirit. A charge of party intrigue struck directly at this self-conception, painting them not as honorable guardians of the public realm but as self-promoting partisans guided by motives of political self-interest. Hamilton quickly clarified his position, arguing that he was not imputing party motives to any of the men. He also reiterated his feeling that all had acquitted themselves well in the previous meeting: "I was satisfied with and sensible to the candour with which I had been treated."[35]

For Hamilton, the prominent names of Monroe, Muhlenberg, and Venable attached to Callender's pamphlet were what demanded a response. He wrote that although he generally chose not "to answer the calumnies which party spirit is so incessantly busied in heaping upon me," he could not ignore the current accusation because "the names of three citizens of political and personal importance in the community appeared to give sanction to the slander."[36] The accusations were linked with other men of honor who had the power to confirm or dispute his own honor, so Hamilton believed that he had to respond. Muhlenberg and Venable complied with Hamilton's request for a statement, but Hamilton thought that Monroe did not offer a satisfactory reply. Monroe did remain equivocal, writing at one point, "Whether the imputations against you as to speculation, are well or ill founded, depends upon the facts & circumstances which appear agnst you & upon yr. defense."[37] While two out of three endorsements would seem to offer a preponderance of opinion in Hamilton's favor, he could not rest there. Given Monroe's stature, Hamilton could only feel that the lack of an endorsement from him would leave his honor tarnished, and even the slightest tarnish was felt to strike at one's claim to any honor. The two entered into a negotiation to attempt to resolve the matter short of a duel.

The negotiation between Hamilton and Monroe showed how complicated honor could be even among gentlemen. When finding themselves embroiled in an affair of honor, men weighed words with the utmost precision to determine the necessary course of action, but, ironically, the rigidity of the honor code frequently served to increase the very ambiguity that it was meant to resolve. That ambiguity was sometimes functional, allowing a man the linguistic room to craft a response that would satisfy his challenger while not humiliating himself, but it was also at times dysfunctional, goading men to a duel when negotiations only led them deeper into an interpretive thicket of misunderstanding. In addition, the code of honor made it difficult for either man to back down, for fear of appearing cowardly. Monroe wrote, "I shall always be equally prepared to vindicate my conduct and character against the attacks of any one who may assail them," which goaded a similar response from Hamilton, who thought that Monroe was questioning his willingness to duel.[38] Instead of safeguarding a man's reputation, the code of honor frequently only heightened insecurities about that reputation.

Invoked in order to resolve ambiguity about a man's character, the honor code demanded an almost obsessive attention to nuance, which

Figure 7. *James Monroe*, painted by John Vanderlyn, 1816. Courtesy of the National Portrait Gallery, Smithsonian Institution.

transformed even the most straightforward statements into complicated texts open to various interpretations. Hamilton's negotiations with Monroe were murky enough that Hamilton was not even sure which one of them was the insulted party. When he turned to his friends for advice, they found themselves almost as bewildered as he was. One friend commented, "It is certainly a question of feeling which of you is to consider yourself as the Party injured by the correspondence."[39] He decided that Hamilton had already called Monroe's conduct "malignant and dishonourable," so that "it [rested], in my opinion, with Mr. Monroe either to submit to, or to resent these expressions," a sentiment with which others concurred.[40] Hamilton and Monroe even found themselves unsure if the other had issued a challenge. Monroe wrote, "If your object is to render this affair a personal one between us you might have been more explicit."[41] Expressing similar feelings, Hamilton wrote, "In my opinion the idea of a personal affair between us ought not to have found a place in your letters or it ought to have assumed a more positive shape." Thinking that perhaps Monroe had challenged him, Hamilton added, "If what you have said be intended as an advance towards it, it is incumbent upon me not to decline it."[42] Monroe denied the challenge but thought that perhaps Hamilton was trying to challenge him, writing, "If on the other hand you meant this last letter as a challenge to me, I have then to request that you will say so."[43] Their misunderstandings reveal the interpretive difficulties sometimes created by the code of honor, which was supposed to clarify, not confuse.

Their negotiations underscored a central problem of politics in the early republic: the impossibility of separating measures from men, public from private, political from personal. Given the fluid state of national politics, in which the boundaries between public and private were not at all self-evident, politicians struggled to define the boundaries between acceptable political criticism and unacceptable personal insult. As one political figure wrote, "It is impossible to censure measures without condemning men."[44] To call a man a liar gave instant grounds for a challenge, but often matters were not that simple, especially in the political world. Did criticism of a man's politics constitute a challenge to a man's honor? The answer was ambiguous. Hamilton certainly thought that his own politics, rather than any personal failing, was the cause of his troubles: "Merely because I *retained* an opinion once common to me and the most influential of those who opposed me, *That the public debt ought to be provided for on the basis of the contract upon which it was created*, I have been wickedly accused with wantonly increasing the public burthen many millions, in order to promote a stock-jobbing interest of myself and friends."[45] Perhaps Monroe best expressed the nature of the difficulty both between the two men and, more generally, for early American politics when he wrote, "The issue is quite uncertain as to the mode of adjusting what is personal in the business."[46]

Hamilton's difficulties in negotiating a settlement with Monroe were not unusual. In fact, his fatal duel with Aaron Burr illustrated even more forcefully the tangled blend of personal and political motives that guided behavior. The grounds of Burr's challenge were ambiguous, and much of their correspondence was, in effect, a debate about where to draw the line between political disagreements and personal insults. Ultimately, their correspondence itself served as much as anything as a spur to their combat, as had been the case in the Monroe-Hamilton exchange. As with his defense pamphlet, Hamilton agreed to the duel with Burr because, according to his second, "his Sensibility to public opinion was extremely strong, especially in what related to his conduct in Public Office."[47] In justifying his decision to duel despite his moral objections, Hamilton made clear his own belief in the interdependence of honor and politics, with its problematic blend of public and private life. He wrote, "I answer that my relative situation, as well in public as private aspects, enforcing all the considerations which constitute what men of the world denominate honor, impressed on me (as I thought) a peculiar necessity not to decline the call. The ability to be in future useful, whether in resisting mischief or effecting good, in those crises of our public affairs, which seem likely to happen, would probably be inseparable from a conformity with public prejudice in this particular."[48]

In the end, a duel with Monroe did not take place only because Hamilton chose to write a defense pamphlet. He wrote to Monroe, "The public explanation to which I am driven must decide, as far as public opinion is concerned, between us," once again revealing how ostensibly private quarrels about honor were largely matters of public opinion.[49] Monroe recognized this as well, remarking that the public would have to decide the affair between them. Although avoiding a duel, Hamilton now faced a much more complicated task—convincing the public.

"So vile an instrument"

Elitist Honor

After a number of pages in the pamphlet in which he blasted the Jacobin spirit of his opponents, Hamilton eventually came to the heart of the matter, his affair with Maria Reynolds. Facing this unpleasant revelation, he addressed it simply and directly: "The charge against me is a connection with one James Reynolds for purposes of improper pecuniary speculation. My real crime is an amorous connection with his wife" (243).[50] Forced to defend his public character by admitting to adultery because of honor's centrality to political life, Hamilton's defense revealed not just the grounds of his own honor but his vision of a nation shaped by honor.

To defend himself, Hamilton tried to build a barrier between his private infidelity and his public rectitude, insisting that any lapses in his private life should not reflect on his public character. Hamilton repeatedly offered proof of how stringently he had discharged his public responsibilities.[51] For instance, he had refused to give Reynolds a job in the Treasury Department and used that fact to argue for his public fidelity: "This little circumstance shews at once the delicacy of my conduct, in its public relations" (252). Many undoubtedly found it shameless to insist on one's delicacy even while publicly exposing one's sexual peccadillos, but Hamilton argued that nothing of a private nature was relevant in judging his fitness for public office. According to this distinction, delicacy of conduct was crucial in public life but not necessarily significant (from a political standpoint) in private life. He called the affair simply "the plain case of a private amour unconnected with any thing that was the proper subject of a public attack" (266). Although accused of showing even greater insensitivity for his disclosure, Hamilton was aware of the magnitude of the confession. He noted:

> No man not indelicately unprincipled, with the state of manners in this country, would be willing to have a conjugal infidelity fixed upon him with a positive certainty—He would know that it would justly injure him with a considerable and respectable portion of the society—and especially no man, tender of the happiness of an excellent wife could without extreme pain look forward to the affliction which she might endure from the disclosure, especially a public defense, of the fact. (264)

Arguing that his personal life had no bearing on his political life, he erected his own boundaries between public and private life in which his wife and family were without political meaning—a problematic distinction given the mingling of public and private in the honor-based politics Hamilton was trying to create. If Jefferson's problem was keeping his private life separated from the corruption of public involvement (at least rhetorically), Hamilton's difficulty was fashioning a public self independent of and immune to his private foibles (in many ways, a solution diametrically at odds with Jefferson's own attempts to ground his political sincerity in the authenticity of his private self). Jefferson had tried to remake public life in the image of domestic society. In stark contrast, Hamilton wanted a complete separation, a world in which private life was without political meaning.

As partial exculpation for his affair and to reinforce his distinction between private conduct and public character, Hamilton relied on familiar gender norms in which he was the victim of the seductive arts of a woman, who took advantage of his sensibility.[52] Hamilton first met Maria Reynolds in 1791 when she appeared at his door asking for money. She told him that her husband had deserted her for another woman and had left her penniless. Hamilton was touched by her story and promised to give her money. That same day, after entering her lodgings, he wrote, in one of the great laconic statements of early American politics, "Some conversation ensued from which it was quickly apparent that other than pecuniary consolation would be acceptable" (251). In his draft (but not the published text), Hamilton followed that statement by writing, "It required a harder heart than mine to refuse it to Beauty in distress." When he later tried to end the relationship, according to the pamphlet, he still found himself bewitched by her charms. "Her conduct made it extremely difficult to disentangle myself," he noted (252). Even as he wrote the pamphlet in 1797, after having been blackmailed by James Reynolds about the affair and finding himself facing trumped up accusations, Hamilton still seemed befuddled by Maria. "The variety of shapes which this woman could assume was endless," he wrote (262).[53] He credited her with what he termed "a most imposing art" (252).

The female body was supposed to embody, literally, the truth. Blushes, hesitations, sighs, and the like were thought to provide the unshuttered windows to a woman's heart, so much so that Samuel Richardson's Sir Charles Grandison confidently claimed that "a man of common penetration may see to the bottom of a woman's heart."[54] Maria's "most imposing art" marked her as a victimizer, not a victim. Hamilton was attempting to tell a story in which he was not the seducer but the seduced, a gentleman of sensibility taken advantage of by a designing woman. This story relied on the familiar juxtaposition of feminine corruption and masculine virtue, corresponding to and reinforcing Hamilton's distinction between public life as the domain of male political activities and private life as the purview of women.

The world of honor itself, though, undermined Hamilton's neat distinction. For example, women did play a role, though largely unacknowledged, in maintaining this world. Displays of sensibility demanded an audience to judge and value the performance, allowing women, as the exemplars of sensibility, a role in the production of the honorable self.[55] Hamilton himself had teasingly revealed this when he played the gallant during the war. In a 1779 letter to Susanna Livingston, who requested special permission to travel from New York, Hamilton chided her for appealing to something as impersonal as his humanity, writing that if she had appealed to his "gallantry, it would have been irresistible." He then created an alternative scenario straight from fairy tale: "I should . . . even to have attacked *windmills* in your Ladyship's service. I am not sure, but my imagination would have gone so far, as to have fancied New York an *inchanted castle*—the three ladies, so many fair damsels, ravished from their friends and held in captivity, by the spells of some wicked magician—General Clinton a huge giant placed as keeper of the gates, and myself a valorous knight, destined to be their champion and deliverer."[56] Hamilton's chivalrous scenario revealed honor's reliance on women as both object and judge of chivalrous action. Although Hamilton's battles to retain his political honor were seemingly removed from this sort of chivalry, the use of honor invoked, even if implicitly, ideas about gender.

Thus, exclusively male activities still relied for their meaning on gendered relationships, and women served as the linchpin, if unseen, of this world. Hamilton himself revealed the implications of gender for constructions of masculine political identity when he complained of Madison and Jefferson, "*They have a womanish attachment to France and a womanish resentment against Great Britain*," delineating the proper behavior of political leaders along gendered lines.[57]

Hamilton's true villain, though, was not Maria but her husband, James Reynolds. A man of honor perceived insult not simply by the challenge issued but also by the nature of the challenger, and Hamilton was mortified that his own attacker was the "reptilian" Reynolds. Hamilton spent a good portion of the pamphlet attempting to demolish Reynolds's character and ridiculing the possibility of pecuniary involvement with him. Hamilton wrote, "I should have been foolish as well as depraved enough to employ so vile an instrument as Reynolds for such insignificant ends. . . . Reynolds was an obscure, unimportant and profligate man" (244). When not ridiculing the man, he ridiculed the allegations, particularly noting the paltry sums Reynolds claimed were involved: "The scale of the concern with Reynolds, such as it is presented, is contemptibly narrow for a rapacious speculating secretary of the treasury" (245). Hamilton found the very fact of Reynolds's challenge offensive. "Could it be expected," he wrote with disgust, "that I should so debase myself as to think it necessary to my vindication to be confronted with a person such as Reynolds? Could I have borne to suffer my veracity to be exposed to the humiliating competition?" (266). Throughout the pamphlet, Hamilton tried not merely to disprove the charges but to vanquish his enemies completely. One could not save part of one's honor. To be partially successful would be to fail. He himself cast it as an either/or proposition: "If they are worthy of credit I am guilty; if they are not, all wire-drawn inferences from parts of their story are mere artifice and nonsense" (263).

Hamilton's unbridled attack on James Reynolds was not simply part of his defense—it was an outgrowth of his elitist conception of honor as a means of separating those worthy of wielding political power from the rest of society. His proposed distinction between private and public life revealed his conception of the national polity, a conception that excluded the vast majority of citizens from political life. According to Hamilton, only those who held political office could even *have* a public character to uphold. Using his distinction, most of day-to-day life was not part of this public realm, so only men privileged enough to have the resources to put aside such mundane concerns could participate. In other words, Hamilton's distinction was implicitly a justification for a polity peopled solely by elite men.

Considered an attribute of the higher classes, honor provided a standard to distinguish the worthy from the masses.[58] Calling attention to honor's usefulness in distinguishing a worthy elite, one commentator remarked, "The idea of honor . . . [is] something distinct from mere probity, and which supposes in gentlemen a stronger abhorrence of perfidy, falsehood, or cowardice, and a more elevated and delicate sense of the dignity of virtue, than are usually found in more vulgar minds."[59] This standard was firmly tied to wealth. Humorously discussing sensibility, honor's key attribute, Thomas Monroe in *Olla Podrida* wrote, "No man should be permitted to moisten a white handkerchief at the *ohs* and *ahs* of a modern tragedy, unless he possessed an estate of seven hundred a year."[60] Ironically, the reliance on sensibility to guard the elite domain of honor also played a role in subverting it. The widespread popularity of novels of sensibility, such as *Charlotte Temple*, revealed the quick diffusion of sensibility to a much broader audience in the new republic, an audience who felt perfectly capable of judging elite political leaders. As always more in tune with popular sentiment, Jefferson saw sensibility as the foundation for a brotherhood of all citizens, in contrast to Hamilton's use of it as a barrier to the common people's political involvement.

Hamilton's experiences during the Revolutionary War had left him with little confidence in the ability of average citizens to govern themselves, and he showed a lack of regard for the people. "Take mankind as they are, and what are they governed by?" he asked at the 1787 Constitutional Convention, answering "their passions."[61] In the *Federalist*, he described mankind as "ambitious, vindictive, and rapacious."[62] Often quoting Hume's remark that "*every man* ought to be supposed a *knave*," the New Yorker had little hope that Americans could judge a matter according to its merits, because they were "turbulent and changing," so that they "seldom judge or determine right."[63] By 1782, he already feared that the people had gained too large a role in government. "Here we find the general disease which infects all our constitutions, an excess of popularity," he wrote. "The inquiry constantly is what will *please* not what will *benefit* the people. In such a government there can be nothing but temporary expedient, fickleness, and folly."[64] For Hamilton, democracy promised nothing but disorder, and he warned that most were "not duly considering the amazing violence and turbulence of the democratic spirit. When a great object of government is pursued, which seizes the popular passions, they spread like wild fire, and become irresistible."[65] Many of the pseudonyms that Hamilton used in the newspapers (Phocion, Tully, Camillus, and Pericles, for example) revealed, at least symbolically, a profound contempt for the people.[66]

Hamilton's answer was for a worthy elite, honorable men such as himself, to conduct the country's government.[67] In a speech at the Constitutional Convention, he remarked: "There may be in every government a few choice spirits, who may act from more worthy motives. . . . Perhaps a few men in a state may, from patriotic motives, or to display their talents, or to reap the advantage of public applause, step forward."[68] Writing as "the Continentalist," he understood that such leadership would not necessarily be popular, noting the tendency for the influence of good men to be "too commonly borne down by the prevailing torrent of ignorance and prejudice," by "the passions of the vulgar."[69] But he had little respect for popularity. He dismissively called the Republicans "LITTLE POLITICIANS" and attributed their success to the low arts of winning popular favor. "Consummate in the paltry science of courting and winning popular favor," he wrote, "they falsely infer that they have the capacity to govern, and they will be the last to discover their error."[70]

In the *Federalist*, Hamilton argued for a senate precisely because he hoped that it would be a place where men would be guided by honor rather than popularity. If the national government did not have a senate, he argued that "the national councils will not possess that sensibility to the opinion of the world, which is perhaps not less necessary in order to merit, than it is to obtain, its respect and confidence." A large legislature based on frequent elections would never answer the purpose. He wrote, "Yet however requisite a sense of national character may be, it is evident that it can never be sufficiently possessed by a numerous and changeable body. It can only be found in a number so small, that a sensible degree of the praise and blame of public measures may be the portion of each individual; or in an assembly so durably invested with public trust, that the pride and consequence of its members may be sensibly incorporated with the reputation and prosperity of the community."[71] Members of a small, elite body would feel that their own individual honor was tied to any decisions and, thus, would be more likely to act honorably both as individuals and as a group, according to Hamilton. He viewed the presidency in similar terms. Arguing against "the maxim of republican jealousy which considers power as safer in the hands of a number of men than of a single man," Hamilton claimed that the president would feel greater personal responsibility for his actions than a group of men and that the people would have an easier time holding him accountable.[72]

Hamilton's willingness to use force against the nation's own citizens reveal his disregard for the demands of popular government. Three times during the 1790s—the Whiskey Rebellion in 1794, the Virginia resistance to the Alien and Sedition Acts in 1798, and Fries Rebellion in 1799—he argued for the use of the army. By doing so, he hoped to create the kind of respect that he thought the government should command from its own citizens. He wrote in 1794, "The force ought, if attainable, to be an imposing one, such . . . as will deter from opposition, save the effusion of the blood of citizens, and secure the object to be accomplished."[73] His larger objective was to instill feelings of respect for the national government.

Figure 8. "A Peep into the Antifederal Club," political cartoon. Courtesy of The Library Company of Philadelphia. This 1793 etching, the earliest known anti-Jefferson cartoon, shows Thomas Jefferson presiding over a meeting of the "Antifederal Club" as the devil looks on approvingly. The cartoon revealed the fears of Federalists if Jefferson and his followers managed to gain power—an end to law and order as the enlightened rule of elites proposed by Hamilton would be replaced by mob rule.

"Whenever the government appears in arms," he wrote, "it ought to appear like a *Hercules*, and inspire respect by the display of strength."[74]

Even as Hamilton recommended the use of the army against American citizens, though, he thought the people's honor was so inextricably tied to national honor that he considered the use of force by the government against the people as government *for* the people. In appealing to the public to support the forces used to quell the Whiskey Rebellion, he called on citizens to recognize that the army was not an instrument to blunt the will of the people but an expression of that will. "Ye cannot but remember that the government is YOUR OWN work—that those who administer it are but temporary agents; that YOU are called upon not to support their power, BUT YOUR OWN POWER," he wrote.[75] Just as he identified his own honor with the nation's, he also collapsed the people's honor into national honor. The increased power and respect accorded to such a government, he thought, redounded to the people themselves. Hamilton argued in 1792 that the people's "own importance is increased by the increased respectability of their country, which from an abject and degraded state, owing to the want of government, has, by the establishment of a wise constitution and by the measures which have been pursued under it, become a theme for the praise and admiration of mankind."[76]

What Hamilton could not abide was a nation without honor. A theme throughout Hamilton's contributions to the *Federalist Papers* was his belief that a weak Union would never be able to demand respect from the world or even from its own citizens.[77] In *Federalist #15*, he could scarcely restrain his disgust with the nation. "We may indeed with propriety be said to have reached almost the last state of national humiliation," he wrote, "There is scarcely any thing that can wound the pride or degrade the character of an independent nation which we do not experience."[78] All the requirements of a national government were sorely lacking. He continued, "We have neither troops, nor treasury, nor government for the Union."[79] These deficiencies undermined the government not simply at home but abroad. Hamilton called the nation's ambassadors "the mere pageants of mimic sovereignty."[80] As a man without honor could not exert any influence, so a country without honor could not protect its interests. Only a powerful nation could command respect. "The rights of neutrality will only be respected, when they are defended by an adequate power. A nation, despicable by its weakness, forfeits even the privilege of being neutral," he noted in *Federalist #11*.[81] Although no proponent of quixotic battles, he believed that a challenge to national honor required the same response as a challenge to personal honor—vindication: "An evasive conduct . . . is never dignified—seldom politic." He argued that a nation "had better hazard any calamities than submit tamely to absolute disgrace."[82]

Hamilton's most important public policies, those related to the nation's finances, were made not only for financial reasons but also for reasons of honor. Credit stood as a proxy for faith in a person's or a government's power. Hamilton's efforts to establish the nation's creditworthiness had a great deal to do with establishing the nation's honor, a creditworthiness akin to national dignity itself. Like personal honor, it was largely a matter of reputation, of others' opinions. As secretary of the treasury, he wrote, "In nothing are appearances of greater moment, than in whatever regards credit. Opinion is the soul of it, and this is affected by appearances, as well as realities."[83] For Hamilton, funding the national and state debts was the preeminent issue of the early republic. To succeed at this task would go a long way not just to establish the nation's credit but to establish its honor.[84]

But Hamilton's elitist stance left him out of touch with the emerging political realities of national politics. Unleashed by the Revolution, a variety of forces began to create a political world vastly different from the kind of deferential politics that Hamilton sought.[85] His understanding of the Revolution failed to take into account what most considered one of the fundamental legacies of that Revolution—popular sovereignty, a government responsive to the desires of the people. In his quest to create an honorable national government, he sometimes seemed to forget the very people for whom that government was being created.

"Respectable men of whatever political party on whose delicacy reliance may be placed"

Hamilton's Audience

In judging the success or failure of Hamilton's defense of his character, it is crucial to keep in mind the question of audience. In the first place, we must determine what audience he thought he was addressing. In the pamphlet itself, there is a clue that reveals that his intended audience was his political peers, not the public at large. To clinch his case in the pamphlet, Hamilton made use of a private letter. He refused to name the author, but he extended an offer to his fellow citizens: "Though I am not permitted to make a public use of [the letter], I am permitted to refer any gentleman to the perusal of his letter in the hands of William Bingham, Esquire" (262). Obviously, all men were not invited to invade the home of William Bingham, Esquire—the offer applied only to the political elite. In a 1797 letter to John Fenno, he confirmed this intention. He wrote that he wanted "to place in the hands of my friend a particular narrative of the affair and the original papers which support it, with permission to communicate them to respectable men of whatever political party on whose delicacy reliance may be placed."[86]

How did the political elite respond to Hamilton's defense? Federalists generally rallied behind Hamilton, implicitly accepting the division between public and private life that the New Yorker proposed, although even men of his own party expressed misgivings about his revelations. His friend Robert Troup complained that Hamilton's "ill judged pamphlet has done him incomparable injury."[87] While some Federalists did defend Hamilton in writing, others attempted to shift the public's attention to different matters. Unsurprisingly, Republicans became almost giddy with the opportunity presented to them by their archfoe. They wasted no time in pouring out execrations upon him and argued that his private adultery had direct ramifications for his public character. As one man wrote to Jefferson, "Mr. H——has assuredly, reduced his Consequence, to the most degrading and Contemptible point of view. . . . as if, it were possible—by that means to justify his public Conduct, by a *simple* confession of his private ridiculous Amour, at the expense of both—his Reputation and future peace of mind."[88] Madison dismissed Hamilton's pamphlet as a poor rhetorical performance that undermined itself, "Next to the error of publishing at all, is that of forgetting that simplicity & candor are the only dress which Prudence would put on innocence. Here we see every rhetorical artifice employed to excite the spirit of party to prop up his sinking reputation."[89] And Callender told Jefferson, "It is worth all that fifty of the best pens in America could have said agt. him."[90]

The mixed responses reveal the shifting grounds of the politics of character in the early republic. Even within Hamilton's more narrowly conceived public of elite men of honor, politics was becoming the grounds by which honor was judged, rather than honor serving as the grounds by which to judge politics, a shift that ran counter to the honorable political world he was attempting to fashion. Even more problematically, Hamilton's defense ran afoul of the code of honor itself, which made no distinction between public and private behavior and demanded that both private and public selves cohere in an honorable whole. Even Hamilton's place within the narrowly circumscribed world of the political elite was changing in ways that he seemed unwilling to recognize. His almost reflexive and in the end self-destructive turn to writing was understandable, given the great triumphs that he had achieved with his earlier newspaper writings. Along with Madison, Hamilton as Publius had outlasted and outargued all his Antifederalist opponents. Under other pseudonyms, Hamilton had also successfully defended Washington's administration on numerous occasions. The context of those performances, though, was entirely different. In the early 1790s, Hamilton had been defining and defending the administration's position, a task made easier by Washington's moral authority, and his efforts had been directed mainly at convincing key congressmen.[91] The political landscape of the late 1790s was radically different. No longer speaking for the administration, Hamilton found himself in the anomalous and potentially dishonorable position of a quasi oppositionist, one whose efforts served primarily to divide and demoralize his own allies and to give the Republicans a desperately needed boost. Leaving aside his general disdain for a public who no longer acted with proper deference, the situation within the national elite and Hamilton's position in that elite were radically different by the end of the 1790s.

Despite the varied reactions, his pamphlet was at least a qualified success with his chosen audience. Only a short time later, Hamilton would be appointed second-in-command to the army. His reputation had, in a sense, been successfully defended, at least among his peers. Simply put, honor was not tied to a man's sexual fidelity, only to a woman's.[92] Daniel Defoe's aphorism neatly illustrated the double standard: "A Tradesman's credit, and a maid's virtue, ought to be equally sacred from the tongues of men."[93] As one politician wrote, "Hamilton is fallen for the present, but if he fornicates with every female in the cities of New York and Philadelphia, he will rise again."[94] Confessing to adultery to disprove charges of financial impropriety did not destroy his character, although it certainly did not improve it.

But Hamilton's pamphlet was read far beyond the narrow circle that he envisioned. In this larger public, he was pilloried in the press and from pulpits across the nation. As one writer noted, Hamilton's confession had failed to reassure the public, who now believed that Hamilton was "incapable of sharing in the management of the finances of the country, because an infamous debauchee; [and] unworthy of eminent station in a republic, because a brutal tyrant in his house."[95] The comment once again revealed a gendered component to the construction of character, relying on Hamilton's treatment of women to determine the fitness of his political character—a judgment likely shared by the main audience for those pulpit denunciations, women, who were seen as the guardians of precisely those qualities Hamilton flouted. The writer also rejected Hamilton's attempt to distinguish between his private infidelity and his public rectitude, a reaction likely shared by many who saw his confession as grounds for questioning his character. Although not overly concerned about the opinions of average citizens, Hamilton ignored them at his peril, because of their increasing importance for political success.

The defense pamphlet was not a precise tool. Pamphlets circulated promiscuously, finding their way to audiences unimagined by the writer. The differing reactions to the pamphlet revealed not simply the hardening political divisions in the nation but an increasingly diverse national audience as well. Hamilton's difficulty in defining his public, a definition that walked a fine line between acknowledging a broader audience and trying to limit that audience to a certain elite, was, in many ways, a difficulty inherent in the political culture, which carried traces of an earlier, deferential politics and harbingers of the emerging democratic political culture. Subjected to the vagaries of public opinion, the code of honor simply did not translate well into the newly created and expanding polity. The audience was too diverse to be persuaded by appeals to an elite code of conduct practiced by a small body of men, especially when men of a different political persuasion saw a pamphlet such as Hamilton's as an opportunity to promote their own political cause, rather than as a means of judging a man's character. Complicating that already difficult task, Hamilton relied on a firm distinction between his public character and his private actions, a distinction that had little support in the code of honor, in the political realm, or in society. Was Hamilton out of touch with the new political realities? The Reynolds pamphlet offered warning signs.

"The evil genius of this country"

The End of Honor

Despite the pamphlet's mixed reception, Hamilton was not hesitant to enter the arena again. Although not a defense pamphlet, his open letter to John Adams in 1800 represented a similar rhetorical endeavor.[96] Hamilton believed that he had received ample provocation. Convinced (correctly) that the majority of his cabinet was more loyal to Hamilton than to himself, Adams became increasingly enraged at the New Yorker's influence. Worse, as the election of 1800 approached, Hamilton began toying with a scheme to put Federalist Charles Cotesworth Pinckney in the presidency ahead of Adams. Adams loosed his frustration in a torrent of abuse. According to one correspondent, he called Hamilton "the greatest intrigu[er] in the World—a man devoid of every moral principle—a Bastard, and as much a foreigner as Gallatin."[97] Eventually, word began to spread of Adams's rough usage.[98] Although Adams later denied these imputations, Hamilton had heard enough to believe that his honor had been wounded.[99]

Hamilton feared that the private slanders would eventually ruin his reputation and had to be refuted. He complained that if no response was given to Adams's slanders, "Mr. Adam's personal friends seconded by the Jacobins will completely *run us down in the public opinion.*"[100] An ally agreed: "Still it is probably fit & it may be indispensable to expose Mr. Adams fully to the public; the countenance & authority given by him & his friends to the vile calumnies against us may strengthen their credit so much as to render them irrefutable without such an exposition."[101] His first impulse was to handle the affair in the standard way between men of honor, man-to-man. He told Oliver Wolcott: "I have serious thought of writing the *President* to tell him That I have heard of his repeatedly having mentioned the existence of a British Faction in this Country & alluded to me as one of that faction—requesting that he will inform me of the truth of this information & if true what have been the grounds of this suggestion."[102]

Hamilton did, in fact, write the president a private letter on the matter. He followed the usual etiquette. First, he repeated the accusation: "It has been repeatedly mentioned to me that you have, on different occasions, asserted the existence of a *British Faction* in this Country . . . and that you have sometimes named me . . . as one of this description of purposes." Second, he asked for an avowal or disavowal of the statement: "I must, Sir, take it for granted, that you cannot have made such assertions or insinuations without being willing to avow them, and to assign the reasons to a party who may conceive himself injured by them." Finally, because of these considerations, Hamilton asked for his authority, "whether the information, I have received, has been correct or not, and if correct what are the grounds upon which you have founded the suggestion."[103] Despite making it clear that this was an affair of honor, Hamilton received no reply.

By refusing to follow the prescribed etiquette between gentlemen, Adams forfeited, in Hamilton's mind, any claim to honor. Hamilton wrote another letter to Adams in which he barely disguised his contempt. "From this silence, I will draw no inference; nor will I presume to judge the fitness of silence on such an occasion, on the part of The Chief Magistrate of a Republic, towards a citizen, who without a stain has discharged so many important public trusts," he wrote. Of course, Hamilton made it clear that he did judge Adams's silence, and he judged it harshly. Without ever referring to Adams by name, Hamilton insulted him in the clearest manner possible. "But this much I will affirm," he wrote, "that by whomsoever a charge of the kind mentioned in my former letter may, at any time, have been made or insinuated against me, it is a base wicked and cruel calumny; destitute even of a plausible pretext to excuse folly or mask the depravity which must have dictated it."[104] Adams's failure to respond left Hamilton in a quandary. Given Adams's age and his office, challenging the president to a duel was not an option.[105] If Adams chose to ignore Hamilton's letters, though, Hamilton could only vindicate himself by turning to the court of public opinion.

Typically, for any action that would affect his honor, Hamilton canvassed his friends and confidants before making a decision. He first mentioned his idea of taking his case to the public and writing a pamphlet to defend himself in a 1 July letter to Wolcott. He argued that Adams's "friends are industrious in propagating the idea [of a British faction] to defeat the efforts to unite for Pinckney. The inquiry I propose may furnish an antidote and vindicate character."[106] He hoped both to "vindicate" his character and to unify Federalists behind Pinckney. As with the Reynolds pamphlet, personal and political motives were closely linked.

Protecting one's honor was a complicated business under any circumstances, but Hamilton also had to consider the larger political ramifications. While he considered whether or not to write the open letter, his friends offered words of caution. Recognizing that Hamilton's pamphlet would likely reach unintended readers, George Cabot advised Hamilton against signing his own name to it, because "this might give it an interest with men who need no such interest but it will be converted to a new proof that you are a *dangerous man*. Ames & I agree that you will give the enemy an advantage to which he has no claim."[107] Fisher Ames made the case for political caution even more strongly, arguing that both Pinckney and Adams needed to be supported equally "because any other arrangement would, by dividing the party, inevitably exclude *both* and absolutely secure the success of Mr Jefferson." That did not preclude, Ames argued, Hamilton's proposed pamphlet, but it did necessitate a great deal of discretion. "I am therefore clear that *you ought not with your name, nor if practicable in any way that will be traced to* you, to execute your purpose of exposing the reasons for a change of the executive," Ames wrote.[108] Despite the words of caution, Hamilton decided to write the letter and publish it in the form of a pamphlet. This decision, as much as any during his career, reveals his excessive attachment to honor, sometimes to the detriment of his political objectives.

The letter criticized Adams's policies and his character, perfectly in keeping with the commingling of these two in the early republic. Not surprisingly, Hamilton argued that Adams lacked the qualities essential in an honorable man. He wrote, "He is a man of an imagination sublimated and eccentric; propitious neither to the regular display of sound judgment, nor to steady perseverance in a systematic plan of conduct; and I began to perceive what has been since too manifest, that to this defect are added the unfortunate foibles of a vanity without bounds, and a jealousy capable of discoloring every object."[109] Given Hamilton's view of the tie between a leader's personal honor and national honor, Adams's defects threatened the nation.[110] Hamilton claimed that Adams's character "has sunk the tone of the public mind . . . sown the seeds of discord at home, and lowered the reputation of the Government abroad" (207–8). He justified his savage attack on the ostensible head of his party through his need to defend his public reputation with "those who have been spectators of my public actions." He willingly offered to compare himself "in the cardinal points of public and private rectitude" (229), a claim that showed honor's role in both public and private life despite his arguments to the contrary in the Reynolds pamphlet.

Hamilton hoped to confine his incendiary open letter to a small group of readers. Taking notice of his friends' advice, he decided to limit the circulation of the letter, originally planning to print two hundred copies. He wanted to reach a limited number of Federalist leaders (as he wrote in one letter, only "the most discreet")[111] who could strongly influence the course of the election. He commented, "Indeed, it is much my wish that its circulation could forever be confined within narrow limits" (234). He intended it, in other words, only for men of honor in his own party, in effect his public as he viewed it (elite leaders from the other party having long since been condemned as a Jacobin faction). Hamilton miscalculated once again, though, revealing a lack of awareness about the realities of the early American political world and the impossibility of circumscribing the public within such narrow confines. With the help of savvy and active political operatives such as Beckley, the letter almost inevitably found its way to a wider public. When the letter escaped the narrow readership that Hamilton had intended, he felt compelled to publish it himself.[112]

In this case, widespread circulation of the letter, now essentially a pamphlet, immediately doomed it to failure. The results were disastrous, since the public, especially Republicans, could hardly be expected to interpret his pamphlet according to the strictures of honor when it presented such an overwhelming political opportunity to them. Hamilton had written the letter as if he could "fix" not just his character but his readership, limiting it to elite Federalists who accepted the dictates of honor and held similar political beliefs. This vision was almost ludicrously out of touch with the political realities of the early republic in 1800, in which he had to address not a homogeneous audience of peers but a diffuse and varied audience of average citizens.[113]

After Hamilton published his letter, his enemies rejoiced, and his allies lamented what he had done. One Republican operative wrote that Hamilton's "career of ambition is passed, and neither honor or empire will ever be his."[114] Madison exalted, "What an important *Denouement* has lately been made!. . . . It will be a Thunderbolt. . . . I rejoice with you, that Republicanism is likely to be so *completely* triumphant."[115] Even his fellow Federalists generally condemned him.[116] Jedediah Morse wrote Wolcott, "I can only lament, (as I do most sincerely) the conduct that provoked the publication, & the too great warmth that dictated some parts of it. Of the patriotism & integrity of Genl. H. I have never entertained a doubt . . . but of his *prudence* in a former publication, & in the present, many good men will have their doubts."[117] Robert Troup concurred. He wrote that New York Federalists "lamented" its publication: "I find a much stronger disapprobation of it expressed every where. In point of imprudence, it is coupled with the [Reynolds] pamphlet. . . . Our enemies are universally in triumph. I have little or no doubt the latter will lay the foundation of a serious opposition to General Hamilton amongst the federalists, and that his usefulness hereafter will be greatly lessened."[118] Troup wrote to Rufus King, "The influence . . . of this letter upon Hamilton's character is extremely unfortunate. An opinion has grown out of it, which at present obtains almost universally, that his character is *radically deficient in discretion*, and therefore the federalists ask, what avail the most preeminent talents—the most distinguished patriotism—without the all important quality of discretion? Hence he is considered as an unfit head of the party."[119] Noting Hamilton's greatest fatal blind spot, Noah Webster wrote that Hamilton's letter showed that he "disdains public opinion and overleaps all the ordinary maxims of prudence."[120]

In 1800, it was virtually impossible for Hamilton to keep his letter's circulation tightly circumscribed. Hamilton should have known that it would reach a wider audience who would not accept either his arguments or his political goals. Hamilton's failure to realize this meant not simply that the publication backfired but that Hamilton had dishonored himself, so that even his allies judged him harshly. "Too much warmth," doubts about his "prudence" and his "discretion"—such words revealed that Hamilton had failed to conduct himself in the proper manner. He had acted imprudently and with too much personal feeling. He had written the letter, it seemed, out of personal enmity, displaying to his friends as well as his enemies a distressing lack of the qualities necessary to a character based on honor.

His miscalculation rested in part on the impossibility of separating private and public actions under the rules of honor, the impossibility of being able to criticize measures without condemning men. Even as honor provided a platform on which Hamilton tried to erect a carefully circumscribed polity, it also melded the personal and the political inseparably. Although honor was supposed to be an all-or-nothing proposition, there was an art to deploying it, an ongoing performance in which personal, political, and even national claims were negotiated in a fluid and dynamic fashion. As the public grew, maintaining honor involved more than a simple vigorous defense but rather a balance, an ability to moderate and adjudicate a variety of claims, a new "sensibility" by which to judge.

When others said that they felt Hamilton's usefulness would be greatly lessened, they made explicit the link between honor and political power, as well as Hamilton's slipping grasp on both. Graphic illustration of Hamilton's fall from grace was given a short time later when he spoke on behalf of his brother-in-law's campaign for governor of New York. Robert Troup described Hamilton's reception at his speeches to different wards. "At one of the polls General Hamilton, with impunity by the populace, was repeatedly called a thief," Troup wrote, "and at another poll with the same impunity he was called a rascal, villain, and every thing else that is infamous in society!"[121] Hamilton's reception offered clear proof of the electorate's public and humiliating refusal to ratify through deference his pretensions to honor and public leadership. At one time, such words would have roused Hamilton to defend himself. Instead, he declared to Troup that he would never show himself in public life again.

Figure 9. *John Adams*, painted by Gilbert Stuart, 1800/1815. Courtesy of the National Gallery of Art.

THREE

Virtue

Shortly after starting his diary, John Adams reflected on his new role as schoolmaster. Far from feeling limited in his new position, he thought that he sat at the head of the world in miniature:

> I sometimes, in my sprightly moments, consider my self, in my great Chair at School, as some Dictator at the head of a commonwealth. In this little State I can discover all the great Genius's, all the surprizing actions and revolutions of the great World . . . Generalls but 3 feet high . . . deep-projecting Politicians in peticoats . . . Virtuouso in the royal society. . . . Alexander. . . . Cesar. . . . Mr. Insipid . . . the polemical Divine. . . . my little school like the great World, is made up of Kings, Politicians, Divines, LD., Fops, Buffoons, Fidlers, Sychophants, Fools Coxcombs, and every other Character drawn in History or seen in the World.

Adams saw his own role in all of this as the judicious spectator, rewarding the just and punishing the wicked. "Is it not then the highest Pleasure my Friend to preside in this little World, to bestow the proper applause upon the virtuous and generous Actions, to blame and punish every vicious and contracted Trick," he wrote in his diary.[1] Adams admitted that this view seemed somewhat out of character: "Methinks I hear you say, this is odd talk for J. Adams." To explain his attitude, he offered a story that revealed the attraction of working with the undisguised characters of schoolchildren:

> About 4 months since a poor Girl in this neighbourhood walking by the meeting H[ouse] upon some Occasion, in the evening, met a fine Gentleman with laced hat and wast coat, and a sword who sollicited her to turn aside with him into the horse Stable. The Girl relucted a little, upon which he gave her 3 Guineas, and wished he might be damned if he did not have her in 3 months. Into the horse Stable they went. The 3 Guineas proved 3 farthings—and the Girl proves with Child, without a Friend upon Earth that will own her, or knowing the father of her 3 farthing Bastard.[2]

The entry contained in embryo concerns that would dominate Adams's life.

In his miniature world, he reigned supreme in a godlike position of omniscience, and he found the task of judging the characters of his pupils a relatively simple one. As he understood them, children's characters were transparent and hid no ambiguity about their ultimate motivations or designs. The real world presented a much more complicated picture, though, even to the most observant of spectators. The girl was accosted by a "fine Gentleman with laced hat and wast coat, and a sword." Such accoutrements were supposed to denote not simply polished manners but an inner refinement.[3] Instead, they proved mere stage props, as false as the three guineas the gentleman promised.

Adams would spend his life attempting to see beneath the laced hats and fine waistcoats of society, to strip away the false trappings of men in his search for virtue, vexing as that search often was for him. In his reading, he noted a passage from Bolingbroke: "True moral virtue is something very real. It is the cause of our happiness." Adams scribbled beside it: "This is divine and eternal truth. But alas! how shall we define true moral virtue? And where shall we find it?"[4] As he wrote in another margin, "There is a voice within us, which seems to intimate that real merit should govern the world; and that men ought to be respected only in proportion to their talents, virtues, and services. But the question always has been, how can this arrangement be accomplished? How shall the men of merit be discovered? How shall the proportions of merit be ascertained and graduated?"[5] Adams's obsessive search for virtue served not so much to identify and protect it as to call it into question. Engaged in an almost paranoiac quest of unmasking, he could never rest secure. He could never be sure that he had peeled back the last layer of disguise. "Who shall judge?" he asked, unsure if even he exhibited the necessary virtue.[6]

In search of characters of virtue, Adams would find himself entangled in the ambiguities surrounding the distinction between public and private. Distrusting the public masks that men wore to hide their true motives, Adams attempted to penetrate to a deeper level by uncovering his and others' private motivations. The code of conduct to which Adams's sense of virtue committed him was strikingly different from Hamilton's sense of honor or Jefferson's use of friendship. If Jefferson struggled to maintain a private self, uncorrupted by politics and insincerity, and if Hamilton struggled to fashion a public self based on honor, Adams disdained the very idea of fashioning a self, seeing it as one more duplicitous attempt to mask one's true motivations. While Jefferson and Hamilton spent a great deal of energy on their self-presentations, Adams spent his energy judging those presentations, probing beneath them to the "truth." But his pervasive mistrust of all public representations of virtue tended to undermine not just the distinction between public and private life but his belief in virtue itself. Skeptical to the end, he would attempt to create a government that harnessed the "passion for distinction" in order to persuade people to act with at least a semblance of virtue, even if they failed to possess the austere virtue that he claimed as his own standard. Before he could begin proposing national remedies, though, he would first have to examine himself.

"Do I know my own heart? I am not sure"

Adams's Attempt to Lead the Virtuous Life

Adams struggled throughout his life to maintain a virtuous character. Those struggles were constantly monitored in his diary, which he kept with varying degrees of rigor from 1755 to 1804. It was the essential genre for Adams in his never-ending quest to determine true from false virtue.[7] The diary provided a forum in which to judge the virtue of himself and others, far from the distorting lens of public approval. It embodied a certain attitude about the self and its place in the world, a skeptical vantage point much like his days as a schoolmaster from which to view the successes and failures in the daily battle to subdue the unruly passions of the self.

By choosing a genre in which he was both writer and reader, Adams freed himself from the necessity of tailoring his writing for an audience, of creating the kind of public mask that he distrusted. Adams despised the kind of role playing occasionally demanded by honor, seeing that behavior as the worst kind of falsehood. He ridiculed the public recognition and validation that honor required. Adams's use of the diary also highlights significant differences between him and Jefferson. For Adams, Jefferson's attempt to create harmony was really an exercise in "trimming," of altering his views for the sake of popularity, a sacrifice of principle to relationship; instead, Adams sought conflict as a sign of his independence. Adams would have been appalled at the quid pro quo that often lurked behind Jeffersonian gestures of friendship. Adams was against blatant political maneuvering, but politics masquerading as friendship horrified him even more.

Adams's political character would emerge from the lessons that he learned in his diary. In fact, his diary writing, with its emphasis on unfettered and unedited expression, probably influenced his other writings, which exhibited certain diaristic tendencies. His writings were almost always disorganized (about which his contemporaries frequently complained). They also exhibited a certain self-involved obsessiveness, sometimes continuing for an interminable length, such as his essays in the *Boston Patriot* from 1809 to 1812 defending his conduct in public life, and sometimes abandoned for no apparent reason, such as his autobiography.[8]

Perhaps most important, the distrust of public approval explored in his diary informed his public writings as well, and he refused to modify his remarks, even when they threatened to become a source of misunderstanding and criticism. Virtually all his public writings, Adams argued, were unpopular (which he took as further confirmation of his own virtue). So, despite the diary's private nature, its influence extended into the public realm.[9]

Even as the diary provided an ideal forum for Adams to judge his efforts to create a virtuous character for himself undisturbed by considerations of public approval, though, it exacerbated his most significant problem, determining true from false virtue. Because the genre created a closed circuit between writer and reader, Adams could rely only on himself to impose a just standard, but as he recognized, one could not trust even one's self.[10] Adams called self-deceit "the source of far the greatest and worst part of the vices and calamities among mankind."[11] Although he would attempt to strip away the public masks of deception, his corrosive skepticism left him unsure if he had uncovered true virtue. Far from providing the generic means to answer that question, the diary contributed to Adams's chronic uncertainty, leaving him anxious about his own virtue and deeply pessimistic about everyone else's.[12]

Increasing his difficulties, the meaning of virtue itself was undergoing a transformation during Adams's lifetime.[13] Similar to honor and friendship as foundations for the polity, virtue uneasily straddled the boundary between public and private life. In classical republican terms, virtue was thought to be a public quality, the sacrifice of one's private interests for the public good. In Protestant religious thought, virtue was conceived of in private terms, involving domestic traits such as temperance, frugality, and hard work. Adding to the confusion, the two types of virtue were closely related. Frugality and hard work laid the groundwork for the kind of economic success that permitted a man to sacrifice self-interest for the public good. Given this intermingling within the concept itself, Adams's politics of virtue led him into the labyrinth of distinguishing public and private in the early republic.

In his personal struggle to fashion himself into a virtuous character, Adams attempted to achieve both public and private virtue. His diary provided the crucial staging ground for his own personal battle against his infirmities, particularly during his youth. Self-government was a greater challenge than the government of nations, according to Adams, and he lamented, "Oh! that I could *wear out* of my mind every mean and base affectation."[14] There was no middle path of attainable, if flawed, virtue. The choice lay solely between dissipation and stern self-discipline. For Adams, only such a total subjugation would render him truly worthy. "He is not a wise man and is unfit to fill any important Station in Society, that has left one Passion in his Soul unsubdued," he told himself.[15] Given the constant danger of straying from the path of virtue, Adams brought a sense of accountability to all his actions, which his diary allowed him to monitor incessantly. His entries as a young man were filled with exhortations to himself: "Rose not till 7 o clock. This is the usual fate of my resolutions!"[16] He berated himself when he "smoaked, chatted, trifled, loitered away this whole day almost."[17]

Revealing the difficulty of separating true virtue from mere self-interest, though, Adams had eminently practical reasons for his attempts at self-discipline—such habits were not simply the way to virtue but the path to success. Already somewhat guilty about his choice of a legal career in defiance of his father's wishes and fearing that other young, aspiring lawyers in his district had various advantages over him, he believed that he could succeed only through rigorous study and unceasing application. His early experiences did not ease his mind. He lost his first case after preparing a defective writ and had only a couple of clients during the first year that his law office was open.[18] His pursuit of virtue was not some bloodless spiritual quest but was inextricably tied to more worldly goals, such as ambition. This personal experience with the commingling of virtue and baser motives gave him a lifelong distrust of the motives that could masquerade behind a rhetoric of virtue.[19]

Adams's diary allowed him to peel back the layers of his own motives, an experience that left him distrustful of any claims to virtue, particularly when those claims were public. As he warned himself in his diary in 1761, "So subtle are our Hearts in deceiving ourselves. . . . It must be confessed, that the most refined Patriotism with human Nature can be wrought, has in it an alloy of Ambition, of Pride and avarice that debases the Composition, and produces mischievous Effects."[20] He would carry his concerns as a youth throughout his life. When Adams did "scheme," he did so with an uneasy heart, disparaging what he did. "Intrigue, and making Interest, and Asking favors is a new employment to me," he wrote in his diary. "I'm unpractised in Intrigues for Power." Even with a small taste of political maneuvering, he felt the need to warn himself, "I begin to feel the Passions of the World. Ambition, Avarice, Intrigue, Party, all must be guarded."[21] Adams would never dispel this early mistrust. Years later, as he waited to hear the results of the 1796 election, he fretted about his own motivations. "It really Seems to me as if I wished to be left out," he wrote. "Let me See! do I know my own heart? I am not Sure."[22] Adams's skepticism of his own motives escalated when he was trying to exercise public virtue (as in the above case, when he anxiously wondered if he embodied the classical republican belief that only those who did not seek power were fit to hold it). One could achieve private virtue through a regimen of self-discipline, according to Adams, but achieving public virtue demanded the far more difficult regimen of defending against self-deception.

The introspection fostered by his diary did give Adams a better understanding of himself. He would come to recognize one fault in particular: vanity. He wrote, "Vanity I am sensible, is my cardinal Vice and cardinal folly, and I am in continual Danger, when in Company, of being led an *ignis fatuus* Chase by it, without the strictest Caution and watchfulness over my Self."[23] His self-recognition reveals why his attempts at public virtue occasioned personal distrust. Susceptible as he was to approval and praise, claims of public virtue would always be shadowed in his mind by the worry that his actions were really motivated not by his virtue but by his vanity. Adams once again had practical reasons for his self-criticism, worrying that vanity could blot out a man's virtues (and the greater the talent, the greater the danger of vanity). "A puffy, vain, conceited Conversation, never fails to bring a Man into Contempt," he wrote. He admitted being "to a very heinous Degree, guilty in this Respect. . . . but instead of shining briter I only clouded the few Rays that before rendered me visible." For men of great talent, the love of fame "is generally much stronger than in other People, and this Passion it must be confessed is apt to betray men into impertinent Exertions of their Talents."[24] He would turn these lessons to use in his understanding of political motivation and his own ideas about the type of government America should have. Recognizing the universal "passion for distinction," Adams would later attempt to harness man's inherent vanity and need for recognition to good ends, even as he attempted to subdue their hold upon him.

Given his distrust of public facades (and, consequently, of public approval), Adams claimed to trust not praise but criticism. Long before he would experience the vicissitudes of popularity as a politician, he wrote to himself in 1759, "Good treatment makes me think I am admired, beloved, my own Vanity will be indulged in me. So I dismiss my Guard and grow weak, silly, vain, conceited, ostentatious. But a Check, a frown, a sneer, a Sarcasm . . . makes me more careful and considerate."[25] Such contrarian ways were essential, he thought, to maintaining his virtue. When Adams acted in ways that were unpopular, he felt such actions proved his virtue, and he recalled them with great pride. For example, he sent Elbridge Gerry as a minister to France against the wishes of his entire cabinet. After his retirement from public life, he wrote that he viewed Gerry's nomination "with infinite satisfaction, and which will console me in my last hour."[26] For Adams, the path of true virtue was always marked by neglect, if not outright hostility. "If virtue was to be rewarded," Adams wrote, "it would not be Virtue. If Virtue was to be rewarded with Fame, it would not be Virtue of the sublimest Kind." Unpopular actions reassured Adams that public approval had not seduced him from the right course.[27] Despite his claims, Adams's words proved to be no match for his vanity. When he won his first case before a jury, he noted with pride in his diary that observers praised his "saucy" performance. In another diary entry, he bragged that spectators were swept away by his courtroom rhetoric. And throughout his life, Adams complained that his efforts on behalf of the Revolution were overlooked.[28]

Although personal virtue was the product of an arduous and never-ceasing struggle, Adams believed that his self-scrutiny had indeed helped him achieve it, which in turn allowed him to stand before others free of any dissimulation. In looking back over his public life, he wrote to Mercy Otis Warren in 1807, "I have never practised simulation or dissimulation with my countrymen. My principles and opinions have always been as public as arguments before the most numerous popular assemblies, and even as dissemination from the press could make them; and they have always been uniformly the same in matters of government."[29] He later wrote to her again on the point: "I have never sacrificed a principle, nor even concealed an opinion, from a motive of ambition or an affectation of popularity."[30] The language that he used—"dissimulation," "concealed"—shows his fear of the hidden motives of men. Virtue was supposed to govern all the way to the core. If not, was there true virtue underneath, or was it only self-interest masquerading as virtue? For Adams, the only solution seemed to be to strip away all masks and disguises, beginning with his own.

"To strip off the gilding and false lustre"
Adams and the Theater of Virtue

In the political arena, Adams extended to others the same careful scrutiny that he practiced on himself in his diary. Recapitulating on the national stage his earlier experience as a schoolmaster rewarding the just and punishing the wicked, Adams challenged himself to refine his ability to discern others' hearts. In his diary, he praised a history book for performing a similar task. "It is calculated to strip off the Gilding and false Lustre from worthless Princes and Nobles," he wrote, "and to bestow the Reward of Virtue, Praise upon the generous and worthy only."[31] He would attempt the same task with his contemporaries. In 1775, deeply immersed in his activities as a member of the Continental Congress, Adams wrote James Warren on the importance "of a Faculty of Searching Hearts," arguing that "there is a Discernment competent to Mortals by which they can penetrate into the Minds of Men and discover their Secret Passions, Prejudices, Habits, Hopes, Fears, Wishes and Designs, and by this Means judge what Part they will act in given Circumstances for the future and see what Principles and Motives have actuated them to the Conduct they have held in certain Conjunctures of Circumstances which are passed."[32] A short time later, he promised "to draw the Character of every new Personage I have an opportunity of knowing. . . . My View will be to learn the Art of penetrating into Men's Bosoms."[33] He hoped to see beneath the public characters of his fellow leaders to determine if true virtue lay beneath their facades.

As Adams himself recognized, though, discerning the hearts of his fellow revolutionaries was a far more complicated task than what he had faced as a schoolmaster. Given the complexity of bringing thirteen separate colonies together to act as one body in the Continental Congress, he despaired of achieving his goal. He wrote in 1775:

> A Mind as vast as the Ocean or Atmosphere is necessary to penetrate and comprehend all the intricate and complicated Interests which compose the Machine of the Confederate Colonies. It requires all the Philosophy I am Master of, and more than all, at Times to preserve the Serenity of Mind and Stediness of Heart which is necessary to watch the Motions of Friends and Enemies, of the Violent and the Timid, the Credulous and the dull, as well as Wicked.[34]

The creation of a national political sphere increased Adams's difficulties exponentially. "In a Provincial Assembly, where we know a Man's Pedigree and Biography, his Education, Profession and Connections, as well as his Fortune, it is easy to see what it is that governs a Man and determines him to this Party in Preference to that, to this System of Politicks rather than another, etc.," he noted in a letter written to James Warren in 1775. "But here it is quite otherwise. We frequently see Phenomena which puzzles us. It requires Time to enquire and learn the Characters and Connections, the Interests and Views of a Multitude of Strangers." Despite the herculean task facing him, Adams viewed it as essential to his success: "A Dexterity and Facility of thus unraveling Mens Thoughts and a Faculty of governing them by Means of the Knowledge we have of them, constitutes the principal Part of the Art of a Politician."[35] With his emphasis on his own lack of guile, Adams thought himself entirely legible to the political world. Others, he thought, needed to be unmasked.

Adams's search into the hearts of other men sounded a recurrent theme: most men were driven by selfish and even wicked motives. His distrust sprang from his constant fear that public representations of virtue masked private iniquity. When he judged public officials, his pervasive distrust would lead him to find, almost always, "false gilding." On the eve of the Revolution, Adams unmasked what he saw as the duplicitous public facade of British officials. He faulted them, particularly Massachusetts governor Thomas Hutchinson, with engaging in a vast and nefarious plot.[36]

Responding to a series of Loyalist newspaper essays, Adams painted a picture of an immense conspiracy by the British to dupe the colonists. Writing a series of essays under the pen name "Novanglus," Adams repeatedly conjured up a dark and sinister picture of British actions. Claiming to "penetrate arcana" and "show the wicked policy of the tories," Adams told readers that he would reveal the "secret springs of action." He wrote of "dark intrigues and wicked machinations" aimed at "enslaving this country" and hunted them down in "all their disguises."[37]

Adams found few public figures worthy, though, and criticized even the heroes of the Revolution.[38] Given his distrust of the true motivations behind the public actions of men, it is unsurprising that he would so frequently dispute the virtuous "characters" that they proclaimed for themselves. Benjamin Franklin, in particular, excited his detestation, and Adams often referred to him as cunning—a word he used only when he wanted to show the deepest opprobrium.[39] The cunning man manipulated appearances and deceived others with his public facade. Later in life, he disparaged Franklin's personal charm in his *Autobiography*: "He has the most affectionate and insinuating Way of charming the Woman or the Man that he fixes on. It is the most silly and ridiculous Way imaginable, in the Sight of an American, but it succeeds, to admiration, fullsome and sickish as it is, in Europe." By attempting to make Franklin's popularity merely a European phenomenon, Adams hoped to show both its un-American quality and its link to corruption, the antithesis of republican virtue's transparency. Adams's tenure in France as one of America's ministers, along with Franklin, shaped his opinion. While diligently fulfilling his duties and attempting to keep his expenses at a minimum, Adams watched Franklin engage in an endless round of socializing at the expense of both austerity and duty (a failure to exhibit both private and public virtue). Franklin's behavior courted precisely the kind of popularity that Adams mistrusted (and envied as well), because it relied on superficial manners, a public facade, rather than true virtue. Adams complained about Franklin's efforts to burnish his own reputation, "He has a Passion for Reputation and Fame, as strong as you can imagine, and his Time and Thoughts are chiefly employed to obtain it, and to set Tongues and Pens male and female, to celebrating him. Painters, Statuaries, Sculptors, China Potters, and all are set to work for this End."[40] He considered Franklin's reputation as a diplomat "one of the grossest impostures that has ever been practiced upon mankind since the days of Mahomet."[41] Adams once again had more personal motives for his criticisms. Franklin persuaded Congress in 1781 to strip Adams of his exclusive commission to negotiate peace with the British, an act that probably triggered a nervous breakdown in Adams. Most of Adams's harshest comments came from the period after this occurred.

Figure 10. *Benjamin Franklin*, painted by Joseph Siffred Duplessis, c. 1785. Courtesy of the National Portrait Gallery, Smithsonian Institution.

For a number of years, particularly after he lost the presidential election, Adams also described Jefferson as "cunning."[42] Adams's criticisms were again complicated by personal motives, as his onetime friend increasingly opposed his presidency and eventually supplanted him, achieving much greater popularity than Adams along the way. Adams spoke contemptuously of Jefferson as a "party man" and "an intriguer."[43] He claimed to "shudder . . . at the calamities, which I fear his conduct is preparing for his country: from a mean thirst for popularity, an inordinate ambition, and a want of sincerity."[44] Adams's complaints all focused on Jefferson's lack of public virtue. A party man did not uphold the public good. A thirst for popularity bespoke a desire for personal aggrandizement. Ambition marked Jefferson as someone unfit to hold power. Unsurprisingly, Adams also found Jefferson lacking in sincerity, precisely what Jefferson himself had feared when composing his letter to Adams. Adams found Jefferson's attempts to reach out to political allies as the kind of "intriguing" that duplicitous politicians pursued.[45]

Assessing Jefferson in 1807, Adams explicitly compared his own virtue with Jefferson's. Adams noted in a letter to Mercy Otis Warren that he had "crossed the Atlantic Ocean three times, and run the gauntlet through successions of British men-of-war, at a time when the spirit of the British government was so high, and the passions of the nation so exasperated, that I had every reason to apprehend, if they once had me in their power, they would make of me an example of their vengeance by executing upon me their punishment of treason in all its horrors." Of Jefferson's own efforts during the Revolution, Adams wrote, "You knew that I had undertaken all these hazards, after your philosophical friend Jefferson had not dared to accept them."[46] The snide description of the "philosophical" Jefferson revealed Adams's opinion that the great friend of the people was not willing to make the kind of sacrifices for the public good that Adams himself had so willingly made and that were the sign of true virtue.

In one of his many letters to Mercy Otis Warren refuting her history of the American Revolution, Adams disclaimed any improper ambition for himself: "If by 'ambition' you mean a love of power or a desire of public offices, I answer, I never solicited a vote in my life for any public office. I never swerved from any principle, I never professed any opinion, I never concealed even any speculative opinion, to obtain a vote. I never sacrificed a friend or betrayed a trust. I never hired scribblers to defame my rivals. I never wrote a line of slander against my bitterest enemy, nor encouraged it in any other." The statement showed whom Adams had in mind as the prototypical man of improper ambition—Thomas Jefferson. Although Adams excessively disclaimed any sense of thwarted ambition, he clearly harbored considerable anger toward his presidential successor. All the activities he listed were thinly veiled criticisms of Jefferson (hiring Freneau to write and edit a newspaper, instigating friends to write for his cause, telling people what they wanted to hear, and betraying his longtime friend Adams). Adams's implicit critique became explicit a few paragraphs later when he complained of the effort "to cry up Jefferson as the great republican,—Jefferson, who is not half so much of a republican as I am, and whose administration has not been so conformable to republican principles or manners as mine was."[47] Although Jefferson and other popular politicians served as the focus of much of Adams's anger, the truth was that few, if any, political leaders seemed to merit praise as virtuous leaders in Adams's eyes. The very nature of their public roles made him distrust their public virtue as mere window dressing.

"The Furnace of Affliction may refine them"
America as Virtuous Nation

Adams's most important search for virtue was into the virtue of the nation's people. He believed the success or failure of America would depend on it. As Adams noted in his diary in 1772, "The Preservation of Liberty depends on the intellectual and moral Character of the People. As long as Knowledge and Virtue are diffused generally among the Body of a Nation, it is impossible they should be enslaved. This can be brought to pass only by debasing their Understandings, or by corrupting their Hearts."[48] Given his personal struggles and his deep distrust of the virtue of other politicians, though, he struggled with the question of how to ensure a virtuous people to sustain America's republican government.

From his youth to his final years, he exhibited an ambivalence about the people's virtue, as his mercurial emotions carried him from one extreme to the other—Jefferson claimed that Adams "never acted on any system, but was always governed by the feelings of the moment."[49] Occasionally, Adams waxed optimistic. In 1765, he wrote, "America was designed by Providence for the Theatre, on which Man was to make his true figure, on which science, Virtue, Liberty, Happiness and Glory were to exist in Peace."[50] Later, he wrote, "If ever an infant country deserved to be cherished it is America. If ever any people merited honor and happiness that are her inhabitants. . . . they have the most habitual, radical sense of liberty, and the highest reverence for virtue."[51] After the Continental Congress approved the Declaration of Independence, a high point in revolutionary patriotism, he wrote to Abigail, "I am well aware of the Toil and Blood and Treasure, that it will cost Us to maintain this Declaration, and support and defend these States.—Yet through all the Gloom I can see the Rays of ravishing Light and Glory. I can see that the End is more than with all the Means. And that Posterity will tryumph in that Days Transaction, even altho We should rue it, which I trust in God We shall not."[52] In 1789, as he assumed his position as vice president in the new government created by the Constitution, he claimed that America's success would "loosen the chains of all mankind."[53] In 1798, riding a wave of popularity as president for his measured stand against French insults, he wrote, "Our independence will be one essential instrument for reclaiming the fermented world, and bringing good out of the mass of evil."[54]

But he also frequently lamented his countrymen's lack of virtue. A number of weeks after signing the Declaration, he claimed that "human nature will be found to be the same in America as it has been in Europe."[55] Reacting to news of Shays's Rebellion, Adams noted in January 1787, "Our Countrymen have never merited the Character of very exalted Virtue."[56] Perhaps disillusioned by his own political experience as well by the war with Great Britain in which America was embroiled, he argued in 1812 against the idea that America was exceptional: "There is no special Providence for us. We are not a chosen people that I know of, or if we are, we deserve it as little as the Jews. . . . We must and we shall go the way of all earth."[57] Even during the early days of the Revolution, though, he worried that Americans had already fallen from the path of virtue. "Virtue and Simplicity of Manners are indispensably necessary in a Republic among all order and Degrees of Men," he wrote in 1776. "But there is so much Rascallity, so much Venality and Corruption, so much Avarice and Ambition, such a Rage for Profit and Commerce among all Ranks and Degrees of Men even in America, that I sometimes doubt whether there is public Virtue enough to Support a Republic." Adams doubted if such virtue was possible even in America.[58]

His skepticism about virtue extended to private life as well. Although in that case Adams had no need to unmask his fellow citizens, he still found himself extremely doubtful of the private virtue of the people. In a letter to Abigail in 1774, he listed the many ways Americans had already been corrupted by Britain, writing of "the universal Spirit of Debauchery, Disipation, Luxury, Effeminacy and Gaming which the late ministerial Measures are introducing." Adams accused the Tories of acting "the Part of the Devil—they tempt Men and Women into sin, and then reproach them for It, and become soon their Tormentors for it."[59] Forever on the lookout for hidden plots, he made use of a common story of the Revolution, the story of temptation and seduction, of malevolent designs behind ministerial acts. His list of corruptions (debauchery, dissipation, luxury) revealed the private virtues (temperance, self-discipline, and frugality) that he found lacking in the people at large, private virtues that were supposed to lay the foundation for public virtue.

The idea that the people would be drawn into corruption by British measures implicitly identified Americans with the female role of the seduced and its concomitant concerns with private, domestic virtues. When Adams discussed the lack of virtue in America, the centrality of seduction as a trope for understanding revolutionary events (and thus a gendered understanding of the Revolution itself) frequently came to the fore. One of the battles of the Revolution was clearly a rhetorical battle of American men trying to claim their political manhood.[60] He often saw the people in the role of the virtuous but vulnerable woman. "Democracy is

Lovelace, and the people are Clarissa," he once wrote, a formulation that equated American virtue with the passive female virtue of chastity.[61] Such an understanding seemed to leave the people at the mercy of scheming men, a dangerous situation given what he believed about his fellow Americans' "effeminate Appetites."[62]

Those "effeminate Appetites" became the avenue by which Adams extended his corrosive mistrust of virtue to the hearth. The ever present, ever expanding presence of British goods best captured the ubiquity of corruption and the failure of private virtue. Those goods revealed the insidious way that Britain had entered every household and undermined private virtue. Adams complained to Abigail, "There is not a Sin which prevails more universally and has prevailed longer, than Prodigality, in Furniture, Equipage, Apparell and Diet. And I believe that this Vice, this Sin has as large a Share in drawing down Judgments of Heaven as any."[63] Even at the height of revolutionary fervor, it was difficult for him not to see the American scene in a deeply pessimistic light, because no family was free from the taint of commerce. "The Spirit of Commerce, . . . which even insinuates itself into Families, and influences holy Matrimony, and thereby corrupts the morals of families as well as destroys their Happiness, it is much to be feared is incompatible with that purity of Heart and Greatness of soul which is necessary for an happy Republic," he wrote. Even in Adams's New England, such a spirit was "rampant," and "trade is as well understood and as passionately loved there as any where."[64]

Despite the obvious role of women in fostering or undermining virtue through the exercise of domestic economy, Adams dismissed the idea of giving women a public political role. A few months before Congress declared independence, Abigail asked Adams to "Remember the Ladies," adding that his "Sex are Naturally Tyrannical" and promising "to foment a Rebellion," if ignored.[65] Adams laughed at her request, comparing her rebellion to that of "Children and Apprentices . . . Indians . . . and Negroes." Even as he circumscribed women firmly within the domestic world, though, he also called attention to their power, albeit humorously. Claiming that men "have only the Name of Master," Adams told Abigail that "in practice you know We are the subjects" and that, without their legal and political advantages, men would soon be subjected to "the Despotism of the Peticoat."[66] Given his close relationship with his wife, his joking remarks probably held some truth for his own marriage, even if he did not seriously consider her request.[67]

But his political vision simply did not include any significant role for women. He claimed that their "delicacy" rendered then "unfit" for the "great businesses of life" and that their attention was "engaged with the nurture of their children." According to Adams, "nature has made them fittest for domestic cares."[68] Adams was willing to recognize that excluding

Figure 11.   *Abigail Smith Adams*, painted by Gilbert Stuart, 1800/1815. Courtesy of the National Gallery of Art.

groups from political participation would always be based on somewhat ar-bitrary grounds, but he thought that the boundaries were in danger of being drawn too loosely. Rather than imagining the inclusion of women, Adams thought that property qualifications should be used to exclude some men.

Adams did envision an important domestic role for women, though, one with political implications. He saw the role of women as central to the creation of good citizens. When Abigail argued that educated women were crucial if the new nation were to have heroes and statesmen, he remarked that her sentiments were "exactly agreeable to my own."[69] He demonstrated these beliefs in his own life. Besides his relationship with his wife, he encouraged his daughters to read philosophy and history, and he supported Emma Willard in her effort to establish a school of higher education for women. He claimed not to think "either Politicks or War, or any other Art or Science beyond the Line of [the female] Sex."[70] Even though unable to imagine a public role for women, Adams did see a significant role for them in domestic life as republican mothers and wives— no small matter given the importance not just of private virtue but of the reliance of public virtue on private virtues.[71]

But what recourse was there against the preponderant commercial interests working to seduce the people? What hope was there for America? Adams prescribed a course of treatment that mirrored the self-examinations he subjected himself to in his diary. "Every man must seriously set himself to root out his Passions, Prejudices and Attachments, and to get the better of his private Interest. The only reputable Principle and Doctrine must be that all Things must give Way to the public," he wrote in a statement that exposed the inextricable link between private and public virtue.[72] In other words, for the people to achieve the public virtue necessary to sustain republican government, Adams believed that they needed to follow the kind of austere regimen of self-discipline that he practiced.

Although Adams accepted those rigors willingly, he had little confidence in the ability of the people to do the same. Instead, he hoped that the hardships of war might reform his fellow citizens. When the British closed the port of Boston, Adams wrote to Abigail mainly of the advantages of such hardship. In the first place, he thought it would give a boost to the cause of revolution. "I cant help depending on this," he wrote in 1774, "that the present dreadfull Calamity of that beloved Town is intended to bind the Colonies together in more indisoluble Bands, and to animate their Exertions, at this great Crisis in the Affairs of Mankind." Second, he hoped it would benefit the people of Boston. "The Tryals of that unhappy and devoted People are likely to be severe indeed. God grant that the Furnace of Affliction may refine them," he wrote.[73] Adams offered a similar analysis when he wrote to Abigail in 1776. Once again, he recognized the possibility that "America shall suffer Calamities still more wasting and Distresses yet more dreadfull." He embraced these hardships and saw in them the possibility for great good. "If this is to be the Case, it will have this good Effect, at least: it will inspire Us with many Virtues, which We have not, and correct many Errors, Follies, and Vices, which threaten to disturb, dishonour, and destroy Us," he wrote. Linking personal and national virtue to the same process of refinement, Adams commented,

"The Furnace of Affliction produces Refinement, in States as well as Individuals. And the new Governments we are assuming, in every Part, will require a Purification from our vices, and an Augmentation of our Virtues or they will be no Blessings. The People will have unbounded Power. And the People are extreamly addicted to Corruption and Venality, as well as the Great."[74]

Even as Adams hoped the people would refine their virtue, he also knew that they faced an additional task similar to the one he had set for himself upon entering politics—stripping away the false gilding. In order to select the proper leaders, Americans would have to see beneath the false appearances presented to them. If he had little confidence in their ability to act virtuously, though, he had perhaps even less confidence in their ability to reward true virtue. Reacting to Jefferson's embargo and the possibility of war, he wrote Benjamin Rush in 1808, "My friend! Our country is in masquerade! No party, no man, dares to avow his real sentiments. All is disguise, visard, cloak. The people are totally puzzled and confounded. They cannot penetrate the views, designs, or objects of any party, or any individual."[75] The problem was part of the fabric of political life, though, so that, as he noted in the late 1780s (likely thinking of himself), "the real merit of public men is rarely fully known and impartially considered." Instead, Adams foresaw his countrymen falling prey to the same duplicity practiced in every other country. "Our country will do like all others—play their affairs into the hands of a few cunning fellows," he wrote. "Human nature is not ungrateful. But while many rate their merits higher than the truth, it is almost impossible that the public mind should be exactly informed to whom they are really obliged."[76] Adams had little faith in the public representations of politicians and even less faith in the ability of the people to see beneath their disguises.

Despite his pessimism, Adams continued to engage in what he saw as the Sisyphean task of enlightening his fellow countrymen. In his most systematic attempt to discuss government, his massive, three-volume *Defence of the Constitutions of Government of the United States of America*, written in 1787–88 ostensibly in response to the calling of the Federal Constitutional Convention, he attempted to counter what he saw as an overly simplistic faith in a virtuous people. Instead, he intended to offer a more complicated vision of America's revolutionary heritage and of man. The *Defence* recalled his diary in its lack of structure, its obsessive concern with certain issues, and its author's claim that he disdained seeking public approval. His years in Europe as a diplomat had left him increasingly out of touch with the development of American politics, though, and his book seemed to be more a response to Europeans than to his fellow Americans.[77] "This Book will make me unpopular," Adams wrote to James Warren.[78] He was right—the book was misunderstood (unsurprisingly, given Adams's own misunderstanding about his audience) as an argument to roll back the Revolution and install a government more like that of the British, when in fact he meant it as a warning against aristocrats.[79]

In the *Defence*, Adams addressed the problem of the credulous many and the artful few. He returned to one of his central concerns: the public facades of virtue behind which men cloaked their private designs. "Is the disposition to imposture so prevalent in men of experience, that their private views of ambition and avarice can be accomplished only by artifice?" he asked. "Nothing can be inferred from it more than this, that the multitude have always been credulous, and the few are always artful."[80] A republic most closely achieved Adams's ideal of transparency. He complained in the *Defence* that in a simple monarchy, "the ministers of state can never know their friends from their enemies; secret cabals undermine their influence, and blast their reputation." Such a state of affairs encouraged spies and informers, which "poison[ed] freedom in its sweetest retirements." In contrast, a free government required each person in government to "declare his opinion, upon every question."[81] In his *Autobiography*, written late in life, he recounted his own efforts to open the proceedings of the Continental Congress to the public—only to have his efforts foiled by the selfish motives of other members. He wrote that he had supported the motion for opening the debates "with zeal" but that "neither party were willing: some were afraid of divisions among the people: but more were afraid to let the people see the insignificant figures they made in that assembly. Nothing indeed was less understood, abroad among the people, than the real constitution of Congress and the characters of those who conducted the business of it."[82]

Adams's fear of ministerial plots hatched behind closed doors helps explain his lifelong commitment to a truly representative government. He called not for a virtuous assembly, although he would have lauded such a body, but for one that was a perfect mirror of society. In his *Thoughts on Government*, written in 1776, he wrote that the assembly "should be in miniature, an exact portrait of the people at large. It should think, feel, reason, and act like them."[83] In his *Defence*, Adams also called for a representative assembly that mirrored the people. "The perfection of the portrait consists in its likeness," he noted.[84] Although not perhaps the road to the most virtuous legislative body, a perfectly representative assembly would at least be transparent, enacting the people's will openly. This reliance on a representative assembly also helps explain Adams's obsession with creating a government that fostered virtue as much as possible. Because it mirrored the people, his scheme of representation would reveal flaws as well as strengths.

Adams recognized the difficulty of determining the true meaning of events and suggested that such an understanding was, for the people at least, an impossibility. After his own political career had ended, he wrote, "I have sometimes thought that public opinion is never right concerning present measures or future events. The secret of affairs is never known to the public till after the event, and often not then. Even in the freest and most popular governments, events are preparing by causes that are at work in secret."[85] Like the schoolmaster he had once been, though, Adams tried to teach others to see what he saw, to see through the masquerades of other men to the truth hidden below. He wrote his old friend Rush, "I love the people of America and believe them to be incapable of ingratitude. They have been, they may be, and they are deceived. It is the duty of somebody to undeceive them."[86]

Rather than the heroic virtue of the furnace of affliction he had once called for, Adams's solution was for what could be called a more bureaucratic virtue. The solution for the lack of virtue among both the people and their leaders was the form of the government, which could shape the character of a people and steer the actions of the politicians.[87] As the colonies were poised to make the final break from Great Britain and create their own government, he wrote, "It is the Form of Government which gives the decisive Colour to the Manners of the People, more than any other Thing."[88] Adams gave man little chance for virtue, public or private, unless guided by a proper government to foster it. Still holding a similar view more than a decade later, in a digression toward the end of volume 3 of *Defence*, Adams offered a trenchant critique of Montesquieu's views on virtue, the key element of a republic, according to the influential Frenchman. Taking issue with Montesquieu's formulation that virtue in a republic is love of the republic, Adams attacked the very existence of public virtue. "It is not true, in fact, that any people ever existed who loved the public better than themselves, their private friends, neighbors, &c.," he wrote, "and there fore this kind of virtue, this sort of love, is as precarious a foundation for liberty as honor or fear." He argued, "It is the laws alone that really love the country, the public, the whole better than any part; and that form of government which unites all the virtue, honor, and fear of the citizens, in a reverence and obedience to the laws, is the only one in which liberty can be secure, and all orders, and ranks, and parties, compelled to prefer the public good before their own; that is the government for which we plead."[89] Laws not men, government not society, were the only possible means to public virtue.

To expect man to be virtuous voluntarily was to expect the impossible. In the *Defence*, Adams proposed a reordering of cause and effect. Rather than a virtuous people creating a virtuous society, he hoped that a well-constructed government would lead to virtuous behavior. Adams warned, "Mankind have been still more injured by insinuations, that a certain celestial virtue, more than human, has been necessary to preserve liberty.

Happiness, whether in despotism or democracy, whether in slavery or liberty, can never be found without virtue. The best republics will be virtuous, and have been so, but we may hazard a conjecture, that the virtues have been the effect of the well ordered constitution, rather than the cause."[90] From the early days of the Revolution, creating a proper government was, as he wrote in 1776, the "great and indispensable Work" of the Revolution, which he considered "the most difficult and dangerous Part of the Business Americans have to do in this mighty Contest."[91] Under a monarchy, Adams said, the people could be "as vicious and foolish as they please." But a commonwealth demanded more. Under it, he claimed, "the People must be wise and virtuous and cannot be otherwise."[92] Adams set himself the task of constructing a government to shape the character of the people and their leaders according to the dictates of virtue.

"The Passion for Distinction"
The End of Virtue and the Beginning of Politics

Adams's unremitting skepticism disabused him of any simplistic reliance on virtue, public or private, as a foundation for the American government. He faced two related problems as he considered how to construct the American polity. First, he distrusted the public virtue of the men who sought to run the government. Second, he feared that Americans as a people did not have enough virtue to sustain that government. He would attempt to tackle both problems through structural remedies that would make use of the public masks that he disdained.

Who would prove worthy enough to sit at the table of power? Adams had little faith in finding enough men of public virtue to run the government. Writing in his diary in 1772 that "The Body of the People seem to be worn out, by struggling, and Venality, Servility and Prostitution, eat and spread like a Cancer," he lamented that every "young rising Genius, in this Country" was in a worse situation than Hercules in the fable of Prodicus:

> Two Ladies are before him: The one, presenting to his View, not the Ascent of Virtue only, tho that is steep and rugged, but a Mountain quite inaccessible, a Path beset with Serpents, and Beasts of Prey, as well as Thorns and Briars, Precipices of Rocks over him, a Gulph yawning beneath, and the Sword of Damocles [over] his Head.—The other displaying his View, Pleasures, of every Kind, Honours, such as the World calls by that Name, and showers of Gold and Silver.
>
> If We recollect what a Mass of Corruption human Nature has been in general, since the Fall of Adam, we may easily judge what the Consequence will be.[93]

Adams simply did not have confidence in man's ability to lead the virtuous life. Great men were no exception, according to Adams, who noted in his diary how such men stooped to the usual duplicitous tricks to secure their reputation. "No man is intirely free from weakness and imperfection in this life," he wrote. "Men of the most exalted Genius and active minds, are generally perfect slaves to the Love of Fame. They sometimes descend to as mean tricks and artifices, in pursuit of Honour or Reputation, as the Miser descends to, in pursuit of Gold. The greatest men have been the most envious, malicious, and revengeful."[94] Finding men of sufficient public virtue to run the government seemed a quixotic quest.

In addressing this problem, Adams took a radically different approach from the typical republican notion of disinterested public servants and proposed an unusual solution—the professionalization of politics, a solution that was the antithesis of classical republican notions of public virtue.[95] It was also far different from the heroic virtue that he so desperately sought in himself and others. His own unremitting skepticism had left him with virtually no men he considered truly virtuous, even among the most lionized American patriots. In a series of letters in 1785, written while he was minister to England, he addressed the problem that his own mistrust had created by proposing a new foundation for public service. He examined the dangers of the supposedly virtuous practice of holding public office without a salary, seemingly a clear example of public virtue, and instead argued for the recognition of politics as a legitimate occupation. He was reacting against the first Pennsylvania Constitution, which stated, in part, "There can be no necessity for, nor use in, establishing offices of profit, the usual effects of which are dependence and servility unbecoming freemen in the possessors and expectants, faction, contention, corruption, and disorder among the people."[96] While Pennsylvania's Constitution seemed to embrace the will of the people in its purest forms (a unicameral legislature as the undiluted representation of popular sovereignty), Adams questioned whether such a constitution actually served to elevate men of public virtue or to safeguard the gains of the Revolution, concerns that echoed issues raised in his diary. Adams proposed a different path to a virtuous republic, one far removed from his own strenuous striving.

Adams attacked the notion, so central to republican thinking and to the idea of public virtue, that the ideal public figure was a disinterested man who sacrificed his own personal well-being to run the government. He wanted to expose what he saw as the faulty assumptions about human nature embedded in this republican belief and, in its place, propose new grounds on which to base governmental service. Adams argued that public offices engrossed a man's full attention. "For public offices in general require the whole time, and all the attention of those who hold them," he wrote. Given these demands, most citizens would be unable to hold a position in the government. "They must then starve with their families unless they have ample fortunes. But would you make it a law that no man should hold an office who had not a private income sufficient for the subsistence and prospects of himself and his family?" Adams asked (undoubtedly influenced by his own modest circumstances compared with many of the founders). He was questioning a fundamental premise behind the republican idea of virtue: only men of independent economic means would have the necessary independence to act for the public good. Unpaid public service did not promote public virtue, according to Adams. Rather, it meant that offices would be "monopolized by the rich." Adams insisted that the classical republican formula for government would lead eventually and inevitably to "an aristocratic despotism."[97]

Even worse, such a system fostered the kind of hidden corruptions in government that Adams feared. "It is not the legal profit, but the secret perquisites, the patronage, and the abuse, which is the evil," he wrote. "And this is what I complain of in the article [of the Pennsylvania Constitution], that it diverts the attention, jealousy, and hatred of the people from the perquisites, patronage, and abuse, which is the evil, to the legal, honest profit of the office, which is a blessing." He questioned the true motives of serving in public office with no salary, arguing that it pandered to the people's "prejudices, and it will recommend itself to whatever there is of popular malignity and envy, and of vulgar avarice, in every country."[98] Calling such pandering a "vulgar error," he argued that "flattery has done more mischief to society, when addressed to the people, than when offered to kings."[99] The standard republican ideas for a government run by virtuous men threatened to create exactly the kind of government that Adams feared, one that would wear a public mask of virtue while actually seeking private benefit.

To prove his point, he turned his critical gaze on a central word of revolutionary rhetoric, "disinterestedness." Although a key element in the classical republican conception of the public good and public virtue, disinterestedness was really a pose that allowed men to claim public virtue while pursuing their own ends, according to Adams.[100] He wrote, "I know very well that the word 'disinterested' turns the heads of the people by exciting their enthusiasm." He warned, though, "the cry of gratitude has made more men mad, and established more despotism in the world, than all the other causes put together. Every throne has been erected upon it, and every mitre has sprung out of it." Adams thought that simple numbers alone precluded relying too heavily on disinterestedness, for disinterested men "are not enough in any age or any country to fill all the necessary offices, and therefore the people may depend on it, that the hypocritical pretence of disinterestedness will be set up to deceive them, much oftener than the virtue will be practised for their good."[101] Too often, Adams observed, the people were fooled by "the semblance of disinterestedness, counterfeited for the most selfish purposes of cheating them more effectually." By requiring such sacrifices as serving without pay from honest men, the unintended consequence was to drive those very men away from public service, because it promised nothing but "misery to themselves and ruin to their families."[102]

Adams questioned even Washington's disinterestedness. The act that had truly made Washington the hero of his age was his retirement at the end of the war, but Adams offered a contrary interpretation of Washington's return to private life. He argued that the supposed necessity of retirement revealed a weakness in the American character. "Does not this idea of the necessity of his retiring, imply an opinion of danger to the public, from his continuing in public, a jealousy that he might become ambitious?" he asked, "and does it not imply something still more humiliating, a jealousy in the people of one another, that another part had grown too fond of him, and acquired habitually too much confidence in him, that there would be danger of setting him up a king?"[103] The cause of Washington's dangerous popularity, according to Adams, was simple—"his serving without pay." Adams had no patience for such boundless "ecstasies" for one person, claiming that "the people should have too high a sense of their own dignity ever to suffer any man to serve them for nothing."[104] By not paying Washington, the people showed too little care for their own independence, laying themselves under the debt of gratitude, a far more difficult debt to know how to recompense properly. Throughout his argument, Adams attempted to drive a wedge between language and behavior, to reveal that words such as disinterested could be used to fool the people about the true nature of their public officials.[105] Once again revealing his own problematic intermingling of virtue and vanity, though, he was also taking aim at Washington's immense popularity—and what he saw as his own lack of popularity. He frequently complained that he himself was never credited with disinterestedness. He wrote to Rush, "Washington and Franklin could never do any thing but what was imputed to pure, disinterested patriotism; I never could do any thing but what was ascribed to sinister motives."[106]

Adams's solution was to place politics on a professional footing. Rather than relying on the public virtue of disinterested men, Adams wanted to make public service both something less exalted and something more dependable. To John Jebb in 1785, he wrote, "Mankind will never be happy nor their liberties secure, until the people shall lay it down a fundamental rule to make the support and reward of public offices a matter of justice and not gratitude."[107] Echoing classic Puritan thought, he argued that since every free man should have a profession that provided for his subsistence, politics should provide such a subsistence to those who labored in it. He allowed politics a place as a dignified activity, a legitimate career and even vocation—a complete rejection of public virtue based on private sacrifice. "Offices in general ought to yield as honest a subsistence, and as clear an independence as professions, callings, trades, or farms," he wrote, perhaps thinking of his own lack of an independent fortune. When politicians were not paid, Adams argued that the people were placed under an obligation, which created precisely the kind of insidious dependence that Adams abhorred. "I will not lay myself under any obligation to you [the unpaid officeholder] by accepting your gift," he proclaimed. "I will owe you no gratitude any further than you serve me faithfully." To place oneself under such an obligation had dire consequences. Although his countrymen were "stingy" until a politician had "gained their confidence," Adams warned that "their gratitude, when once their enthusiasm is excited, knows no bounds." Far worse than a simple salary, their gratitude "scatters their favors all around the man. His family, his father, brother, son, all his relations, all his particular friends, must be idolized."[108] According to Adams, paying a salary to politicians was "thought by many to be one of the best securities of liberty and equality." Through this device, Adams hoped to place government on a more secure footing: "Government must become something more intelligible, rational, and steady."[109] Sacrificing the exalted idea of virtuous and disinterested leaders, Adams suggested relying on the steady habits of professional government officials—an idea that found little traction in the early republican world of elite politicians, with its dependence on a politics of character.[110]

Adams's proposals addressed the lack of public virtue among political leaders, but he still faced the problem of the lack of a virtuous people. To solve that difficulty, he relied on the understanding of human nature that he had developed in his diary. Beginning in 1790, Adams wrote yet another lengthy treatment of his views on government, his *Discourses on Davila*.[111] Originating as a series of newspaper essays ostensibly discussing the Italian historian Davila's account of the French civil wars of the sixteenth century, the *Discourses* were more of a response to the increasingly radical direction of the French Revolution than a response to the direction of American politics, a fact that ensured that Adams would largely antagonize, rather than persuade, his colleagues. French revolutionaries in 1789 had declared their intention to abolish inequality and, toward that end, had begun calling everyone by the title of "citizen." In the same year, the First United States Congress, particularly the Senate (of which Adams was the president), had held a series of rancorous debates on the issue of titles for members of government. Adams had argued emphatically, although unsuccessfully, that giving titles to members of the government would increase the respectability and legitimacy of the government at home and abroad. He feared that the French revolutionaries (and many of his fellow Americans) completely misunderstood man's true nature and thus misunderstood the kind of government necessary to create a virtuous society. He also feared the influence of French thinking in America, where many citizens were embracing the French Revolution as a counterpart to the American Revolution. He based his critique on his understanding of the psychological foundations of human behavior that he had developed in his diary years earlier. In the essays, he offered an extended analysis of the passion for distinction, a passion with which his own struggles against vanity had made him intimately familiar. He had prescribed stern self-discipline to subdue his own passion, but he proposed a different remedy for the mass of men.[112]

Man's passion for distinction, with its emphasis on differences, seems at first glance to be a rejection of the Revolution, with its emphasis on equality, but Adams actually offered a far more democratic avenue for citizens to achieve status (part of his goal was also to limit the type of instability that he thought would arise from the radical French notions of equality). Even in the early days of the American Revolution, he wrote, "There must be a Decency, and Respect, and Veneration introduced for Persons in Authority, of every Rank, or We are undone."[113] But his attempt to harness the passion for distinction was not simply some reactionary attempt to re-create a deferential society. Republican leaders were obsessed with achieving fame, but fame (and, indeed, leadership itself within a republican framework) was available only to a small elite, despite the importance of equality to republican thinking.[114] Even as leaders preached equality, they hoped to receive special recognition and even immortality. Adams's use of the passion for distinction, despite its rejection of absolute equality, actually offered all citizens far more opportunity to pursue distinction. By creating ranks, he made possible not simply the fame of elites but the status and distinction of other men, albeit on a smaller scale. In effect, he democratized fame.[115]

Using the passion for distinction was also crucial to control the aristocracy, the leaders who would deceive the people with their public facades. In a 1787 letter to Jefferson, Adams made it clear where he thought the danger lay (and where he differed from his friend): "You are afraid of the one—I, of the few. . . . You are apprehensive of monarchy; I, of aristocracy. I would therefore have given more power to the president and less to the Senate."[116] His opinion had not changed when he wrote Jefferson more than twenty years later: "When I consider the weakness, the folly, the Pride, the Vanity, the Selfishness, the Artifice, the low craft and mean cunning, the want of Principle, the Avarice the unbounded Ambition, the unfeeling Cruelty of a majority of those (in all Nations) who are allowed an aristocratical influence; and on the other hand, the Stupidity with which the more numerous multitude, not only become their Dupes, but even love to be Taken in by their Tricks: I feel a stronger disposition to weep at their destiny, than to laugh at their Folly."[117] He also discussed the danger of the aristocracy in the *Defence*. Adams again claimed that aristocrats must be separated from the popular branch of government, or they would soon come to control it. "The rich, the well-born, and the able acquire an influence among the people that will soon be too much for simple honesty and plain sense, in a house of representatives," he wrote. "The most illustrious of them must, therefore, be separated from the mass, and placed by themselves in a senate."[118] This justification of the Senate was the opposite of Hamilton's, which was based on a trust of those same aristocratic leaders. Fearing them even after the national government was well established, Adams thought the only solution was to lure this class of men into a place distinct from other legislative bodies, writing in 1813, "As it is a Phoenix that rises again out of its own Ashes, I know no better Way than to chain it in a 'Hole by itself,' and place a Watchfull Centinel on each Side of it."[119]

For Adams, one of the crucial constitutional mechanisms of control was the separation of the aristocrats into their own legislative branch. He argued against simply barring them from government. He thought that such a remedy would only drive their influence underground. "Exclude the aristocratical part of the community by laws as tyrannical as you will, they will still govern the state underhand," he wrote; "the persons elected into office will be their tools, and in constant fear of them, will behave like mere puppets danced upon their wires."[120] As usual, he feared the hidden exercise of power masked by protestations of public good. He hoped to preserve the balance of the government by luring aristocrats into the Senate through their passion for distinction.

Most of the *Discourses on Davila* is devoted to an exploration of how the government could make use of that passion for its own ends. For Adams, no quality was more crucial to understanding human nature. He wrote, "There is none among them more essential or remarkable, than the *passion for distinction*. A desire to be observed, considered, esteemed, praised, beloved, and admired by his fellows, is one of the earliest, as well as keenest dispositions discovered in the heart of man" (232). Although Adams willingly allowed that human nature also contained benevolence, he saw it as insufficient to "balance the selfish affections" (234). Knowledge was also no antidote. It actually increased the potential dangers since "bad men increase in knowledge as fast as good men" (276). Nature had rectified that imbalance, though, with "the desire of reputation, in order to make us good members of society" (234).[121]

He used "the passion for distinction" not simply to understand the behavior of individuals but to understand the behavior of groups and even nations. He claimed that it was "of equal importance to individuals, to families, and to nations," a notion that he returned to later in his *Discourses* (234). Since such passion was "the texture and essence of the soul," Adams argued, "To regulate and not to eradicate [it] is the province of policy." He hoped to enlist it "on the side of virtue" (246), a far cry from his exhortations to himself in his diary to root out and subdue every passion. For Adams, government's main purpose was shaping this malleable force to positive ends. "It is a principal end of government to regulate this passion, which in its turn becomes a principle means of government," he wrote. "It is the only adequate instrument of order and subordination in society, and alone commands effectual obedience to laws, since without it neither human reason, nor standing armies, would ever produce that great effect" (234). Adams claimed that "when it receives a happy turn, it is the source of private felicity and public prosperity, and when it errs, produces private uneasiness and public calamities." Because the passion for distinction had such vast potential to reshape both private and public life, Adams thought that it was "the business and duty of private prudence, of private and public education, and of national policy, to direct it to right objects" (241).

Dissecting the passion for distinction, Adams revealed its capacity to be both a good and an evil force in society. According to Adams, when one aimed only at "a desire to excel another, by fair industry in the search of truth, and the practice of virtue," one was practicing "*Emulation.*" When one sought power, one was under the influence of "*Ambition.*" When one worried that an inferior would become superior, one was being driven by "*Jealousy.*" When one was mortified at another's superiority and sought to bring him down, one was experiencing "*Envy.*" And when one was under a false impression of one's importance, one was under the influence of "*Vanity*" (233). Adams hoped to shape the passion for distinction so that it would take the form of emulation and result in virtuous action — but of course, Adams's withering skepticism of his peers made it difficult to know whom Americans should actually emulate.[122]

According to Adams, no one had made better use of the passion for distinction than the ancient Romans. He wrote that they had best "understood the human heart" and complimented their use "of the passion for consideration, congratulation, and distinction" (243). He wrote admiringly of the "language of the signs" employed to "attract the attention, to allure the consideration and excite the congratulations of the people." Commenting on a particularly moving spectacle staged by the Romans, he wrote, "It is easy to see how such a scene must operate on the hearts of a nation; how it must affect the passion for distinction; and how it must excite the ardor and virtuous emulation of the citizens" (244). For Adams, such masterful manipulation was nothing less than "the true spirit of republics."

To channel the desire for distinction to positive ends in America, Adams proposed making various public virtues the object of emulation by using titles.[123] "As virtue is the only rational source and eternal foundation of honor," he wrote, "the wisdom of nations, in the titles they have established as the marks of order and subordination, has generally given an intimation, not of personal qualities, nor of the qualities of fortune; but of particular virtues, more especially becoming men in the high stations they possess" (242). Adams saw a danger without such titles, since no order or structure would be provided for society's desire for distinction, a situation that would create something of a free-for-all. "The wisdom and virtue of all nations have endeavored to regulate the passions for respect and distinction," he wrote, "and to reduce it to some order in society, by titles marking the gradations of magistracy, to prevent as far as human power and policy can prevent, collisions among the passions of many pursuing the same objects, and the rivalries, animosities, envy, jealousy, and vengeance which always result from them" (243). If properly managed, such distinctions could spread virtue throughout the young republic.

This reasoning underlay Adams's strong support of the use of titles when the First Congress met.[124] If "honors, offices, rewards" were distributed to "valiant, virtuous, or learned men," the people would seek similar attainments, "as long as the door is left open to succeed in the same dignities and enjoyment, if he can attain to the same measure of desert. Men aspire to great actions when rewards depend on merit."[125] As vice president, Adams presided over the Senate as the issue of titles was debated. Largely following Adams's lead, the Senate committee on titles proposed for the presidency the unwieldy and somewhat ridiculous title, "His Highness the President of the United States of America, and Protector of Their Liberties."[126]

Adams's own finicky concern with his personal authority intermingled itself with his call for titles and led to criticism. Many of his colleagues attacked his proposals as being out of touch with the republican nature of the country and saw, beneath his arguments, his own desire for personal aggrandizement. Even Washington agreed that Adams could be "high toned."[127] William Maclay, a senator from Pennsylvania, wrote of Adams: "His grasping after Titles has been observed by every body. Mr. Izard after describing his air Manner deportment and personal figure in the Chair, concluded with applying the Title of *Rotundity* to him." Others began jokingly referring to him as "the Duke of Braintree." Far from thinking Adams's behavior dignified, Maclay frequently criticized Adams in his own diary, writing of the vice president that "he often in the midst of his most important Airs, I believe when he is at loss for expressions, (and this he often is, wrapped up I suppose in the Contemplation of his own importance) suffers an unmeaning kind of vacant laugh to escape him." Far from lending dignity to himself or his office, his deportment "really to me bore the Air of ridiculing the Farce he was acting."[128] In the battle over titles (and other political matters over the years), many of his colleagues would probably have agreed with Franklin's 1783 remark about his fellow diplomat: Adams "means well for his country, is always an honest man, often a wise one," Franklin wrote, "but sometimes and in some things, absolutely out of his senses."[129] More problematic than Adams's vanity, though, was how out of step he seemed with the emerging political character of the nation. Although he imagined the creation of titles as a progressive government measure that would foster virtue in the young nation, his thinking remained firmly indebted to old, European conceptions of politics that had already fallen into disfavor because of the Revolution. Although not the cryptomonarchist that his opponents accused him of being, Adams could only articulate a vision of the future based on a discredited model from the past. In the end, senators followed their House colleagues and decided not to create titles.

Failing to see the role he himself had unwittingly played in the rejection of titles, Adams thought that the decision was simply more proof of man's capability for self-deception on the subject of public virtue. By rejecting them, Adams argued, Americans had not revealed their superior republican virtue. "After all," he complained, "there is not a country under heaven in which titles and precedency are more eagerly coveted than in this country." Adams worried that the country's citizens would find other ways to seek the passion for distinction, instead of pursuing the kind of virtues beneficial to republican government. He predicted that the passion for distinction would be pursued through material display, complaining that "this species of vanity commonly changes the whole moral and political character of a people, by turning their attention, esteem, admiration, and even their confidence and affection, from talents and virtues, to these external appearances." As always, the public facades of men threatened to mislead the nation.

In his fight to create titles for government officials, Adams offered a far different process than the furnace of affliction that he had once proposed. Emulation was, above all, an attempt to become something that one was not. It was firmly other-directed, in contrast to the searching, introspective regime he had embraced to create his own virtuous character. No longer an essentialized internal quality, virtue was to be promoted by channeling the passion for distinction, which would persuade citizens to choose virtuous roles—not the same as embodying them. For the people, Adams placed his hopes not in faith but in a regimen of works.[130] Instead of attempting to impose his own severe regimen of personal self-discipline (which itself was mired in conflicting motivations), Adams turned to a politics of appearance, in which institutional mechanisms created the incentives for scripted performances of public virtue that could be performed even by men of little virtue. He posed the idea succinctly in his *Defence*: "Perhaps, it would be impossible to prove that a republic cannot exist even among highwaymen, by setting one rogue to watch another; and the knaves may in time be made honest men by the struggle."[131]

Adams's plan was far different from the stern plan he had once outlined for himself and the nation. His corrosive skepticism seemed to leave him with a government based on a paltry idea of virtue, if it even deserved that name. According to Adams, though, public virtue, even if inspired only by the desire to be thought better than one was and even if failing to reveal a deeper, private virtue, was still virtue enough. After fighting to see behind the masks that all men seemed to present, Adams embraced those masks as the means to inspire men to strive to be more than they were. If properly conducted, men would still play roles, but at least they would choose virtuous ones. And if America could not be a virtuous nation, it could at least act like one.

"Corruption!"
Virtue Denied

Bitter from his defeat at the polls and at what he viewed as the libels on his character by both foes and supposed friends, Adams hoped that historians would treat him more kindly by recognizing his virtuous character. When Mercy Otis Warren published her three-volume *History of the Rise, Progress, and Termination of the American Revolution; interspersed with Biographical, Political, and Moral Observations* in 1805, Adams must have hoped for some vindication from his longtime friend.[132] Instead, he received a rude shock. Warren wrote a number of critical remarks on Adams, but none stung as deeply as the charge that he had been corrupted. If Americans had been forced to explain the cause of the Revolution in one word, they would have chosen the term "corruption," with all its rich signification of men who had lost the independence so crucial to republican values and virtue itself. For Adams, that one charge struck at the core of his beliefs about his own virtue and his lifetime of labor for the nation.

Adams responded with ten long, tedious, and self-defeating letters. Choosing to justify himself to an audience of one, rather than to his countrymen, he broke off work on his autobiography to quarrel with Warren. In the first letter, Adams promised to "observe no order in selecting the passages, but take them up as they occur by accident."[133] True to his word and exhibiting his usual diaristic tendencies, he began to offer up a disorganized,

rambling rebuttal of her work. The charge that he had been corrupted flab-
bergasted him. He could scarcely contain himself when he wrote to Warren
on the subject, and throughout his long rant, the word "corruption"
became almost a chorus, as he obsessively repeated it.

Even as Adams began his interminable defense, he seemed to realize its
pointlessness. He noted, "A man never looks so silly as when he is talking
or writing concerning himself."[134] As a lifetime in politics had taught him,
the public rarely judged correctly about who had acted what part. He remained obsessed about his place in history, though, hoping in future
years to be accorded the recognition that his contemporaries had failed to
bestow on him. Even that, he came to realize, was a forlorn hope. Rea-
lizing the futility of his attempt to revise his place in history, he wrote to
Benjamin Rush, "That man is in a poor case who is reduced to the necessity of looking to posterity for justice or charity."[135]

Figure 12. *James Madison*, painted by Gilbert Stuart, c. 1821. Courtesy of the National Gallery of Art.

FOUR

Justice

IN OCTOBER 1787, a month after the Constitutional Convention in Philadelphia had ended, Alexander Hamilton, James Madison, and John Jay joined forces as Publius to explain and defend the new Constitution to the educated public in New York, a crucial battleground for ratification. Due to illness, Jay wrote only five essays. Madison and Hamilton shouldered the burden, frequently turning out as many as four essays a week in a series that would eventually stretch to eighty-five papers and would come to be known as the *Federalist Papers*.

No one had done more to shape the Constitution than Madison, and he was quite clear in the *Federalist* about what sort of government he hoped he had created. In *Federalist #51*, Madison wrote, "Justice is the end of government. It is the end of civil society."[1] The Constitution was supposed to provide that government, one that would act based on considerations of the public good (justice) rather than private interest. While persuading his fellow citizens to ratify the Constitution, Madison also hoped to persuade his readers to adopt new characters for themselves.[2]

The fate of the country itself seemed to be at stake. While the *Federalist Papers* were not the decisive element in securing ratification, the success or failure of Publius's attempt to create a realm of disinterested reflection on the common good offered a trial run of the national government's ability to do the same thing. As Hamilton wrote in the first *Federalist Paper*, "It seems to have been reserved to the people of this country, by their conduct and example, to decide the important question, whether societies of men are really capable or not of establishing good government from reflection and choice, or whether they are forever destined to depend for their political constitutions on accident and force."[3]

Madison's conception of a polity based on justice differed radically from the conceptions of Jefferson, Hamilton, and Adams. Jefferson's politics of friendship created a dichotomized world of friends and enemies that allowed no room for political differences.[4] Hamilton's politics of honor attempted to narrow the political world to a small elite and left no means of resolving certain conflicts other than violence. And Adams's politics of virtue left him mistrustful of everyone. The characters of all three men contributed to a political world of personalized conflict that blurred the distinction between public and private life and undermined their attempts to build a stable and legitimate national polity. By contrast, Madison's solution offered a clear distinction between public and private life that promised to put an end to the politics of character.

Even as he offered new possibilities, though, Madison faced the intractable problem of language, which threatened to undermine his just government by providing an avenue for private interests to find their way into the public deliberations. In *Federalist #37*, he wrestled with this fundamental problem for the proposed Constitution. As he realized even then, ratification would be only the beginning, not the end, of a revolutionary settlement. Recalling Washington Irving's complaint that the United States was a *"government of words,"* the written Constitution did not promise a final resolution; instead, it provided only the framework for an endless interpretive endeavor.[5] Madison knew that in the struggle to secure a just nation, language itself, what Madison called "that cloudy medium," would be the most difficult obstacle. Such was America's blessing and its curse.

"To convert men into republican machines"
The End of the Politics of Character

The ostensible subject of *Federalist #37* was a "survey of the work of the convention."[6] Before delving into that subject, though, Madison spent considerable time calling for the proper spirit in considering the work of the convention. His remarks reveal the qualities with which he constructed his own character. Justifying the attention he lavished on delineating the proper spirit, he wrote, "That this remaining task may be executed under impressions conducive to a just and fair result, some reflections must in this place be indulged, which candor previously suggests" (359). Madison was already pointing to some of the key elements of his political vision and rhetorical mission. "Just and fair result" conflated successful ratification of the Constitution and successful reading of the *Federalist*, a linkage between readership and citizenship of which Madison would repeatedly take advantage. His call for candor was equally significant. The word carried two meanings in the eighteenth century: openness of mind and freedom from malice. Both meanings reinforced Madison's attempt to shape his readership.[7] Immediately after those remarks, he emphasized how rarely citizens approached such matters in the proper manner:

> It is a misfortune, inseparable from human affairs, that public measures are rarely investigated with that spirit of moderation which is essential to a just estimate of their real tendency to advance or obstruct the public good; and that this spirit is more apt to be diminished than

promoted by those occasions which require an usual exercise of it. (359)

His choice of words—spirit of moderation, just estimate, and public good—highlighted the necessary qualities for both proper reading and proper government. Reading the essay, ratifying the Constitution, and creating a just government were tightly linked in Madison's brief remarks, pointing to a much more ambitious project than persuading readers to ratify the Constitution. Madison wanted to redefine the nature of their reading and, ultimately, the nature of citizenship in his own bold attempt to shape the character of the nation.

By pursuing these goals in an anonymous newspaper essay, Madison had chosen the ideal forum to create "that spirit of moderation." He employed a genre premised on readers who would rely on objective reasoning to consider the issues, much as he hoped citizens would do in the proposed nation. The moment for such an ambitious series of political essays was brief. A few decades earlier, the *Federalist* would not have been written, while a few decades after 1787–88, the essays would have been lost in the crowd. The format fostered a tone of civility in the debate and contributed to the larger discursive framework that the authors of Publius were attempting to establish.[8] Madison's well-wrought, carefully reasoned political essays became virtual enactments of the kind of just deliberation he hoped the national government would foster. They also provided a generic means to question conventional wisdom, allowing the author to think outside the constraints of established authority—a perfect medium for Madison as he set out to refashion government. And the genre reflected his own style of writing, which was as circumspect as his person (offering striking contrast to Jefferson, Hamilton, and Adams).[9] Clarity, rather than artistry, was thought to be the purview of the essay. In his lectures on rhetoric and belles lettres, Hugh Blair noted that the philosophical writer "must study the utmost perspicuity. . . . Beyond mere perspicuity, strict accuracy and precision are required in a philosophical writer. He must employ no words of uncertain meaning, no loose nor indeterminate expressions; and should avoid using words which are seemingly synonymous, without carefully attending to the variations they make upon the ideas."[10] Although Blair did allow for a certain amount of embellishment to achieve a pleasing composition, he warned that "all his ornaments be of the chastest kind, never partaking of the florid or the tumid."[11] The genre's self-effacement mirrored Madison's own. Commenting on Madison's meticulous writing style, a nineteenth-century historian wrote, "Full, clear, and deliberate disquisition carefully wrought out, as if the writer regarded himself rather as the representative of truth than the exponent of the doctrines of a party or even of a nation, is the praise of Madison."[12]

The essay embodied the qualities by which Madison constructed his own character. Rhetorically positioned as an impartial advocate of the truth, the essay appealed to men's reason and sense of justice. It enabled Madison to enact in the discursive realm what he hoped the Constitution would enact in the political realm—a nation of readers/citizens who would reason in an impartial fashion and place private interests aside to consider the public good. In contrast to the letter, the defense pamphlet, and the diary, all of which were explicitly tied to an individual, the anonymous essay did not rely on personal reputation but only on the strength of its arguments. In fact, the lack of a link to an individual reputation gave it power—"anonymous" denominated public virtue.[13] Taking advantage of this, the three authors of Publius revealed no details about their identities. Publius wrote in the utmost generality and pretended to have no inside knowledge of the Philadelphia convention.[14] He claimed to be merely an intelligent citizen who gave advice based on the same information available to all. Such a strategy gained power by the refusal to base its worth on the author's character.[15]

Madison altered this persona on only one—revealing—occasion, an alteration that further emphasized his use of the genre to appeal to the public good rather than to private self-interest. In *Federalist #54*, he turned to the subject of the three-fifths clause of the Constitution, a subject sure to raise the ire of northerners because of its regional bias. Instead of defending the clause as Publius, Madison slipped into the voice of a southerner, using quotations to designate what he called in the essay "one of our Southern brethren." At the end of the essay, he returned again as Publius, writing, "Such is the reasoning which an advocate for the Southern interests might employ on this subject; and although it may appear to be a little strained on some points, yet, on the whole, I must confess that it fully reconciles me to the scale of representation which the convention have established."[16] This ventriloquism revealed the importance of maintaining himself as an impartial commentator. When defending a clause that was as blatantly sectional as the three-fifths clause, Madison chose the rhetorical strategy of distancing Publius from the arguments in favor of the clause, a choice that valued the rhetorical guise of disinterestedness over a strong defense. The *Federalist Papers* also almost never mentioned specific Antifederalist writers or complaints, even though those attacks shaped the project.[17] The invisibility of the Antifederalists within the essays was part of a similar rhetorical strategy. Publius attempted to establish himself as a neutral commentator offering an unbiased overview, rather than a partisan responding to specific charges. These tactics reinforced the overall thrust of the *Federalist Papers*. Instead of trying to score every possible debating point, the authors attempted to shift the entire realm of the debate away from considerations of competing interests to considerations of the public good.

Even as the genre of the essay provided Madison with the rhetorical means to fashion a foundation for the new polity apart from the politics of character, it entangled him in a significant problem. Blair called for the essay to exercise "strict accuracy and precision." Much like the Constitution, the essay depended on a rhetoric of transparency, in which perfect consensual understanding would be the product of careful, unbiased reading; however, the essay's emphasis on the importance of linguistic determinacy served only to highlight the impossibility of that determinacy. The more one tried to define words precisely, the more those words seemed to escape perfect definition. As John Locke had warned, language would never offer a medium for perfect understanding unless people became "very knowing and very silent."[18] And unlike the other genres, the essay could not rely on an individual's character to buttress its arguments.

For Madison, that was hardly a drawback. In constructing his character, which relied on the same qualities that governed the anonymous essay, Madison differed markedly from Adams, Hamilton, and Jefferson. For the latter three, their characters shaped their politics indelibly, and they attempted to impose those characters on an unruly political world. Madison offered a different possibility, embodying a spirit of moderation so successfully that he was often described as a colorless figure. His political demeanor seemed bereft of personality. Martha Bland's reaction to the statesman was fairly typical. She wrote disparagingly, "A gloomy, stiff creature, they say he is clever in Congress, but out of it he has nothing engaging or even bearable in his manners—the most unsociable creature in existence."[19] Madison's sense of character led not to the aggrandizement of the individual but to his disappearance, not to an excess of personality but to its extinction, a public character that wholly suppressed the private self.[20]

For Madison, government began with the self. Originally, the word "government" applied as much to the individual as to the state. Samuel Johnson defined it as "regularity of behavior; restraint; self-restraint; self-government." Such an attitude about self-government was a common one, conforming both to codes of gentility and to Scottish Enlightenment thought. Freedom was equated with the supremacy of rationality, and some thought that man should ideally function with the precision of a machine.[21] Benjamin Rush, whose restraining chair was designed to teach self-control, wrote, "I consider it possible to convert men into republican machines."[22]

Madison, according to his contemporaries, maintained self-control at all times. Edward Coles, Madison's personal secretary while he was president, wondered at his forbearance. Coles claimed that "nothing could excite or ruffle him," that he always remained "collected" and "self-possessed," that he was "ever mindful of what was due from him to others, and cautious not to wound the feelings of any one." Even during the War of 1812, despite the myriad problems and aggravations facing Madison, Coles wrote that he never heard the Virginian "utter one petulant expression, or give way for one moment to passion or despondency." Instead, he lived by his own maxim that "public functionaries should never display, much less act, under the influence of passion."[23] Madison himself seemed to view his life solely in public terms, writing in his brief autobiography that his "whole life has in a manner been a public life."[24] Madison expected all public officials to exercise similar self-discipline in separating their private from their public characters.

"A neutral umpire"
The Search for Justice

The word "candor" repeatedly appeared in *Federalist #37*. It acted as a reminder to leave aside personal prejudices (or malice) and consider the Constitution from an unbiased perspective. The word reinforced the essay's repeated appeal to impartiality. According to Madison, both candor and impartiality had guided the deliberations of the convention. At the end of the essay, he noted that the convention "must have enjoyed, in a very singular degree, an exemption from the pestilential influence of party animosities." The participants had embodied Madison's ideal by "sacrificing private opinions and partial interests to the public good" (364). His remarks on their efforts were a blueprint for the character of those who would lead the nation.

For Madison, impartiality was essential to justice, and justice was essential to good government. To achieve justice, the government had to be arranged to remove personal motives as much as possible from the deliberating process. Again and again, he returned to the importance of having a disinterested judge or umpire. Defending the convention's handiwork to Jefferson in 1788, he wrote, "Wherever there is an interest and power to do wrong, wrong will generally be done, and not less readily by a powerful and interested party [in a republic] than by a powerful and interested prince."[25] In *Federalist #43*, he wrote: "In cases where it may be doubtful on which side justice lies, what better umpires could be desired by two violent factions, flying to arms and tearing a State to pieces, than the representatives of confederate States, not heated by the local flame? To the impartiality of judges, they would unite the affection of friends."[26] The underlying courtroom metaphor revealed Madison's conception of the properly ordered society, in which a neutral judge could preside over and settle conflicts. Throughout his life, Madison returned to the importance of this remedy.[27] Madison explained to Jefferson in 1787, "The great desideratum in Government is, so to modify the sovereignty as that it may be sufficiently neutral between different parts of the Society to controul one part from invading the rights of another, and at the same time sufficiently controuled itself, from setting up an interest adverse to that of the entire Society."[28] He made the same argument in a letter to Washington (extolling a national veto of state legislation). "The great desideratum," he wrote, "which has not yet been found for Republican Governments seems to be some disinterested and dispassionate umpire in disputes between different passions and interests in the State."[29]

For government to work in this manner, elected officials had to rise above local, private concerns. In discussing the House of Representatives, Madison wrote in *Federalist #57*, "The aim of every political constitution is or ought to be first to obtain for rulers, men who possess most wisdom to discern, and most virtue to pursue the common good of society; and in the next place, to take the most effectual precautions for keeping them virtuous; whilst they continue to hold their public trust."[30] Madison proposed a similar role for the executive, who would act as an impartial umpire. At one point at the convention, Madison called the executive a "just Judge."[31] Madison thought that he had discovered a method to secure disinterested leaders for the government. Extend the sphere of government, he argued in *Federalist #10*, and you liberate legislators from local partisanship. Size and statesmanship went hand in hand.

In devising a political system, Jefferson's and Madison's thoughts ran in different directions. In discussing his plan for ward republics, Jefferson imagined dividing the political world into progressively smaller districts, so that in the end one was left with the private world of the individual, the authentic self at last revealed, whereas Madison always argued for a larger arena, a world in which the private individual with all of his passions and foibles was at last eliminated. As Madison wrote before the Federal Convention, a large republic with its necessary reliance on large districts would "extract from the mass of the society the purest and noblest characters."[32] He repeated the argument in *Federalist #10*, in which he claimed that elections would "refine and enlarge the public views, by passing them through the medium of a chosen body of citizens, whose wisdom may best discern the true interest of their country, and whose patriotism and love of justice will be least likely to sacrifice it to temporary or partial considerations."[33] Revolutionary Americans had rejected any hint of virtual representation in their constitutional quarrel with Great Britain; instead, they had argued for an agency theory of representation in which representatives carried out the exact wishes of their constituents (one popular method was providing written instructions to representatives).[34] Madison's theory of representation was, if not a renunciation, a revision of that revolutionary standard.

A large republic offered greater protection than a small republic both by offering a greater choice of estimable candidates and by making it "more difficult for unworthy candidates to practise with success the vicious arts by which elections are too often carried."[35] Madison was not naive enough to believe that, with the adoption of the Constitution, government would become the preserve of only disinterested men, so he also tried to build impartiality into the system. For example, because the census would affect both taxation and representation, Madison argued, "The States will have opposite interests, which will control and balance each other, and produce the requisite impartiality."[36] Even representation, if it failed to produce virtuous members, promised potential protection with an extended sphere to govern. In *Federalist #10*, he wrote that an extended republic takes in "a greater variety of parties and interests," making it more difficult for a majority to be put together and to act in unison. He told Jefferson, "*Divide et impera*, the reprobated axiom of tyranny, is under certain qualifications, the only policy, by which a republic can be administered on just principles."[37] He still hoped, though, that the new government would consist of men closer to his ideal of disinterestedness.[38]

Patrick Henry, who became a bitter opponent of Madison, represented the antithesis of what Madison was seeking. Henry's oratory was so effective precisely because it stirred men's passions. Madison wanted to design a government that would limit the machinations of the likes of Henry (one of the great stalking-horses in the *Federalist* is the demagogue with his misuse of oratory, the engine, as it were, of faction). Madison the orator was the opposite of Henry. James Callender, who worked as a stenographer covering House speeches, noted, "To do justice to the speeches of this gentleman [Madison], it would be requisite to print every word exactly as it is spoken; since it is impossible to abridge, without injuring it, the stile of a speaker who is, on every question alike remarkable for the most correct elegance, and the most comprehensive brevity."[39] Henry appealed to men's passions; Madison hoped to convince them to use their reason.

Madison wanted legislators who could rise above local prejudice and embrace the character of impartial judges, providing disinterested solutions based on the public good. Jefferson had perfect confidence in the national will and longed only to see it expressed. Hamilton largely disdained it, hoping that the national councils would be led by honorable men such as himself. Adams distrusted it and hoped to instruct it in virtue. Madison chose a different path, one in which representatives would not perfectly express the national will but would interpret it. But what role did this leave for the people?

"A judicious and impartial examiner"

The Role of the People

Madison spent considerable space in *Federalist #37* describing how read-ers should consider the proposed Constitution in order to achieve, as he called it, "a just and fair result." Much as his description of the work of the convention was a blueprint for how the national government should work, his description of his ideal reader revealed his expectations for citizens. Madison realized that considering the Constitution presented a profound challenge for readers. Given that the proposed Constitution included "so many important changes and innovations" and touched "the springs of so many passions and interests," he worried that many would probably be unable to participate in "a fair discussion and accurate judgment of its merits." Fearing that too many people had already prejudged the Constitution, Madison lamented that they had "scanned the proposed con-stitution, not only with a predisposition to censure; but with a predetermi-nation to condemn." He eschewed even attempting to persuade such read-ers and claimed that the *Federalist* essays were "not addressed to persons falling under . . . these characters." He intended only to speak to those "who add to a sincere zeal for the happiness of their country, a temper favorable to a just estimate of the means of promoting it" (359). Offering a similar exhortation at the end of the essay, he pointed out the "neces-sity of sacrificing private opinions and partial interests to the public good" (364).

Understanding the challenge readers faced, Madison attempted to train them to read in the proper spirit and, by extension, to shape the character of the nation. His first contribution as Publius was *Federalist #10*, and this essay, as much as any, did not simply extol the type of reader he called for in #37—it trained a reader to read in a certain way, teaching him how to read the *Federalist*, how to consider the Constitution, and how to be a political citizen in the proposed nation. Although recent scholarship has taken away some of the luster of *Federalist #10* as original political sci-ence, it remains undiminished (and, indeed, underappreciated) as a mas-terpiece of political rhetoric and political education.

While *Federalist #10* has frequently been examined from the viewpoint of political theory, it would be a serious mistake to overlook the rhetoric and structure of the essay itself, which carried a message that matched its argument. The subject of *#10* is how to control faction, the antithesis, for Madison, of a just government because faction represented the pursuit of private interest at the expense of the public good. Commentators usually emphasize Madison's argument about an extended republic's ability to provide a better control of faction. David Hume had already suggested the same thing, and Hamilton had probably reached a similar conclusion on his own.[40] Although Madison expanded and extended the argument well beyond Hume's brief musings, much of the brilliance of #10 lies not in the argument itself but in the way that the argument is made. Using a variety of rhetorical techniques, *Federalist #10* not only argues the case but also asks to be read in a way that breaks and controls the violence of faction.

How did Madison accomplish this ambitious task? He began by expounding at length on faction, "this dangerous vice," which bred "instability, injustice, and confusion . . . the mortal diseases . . . [of] popular governments."[41] His words echoed his private musings on the "vices" exhibited by state government in the 1780s. Madison attributed the country's "heaviest misfortunes" to the "effects of the unsteadiness and injustice with which a factious spirit has tainted our public administrations," a criticism he returned to repeatedly. Even as he did this, though, he laid the groundwork for a different spirit, a spirit to which he was already implicitly appealing in his readers. Warning against "unwarrantable partiality," a caution to his readers against their own tendencies toward faction, he offered his own analysis as one based on "a candid review" of "known facts" leading to unassailable and axiomatic truths. The thrust of his essay would be an extended lesson in how to reason in a public spirit of justice, rather than a private spirit of faction.

In place of faction or, more accurately, in place of reading and thinking in a spirit of faction, Madison offered a type of reasoning that was of such Euclidean clarity that it seemed to be truth itself.[42] Axiomatic thinking and arguments were a consistent part of the Publius facade. Publius spoke in the voice of unquestionable certitudes, of axioms, maxims, and political truth. Madison's essay functioned the same way that he imagined government should. Every idea was countered with an opposing one in a tightly interwoven rhetorical system of checks and balances. In #10, he used what Garry Wills has called the bifurcative method: offering two alternatives, eliminating one, and then splitting the remaining one. Madison argued that there were only two methods to cure faction: by removing its causes or its effects. To remove the causes, he argued that there were also two methods: by destroying liberty or by giving everyone the same passions and interests. Both were impossible, according to Madison, so he offered his first irrefutable truth: "The latent causes of faction are thus sown in the nature of man."

Madison then turned to the only other available solution, controlling the effects of faction. A republican government, based as it is on majority rule, could easily render a minority faction harmless, but what of a majority? Again, he argued, there were only two solutions: by preventing the existence of a shared, unjust passion in a majority, or by rendering it impossible for the majority to carry into effect its schemes of oppression. Madison placed no faith in moral or religious constraints, and he also argued that a democracy offered no protection against majority oppression. A republic, though, differed in two crucial respects from a democracy: by delegating government to a small number of elected citizens and by the greater number of citizens and the greater extent of the country. Both, he thought, placed crucial restraints on the possibility of a majority oppressing a minority.

Throughout the essay, Madison's tight reasoning based on a canvass of all the possibilities seems to lead with irresistible logic to his conclusion. If a reader accepts Madison's range of possibilities, Madison presents the only possible solution not because the reader is a partisan of that side but because he is considering matters in just and reasonable terms. Giving a reading lesson and a civics lesson at the same time, Madison offers a step-by-step guide on how to reason through crucial constitutional provisions in a disinterested fashion.

Implicit throughout the essay is Madison's judicial model of decision making. He addressed the reader repeatedly with such designations as "an impartial and judicious examiner" or "dispassionate and discerning." Such a reader differed markedly from Jefferson's ideal letter reader. Rather than sympathetic attachment, Madison called for reasoned detachment, a suppression of personal feeling. In discussing legislatures, Madison made the model explicit. He argued, "No man is allowed to be a judge in his own cause, because his interest would certainly bias his judgment, and, not improbably, corrupt his integrity." The same held true for bodies of men and, specifically, legislatures. "What are the different classes of legislators but advocates and parties to the causes which they determine?" he asked. "Justice ought to hold the balance between them. Yet the parties are, and must be, themselves the judges." In such a situation, Madison lamented that the "predominant party" was bound to "trample on the rules of justice."[43] To combat this tendency, Madison hoped to fashion the character of his readers along lines similar to what he hoped for from legislators.

What is crucial to remember, though, is that Madison's model of political justice and his stylistic reliance on axiomatic logic were conscious poses. His rhetorical stance was as implicated in the heated political debate as the most wild-eyed harangue. The difference was that Madison and the *Federalist Papers* attempted to change the ground rules of the debate in their favor by arguing for a civil and restrained exchange that fostered the political values they hoped to create and that implicitly painted their opponents as the irresponsible instigators of faction.

But it was still a pose. Despite the seemingly geometric precision of his arguments, Madison's logic has flaws. For example, Madison at one point extolled elections in large republics as a kind of filtration of talent, a means to elect the kind of men who would act as disinterested judges rather than as parties to their own cause. He rejected this possibility earlier in the essay, though, when he discussed the inability of legislatures to act justly. He wrote, "It is vain to say that enlightened statesmen will be able to adjust these clashing interests, and render them all subservient to the public good. Enlightened statesmen will not always be at the helm."[44] In other words, Madison contradicted himself in *Federalist #10* on one of his most crucial points. That is not to say that his essay fails, though. When one reads and thinks about the essay, even if one disagree with it, Madison has already succeeded in persuading one, if only for a moment, to approach the question as an impartial judge, because his essay places readers in that role. It demands that readers approach it through their reason rather than their prejudice and that they consider a range of possibilities rather than simply cling to preconceived opinions. It turns readers, even if only for a moment, into the kind of enlightened statesmen that Madison sought: impartial judges, not partisan advocates.

Unsurprisingly, given the association of men with reason and women with emotion, the readers that Madison had in mind were clearly male. Unlike the language of the other founders, Madison's language in his political writing is virtually free of any sort of gendered reference. This absence does not mean that Madison did not rely on gender to construct the political sphere; rather, it reveals how completely Madison envisioned public life as the arena solely of men, so much so that he had no need to state explicitly that fact. This does not mean, though, that Madison believed in the programmatic exclusion of women from public life. In fact, his wife, Dolley, played as significant a part in his political life as virtually any first lady in history. Madison was notoriously uncomfortable in large social gatherings, and Dolley had a key role in helping him with the social demands of his office—a service that provided him and other political leaders with the setting to conduct the informal negotiations and communications so essential to politics.[45] Despite his wife's and other high-ranking women's informal role in public life, though, Madison imaginatively peopled his readership solely with other men.

Madison's imagined readers were also white. As a young man in the 1770s and early 1780s, Madison wrestled with the issue of slavery and contemplated various ways to end his dependence on slave labor. His creation of an alternative persona in his defense of the three-fifths clause in *Federalist #54* reveals his discomfort defending slavery. But he also became inescapably dependent on slave labor and comfortable in the role of Virginia planter. His revolutionary fervor on the issue eventually gave way to quiescence. And his youthful musings about slavery gave way to public silence—a silence that nonetheless clearly demarcated a racial boundary to his readership as pronounced as the gender boundary.[46]

Figure 13. *Dolley Madison*, undated engraving after Gilbert Stuart's 1804 oil portrait. Courtesy of the Montpelier Foundation.

Even for this more limited white male readership, Madison envisioned a restricted role. In contrast to Jefferson's optimism, Hamilton's pessimism, and Adams's ambivalence, Madison had a realistic, albeit chastened, view of the potential character of the American people.[47] He had seen the problems when self-interested parties attempted to govern. He had only to look at state governments in the 1780s, swayed to and fro by overweening majorities. In considering the "new and intricate" question of the proposed federal Constitution in 1787, Madison told Jefferson that the question "certainly surpasses the judgment of the greater part" of what he called "the mass of the people."[48] His faith in the people was limited, and he designed a government to limit their direct involvement through the moderating influence of their representatives — "a republican remedy for the diseases most incident to republican government," as Madison wrote in *Federalist #10*.[49]

But Madison also refused to concede that the people were unable to uphold a republican government. In the *Federalist*, he repeatedly emphasized that man was neither all good nor all bad. In *Federalist #55*, he wrote:

> As there is a degree of depravity in mankind which requires a certain degree of circumspection and distrust: So there are other qualities in human nature, which justify a certain portion of esteem and confidence. Republican government presupposes the existence of these qualities in a higher degree than any other form. Were the pictures which have been drawn by the political jealousy of some among us, faithful likenesses of the human character, the inference would be that there is not sufficient virtue among men for self-government; and that nothing less than the chains of despotism can restrain them from destroying and devouring one another.[50]

For Madison, proper representation safeguarded the central premise of the Revolution, that the government's legitimacy rested on the people's consent.

He worried more about a citizenry too engaged in political controversy than one too detached, though.[51] As he had seen in the 1780s, active public involvement in the legislative process caused injustice. Madison had a limited trust in the people and feared involving them too frequently. The stability of government rested on public opinion, and stability was crucial to justice. In *Federalist #37* he wrote, "An irregular and mutable legislation is not more an evil in itself than it is odious to the people." Instead, he argued that "stability in government is essential to national character and to the advantages annexed to it, as well as to that repose and confidence in the minds of the people, which are among the chief blessings of civil society" (361). Although Hamilton also emphasized governmental stability, Madison's emphasis remained on the benefits it would bring to the people, rather than on the additional power a stable government could project. For Madison, the gains were ones of justice to American citizens. Madison argued that no constitutional dispute could be safely remedied through appeal to the people, because they would be swayed by private interests.

Madison's manner of thinking contrasted sharply with Jefferson's.[52] He wrote Jefferson in 1788, "In our Governments the real power lies in the majority of the Community, and the invasion of private rights is chiefly to be apprehended, not from acts of Government contrary to the sense of its constituents, but from acts in which the Government is the mere instrument of the major number of the constituents. This is a truth of great importance, but not yet sufficiently attended to."[53] Less than a month after he penned *Federalist #37*, he offered an extensive refutation in *Federalist #49* of Jefferson's proposed method of constitutional revision, which allowed recourse to a new convention whenever two branches agreed that revision was needed.[54] According to Madison, Jefferson's proposed plan risked involving the nation's citizens too actively in constitutional interpretation. Madison strenuously opposed such easy and potentially frequent recourse to constitutional revision. Frequent conventions, Madison argued, would risk "disturbing the public tranquility by interesting too strongly the public passions." Such experiments were "of too ticklish a nature to be unnecessarily multiplied." By frequent turns to revision, the implicit idea would take root "of some defect in the government," depriving it of "that veneration which time bestows on every thing, and without which perhaps the wisest and freest governments would not possess the requisite stability."[55] From Madison's point of view, Jefferson simply did not understand the dangers of too much popular involvement in government.

Madison's disagreement with Jefferson revealed once again his central concern with a just government. He assumed that the legislative branch would always hold preponderant power and would always look to increase its dominance. Better positioned to argue its case than the other branches, according to Madison, "the legislative party would not only be able to plead their cause most successfully with the people. They would probably be constituted themselves the judges." Violating Madison's fundamental principle of an interested party never judging its own cause, the convention would fail to offer a disinterested verdict on constitutional problems. "It would be pronounced by the very men who had been agents in, or opponents of the measures, to which the decision would relate. The passions therefore not the reason, of the public, would sit in judgment. But it is the reason of the public alone that ought to controul and regulate the government. The passions ought to be controuled and regulated by the government," he wrote.[56]

Given his limited faith in the people, Madison feared even the calling of a second convention to amend the document created in Philadelphia in 1787. He wrote Edmund Randolph in 1788, "There can be no doubt that there are subjects to which the capacities of the bulk of mankind are unequal, and on which they must and will be governed by those with whom they happen to have acquaintance and confidence." He believed that public opinion was arbitrary, and he noted that if the identical Constitution had been drawn up by "an obscure individual, instead of a body possessing public respect & confidence," it would never be met with public approval, but if the respected members of the Virginia elite who opposed the Constitution were to approve of it, it would easily be passed by Virginians.[57] Madison argued that only the revolutionary moment, by stifling "the ordinary diversity of opinions on great national questions," had allowed Americans to create new constitutions "whilst no spirit of party, connected with the changes to be made, or the abuses to be reformed, could mingle its leaven in the operation."[58] He worried that a similar spirit could not be expected during normal times, when, he was sure, private concerns would trump those of the public. He hoped that the Constitution would remedy this by prescribing the proper roles for legislators and citizens. But this only shifted the battle to a different arena, for who would interpret the Constitution?[59]

"The Cloudy Medium"

Interpreting the Constitution

After describing his ideal reader, Madison turned to the ostensible subject of the essay, the work of the convention. Written almost directly counter to the spirit of the rest of the *Federalist Papers*, *Federalist #37* offered not the possibility of a commonsense understanding of the Constitution but the impossibility of that vision.[60] Madison engaged in a clever game of lowering expectations by dwelling on the challenges of writing the Constitution. He claimed that unbiased readers should not only consider the Constitution "without a disposition to find or to magnify faults; but will see the propriety that a faultless plan was not to be expected. . . . but will keep in mind that they themselves also are but men, and ought not to assume an infallibility in rejudging the fallible opinions of others" (360). He catalogued at length the "many allowances [that] ought to be made for the difficulties inherent in the very nature of the undertaking referred to the convention" (360).

With each reason, he led his readers deeper into the morass of constitutional theory. First, he emphasized the "novelty of the undertaking," a situation that left the delegates with only historical models to avoid but none to emulate (360). Second, he noted the difficulty "in combining the requisite stability and energy in government with the inviolable attention due to liberty" and called it "an arduous part" because the two qualities embraced contrary attributes (361). Third, he pointed out the difficult task "of marking the proper line of partition, between the authority of the general, and that of the state governments" (361). At this point in the essay, Madison began to turn not simply to the difficulty of the task but to the impossibility of it. He wrote, "The faculties of the mind itself have never yet been distinguished and defined, with satisfactory precision" (361). The kingdoms of nature afforded a similar proof. What, then, could be expected from man? "When we pass from the works of nature, in which all the delineations are perfectly accurate, and appear to be otherwise only from the imperfection of the eye which surveys them, to the institutions of man, in which the obscurity arises as well from the object itself, as from the organ by which it is contemplated," he advised, "we must perceive the necessity of moderating still farther our expectations and hopes from the efforts of human sagacity" (362). No one had yet been able even "to discriminate and define with sufficient certainty" between "the legislative, executive and judiciary; or even the privileges and powers of the different legislative branches" (362). To these problems, Madison added the difficulties of the competing interests represented at the convention, such as those of large states versus small states. All in all, according to Madison's account, the delegates had faced a daunting task.

Madison turned, then, to the final, insuperable barrier to clarity, language itself. In words recalling Hugh Blair's remarks on the essay, Madison wrote, "The use of words is to express ideas. Perspicuity therefore requires not only that the ideas should be distinctly formed, but that they should be expressed by words distinctly and exclusively appropriate to them." He added, "But no language is so copious as to supply words and phrases for every complex idea, or so correct as not to include any equivocally denoting different ideas" (362–63). Because of this, Madison argued that any escape from linguistic ambiguity was impossible. "Hence it must happen," he claimed, "that however accurately objects may be discriminated in themselves, and however accurately the discrimination may be considered, the definition of them may be rendered inaccurate by the inaccuracy of the terms in which it is delivered. And this unavoidable inaccuracy must be greater or less, according to the complexity and novelty of the objects defined" (363). Language simply could not provide perfect transparency. Even God, when he "condescends to address mankind in their own language," found that his meaning was "rendered dim and doubtful, by the cloudy medium through which it is communicated" (363).

The authors of Publius usually downplayed the inherent imperfections in language by arguing that common usage was sufficient to establish reasonable grounds of interpretation. From this view, problems in inter-pretation were not epistemological but moral (caused by the potential disparity between words and intentions).[61] Throughout the essays, Publius refuted Antifederalist charges of ambiguity by confidently interpreting the Constitution's meaning. The Constitution's opponents, Publius seemed to say, were the ones attempting to misrepresent the document. Madison complained of a "confusion of names," and Hamilton argued that the Antifederalists "but yielding to some untoward bias . . . entangle them-selves in words and confound themselves in subtleties."[62] Providing defi-nitions, suggesting rules for construction, and even resorting once to etymology, Publius seemed to suggest that any potential ambiguities in the document could easily be resolved.[63] This viewpoint helps explain the constant attempts to create a certain kind of reader (moderate, just, rea-soned). If all potential interpreters of the Constitution could be prevailed upon to approach the document from that standpoint, interpretation would cease to be a problem, as all reasonable men could be expected to find common ground. But if Publius generally spoke as the voice of can-dor and reason, extolling a world in which one could get beyond parti-sanship to the truth, Madison attacked such a notion, albeit briefly. In *Federalist #37*, he embraced a Lockean understanding of language in which misunderstandings were an inherent part of language.[64]

Addressing Antifederalist complaints of ambiguity, Madison pushed the criticism even deeper. Cleverly turning the Antifederalists' most powerful criticism into another argument in favor of ratification, Madison argued that such ambiguity was inescapable and, thus, in a sense, acceptable. He wrote admiringly, "The real wonder is, that so many difficulties should have been surmounted; and surmounted with an unanimity almost as unprecedented as it must have been unexpected. It is impossible for any man of candour to reflect on this circumstance, without partaking of as-tonishment. It is impossible for the man of pious reflection not to per-ceive in it, a finger of that Almighty Hand which has been so frequently and signally extended to our relief in the critical stages of the Revo-lution" (364). Attributing both to the benevolence of the Almighty, Madison tied the creation of the Constitution to the Revolution itself. Madison's radical defense did not reject the charge of ambiguity—it embraced it.

Throughout the essays, Publius would grasp the opportunity offered by the ambiguity of language to create a powerful vocabulary for ratifica-tion.[65] The crucial words in the *Federalist* and in the Madisonian vocab-ulary were not defined singly but through linkages with other words, creating juxtapositions that helped define the terms of the debate in favor of ratification. For example, when Publius used a word such as "pru-dence," he usually combined it with another word. He wrote of "wisdom and prudence," "uprightness and prudence," "prudence and propriety," "discretion and prudence," "prudence and firmness," "prudence and industry," "prudence and good sense," "prudence and integrity," and "prudence and efficacy." Prudence was also used in a different construction with moderation. Besides linking it with other key words (moderation and wisdom), Publius established a cluster of positive associations with prudence that kept the word free from virtually any negative connotations. Did prudence perhaps reveal a lack of firm principles? Not when associated with integrity and uprightness. Did it seem overly cautious? Not when associated with firmness and efficacy. Did discretion imply an overly subtle and perhaps slippery character? Not when associated with propriety and good sense. Returning again and again to certain key words, Publius established a vocabulary through association and connotation that was virtually unassailable and that aided in the larger project of creating the kind of discursive climate in which the Constitution would be discussed and with which the Constitution would be associated. In the end, the key words all seemed interrelated and inseparable both in meaning and in governance.

Publius treated other central words in a similar fashion. Reason was used so often that cataloguing it would become monotonous. Moderation was tied to candor and justice and was continually invoked as the proper attitude with which to approach the question of constitutional ratification. Impartial was linked with discerning, right determination, consistent, judicious, fair, upright, and unbiased. "Impartial world" was placed in parallel construction with "friends of mankind," and impartial was also repeatedly offered as the proper attitude toward the question of constitutional ratification. Wisdom was repeatedly associated with virtue, as well as with prudence, regularity, stability, deliberation, experience, and integrity. Wisdom offers a particularly good example of the power of association employed by Publius. By linking it repeatedly with virtue, the authors established its centrality but only as a particular kind of wisdom that was, in effect, an argument for ratification. With the states associated with instability, violent faction, and other political ills, the choice of pairings (stability, deliberation, regularity) all emphasized how wisdom and thus the national government were the opposite of such upheavals. By fixing the vocabulary according to his values, Publius could win the argument largely through the acceptance of his own terms, with definitions providing parameters of debate already skewed to favor his goal.

Justice came to be defined as the central value to be fostered through the proposed Constitution. Although linked with a variety of words such as reason and moderation, justice was most often placed with the public good (through various formulations including the public good, the general good, patriotism, and good faith), coming to seem over time as the literal embodiment of the public good. The vocabulary created a virtually unassailable logic. If the end of government was the public good, and the public good was justice, and justice was a disinterested umpire, the Constitution as positioned rhetorically by the *Federalist Papers* was absolutely essential, because it would create a government of impartial judges. The *Federalist* was a masterpiece of argument through juxtaposition.

Although the Federalists won the battle for ratification, Madison still found himself facing the same problem that Antifederalists had so tirelessly pointed out, the ambiguity of the Constitution. He and his coauthors exploited the ambiguity of language to create a powerful vocabulary for ratification, but Madison ultimately hoped to tame that ambiguity. While language would never yield to perfect interpretation, Madison sought to provide well-defined parameters within which leaders would interpret the Constitution and beyond which they would not stray.

He feared that the Constitution would never be able to offer any stability if it was the object of frequent changes. Instead of liquidating interpretive ambiguity, the Constitution would amplify the ambiguity if it offered itself as a readily changeable text. A Constitution of that nature would fail to provide the requisite stability that he thought was necessary to just government. Madison feared that the experience of the 1780s, with mutable and unjust state legislation, would merely be replayed on the national level. To establish limits, Madison returned again to the central lesson of the Revolution—national legitimacy rested on popular sovereignty. He would rely on the people themselves to maintain the integrity of the Constitution and to ensure a just government.

For Madison, an important aspect of government under the Constitution was the slender reed of popular opinion, something that could not withstand too much buffeting. He elaborated on this idea in *Federalist #49*:

> If it be true that all governments rest on opinion, it is no less true that the strength of opinion in each individual, and its practical influence on his conduct, depend much on the number which he supposes to have entertained the same opinion. The reason of man, like man himself is timid and cautious, when left alone; and acquires firmness and confidence, in proportion to the number with which it is associated. When the examples, which fortify opinion, are *antient* as well as *numerous*, they are known to have a double effect. In a nation of philosophers, this consideration ought to be disregarded. A reverence for the laws, would be sufficiently inculcated by the voice of an enlightened reason. But a nation of philosophers is as little to be expected as the philosophical race of kings wished for by Plato. And in every other nation, the most rational government will not find it a superfluous advantage, to have the prejudices of the community on its side.[66]

What applied to all countries generally applied to America with particular force, according to Madison, because the complexity of the American system "requires a more than common reverence for the authority which is to preserve order thro' the whole." He urged that public opinion "should guarantee, with a holy zeal, these political scriptures from every attempt to add to or diminish from them."[67]

Despite his views on the limited role of the people in public life, Maidson's understanding of popular opinion gave the people a crucial role safeguarding the meaning of the Constitution. He understood that the document and the government would achieve legitimacy only when they became objects of veneration, when there was a "reverence for the laws" (to place limits on possible interpretations).[68] Veneration would involve the people as guardians of the true meaning of the text, the final authority for constitutional interpretation not in the active sense of determining what it did say but in the passive sense of resisting unjust constructions of what it could be made to say. By seeing the Constitution not as a text for active interpretation but for veneration, the people would ensure that any proposed changes would be infrequent and modest.

The events of the 1790s only further confirmed Madison's opinion of the role of the people in establishing limits on constitutional interpretation. During that period, as Madison and Jefferson worried that a minority had managed to seize the reins of government, the use of public opinion in Madison's thinking became even more prominent. Writing in a 1791 piece for the *National Gazette,* Madison made more explicit his vision of the role of the public. "Public opinion sets bounds to every government, and is the real sovereign in every free one," he wrote. He argued that "the stability of all government and security of all rights" could be traced to it.[69] Precisely because they would follow custom and habit, ordinary people would serve as a kind of extraconstitutional reason, limiting the ability of artful demagogues to twist the document, even as the people themselves were also barred from playing an overly active role. If the Constitution was inherently ambiguous, the people would eventually resolve that ambiguity. He wrote, "That in a Constitution so new and so complicated, there should be occasional difficulties and differences in the practical expositions of it, can surprise no one; and this must continue to be the case, as happens to new laws on complex subjects, until a course of practice of sufficient uniformity and duration to carry with it the public sanction shall settle doubtful or contested meanings."[70]

Ambiguity would be resolved through public sanction, public approval (or disapproval) of the actions of the government. If legislators attempted innovations that failed the test of constitutionality, Madison relied on the ballot box to turn them from office and undo their work. The Bank of the United States provided an example of Madison's understanding of how constitutional ambiguities could be resolved. After being accused of flip-flopping by signing into law a national bank when he was president, despite opposing such a bank in the early 1790s, Madison denied "the charge of mutability on a constitutional question." He argued that "in the case of a Constitution as of a law, a course of authoritative, deliberate, and continued decisions, such as the bank could plead, was an evidence of the public judgment, necessarily superseding individual opinions" and could "fix the interpretation of a law." But even precedent failed to offer a completely reliable standard. Madison was careful to distinguish a precedent that resolved an ambiguity from a precedent that altered the Constitution's meaning. In 1821, he countered any easy reliance on the legislative record. "There has been a fallacy in this case, as, indeed, in others, in confounding a question whether precedents could expound a Constitution, with a question whether they could alter a Constitution. . . . None will deny that precedents of a certain description fix the interpretation of a law. Yet who will pretend that they can repeal or alter a law?" he asked.[71] And he warned against accepting uncritically all legislative decisions:

> I am persuaded that legislative precedents are frequently of a character entitled to little respect, and that those of Congress are sometimes liable to peculiar distrust. They not only follow the example of other legislative assemblies in first procrastinating, and then precipitating their acts; but, owing to the termination of their session every other year at a fixed day and hour, a mass of business is struck off, as it were, at short-hand, and in a moment. These midnight precedents of every sort ought to have little weight in any case.[72]

Madison relied on the people to provide a firm but flexible sense of constitutional interpretation, strict enough that politicians would not be allowed to read whatever meaning they chose into the document but supple enough to accommodate modest alterations as long as they were grounded in "authoritative" and "deliberate" precedents and backed by "the public judgment." Indeed, one of the central tenets of Madisonian interpretation was to respect "early, deliberate and continued practice under the Constitution."[73] Under these guidelines, the interpretive difficulties surrounding the Constitution would be increasingly limited in scope, as the growing authority of the document itself and an established record of legislative precedents would limit further changes.

Even in his arguments about the original intent of the document, Madison relied on the views of the people, not the framers. In 1824, to protect the Constitution from future misreading, he called for "unbiased" inquiries into "the history of its origin and adoption."[74] The challenge of preserving an accurate historical understanding of the Constitution became, in many ways, the work of his final years. During this time, he became more careful about safeguarding his correspondence in order to create the kind of historical record that he hoped would help others remain true to the Constitution's meaning.[75] Madison rejected the idea that the deliberations of the Constitutional Convention itself could serve as a guide to interpretation, tempting as the possibility might have been. Besides "the difficulty of verifying [the Convention's] intention," Madison did not believe that the delegates' intentions should play a deciding role.[76] He also refused to release his own voluminous *Notes on the Federal Convention*, precisely because he feared the tendency to use that document as the means of interpreting the Constitution (he also hoped to increase veneration for the *Notes* by removing them from any association with partisan political purposes). He wrote that publication of them "should be delayed till the Constitution should be well settled in practice & till a knowledge of the controversial part of the proceedings of its framers could be turned to no improper account. . . . As a guide in expounding and applying the provisions of the Constitution, the debates and incidental decisions of the Convention can have no authoritative character."[77]

Madison placed the issue of original intent not on the Constitutional Convention but on the far broader, if more ambiguous, grounds of the document's ratification, a standpoint that again gave honored place to the role of the people, rather than to an elite group of men deliberating behind closed doors. "If the meaning of the Constitution is to be sought out of itself," he wrote in 1831, "it is not in the proceedings of the body that proposed it, but in those of the State Conventions, which gave it all the validity and authority it possesses."[78] As he noted in a speech to Congress, "Whatever veneration might be entertained for the body of men who formed our Constitution, the sense of that body could never be regarded as the oracular guide in expounding the Constitution. As the instrument came from them it was nothing more than the draft of a plan, nothing but a dead letter, until life and validity were breathed into it by the voice of the people, speaking through the several State Conventions."[79] He reiterated that belief on many occasions, noting that the only "key" to the "legitimate meaning of the instrument" beyond the text itself was to be found "not in the opinions or intentions of the body which planned and proposed the Constitution, but in the sense attached to it by the people in their respective State Conventions, where it received all the authority it possesses."[80] This understanding remained true to his views of America's revolutionary legacy, emphasizing the central importance of the people in establishing the government's legitimacy. But it provided an imperfect guide at best to constitutional interpretation, because the shifting and complicated sentiments of the various state ratifying conventions could never be used to establish a definitive interpretation.

Madison hoped that "the aid of time and habit" would lead to a "just construction" of the Constitution and "put an end to the more dangerous schisms otherwise growing out of it."[81] He claimed that the Constitution's ambiguities were "such as time, usage, and the gradual incorporation of the vital maxims of free Government into the national sentiment, must tend to diminish."[82] He evidently meant a great deal of time, as evidenced by the fact that he made that statement in 1827. The achievement of veneration was no easy task, though, especially given America's revolutionary impulse to question traditional ways. Madison himself wrote in *Federalist #14*, "Is it not the glory of the people of America that whilst they have paid a decent regard to the opinions of former times and other nations, they have not suffered a blind veneration for antiquity, for custom, or for names, to overrule the suggestions of their own good sense, the knowledge of their own situation, and the lessons of their own experience?"[83]

"The silent innovations of time"

Untamed Ambiguity

Madison had hoped that the veneration of the nation's citizens for the Constitution would eventually confine constitutional interpretation within acceptable boundaries. Republican domination of the national political scene after Jefferson's "Revolution of 1800" laid the issue to rest temporarily. For the next two decades, although issues of constitutional interpretation would occasionally arise, Madison could take comfort in the fact that they were relatively minor. During the inaptly named "era of good feelings," though, issues of constitutional interpretation again moved to the fore, and Madison spent the last years of his life trying to defend the labor of his early years.[84] He battled again the same indefatigable foe that he had named in *Federalist #37*, language. Legislative precedent had proved no match for the ambiguity of words, as each precedent seemed to provide only further text for interpretation, re-creating on the national level the problems that he had criticized on the state level in his 1787 "Vices of the Political System of the United States."

Ironically, increasingly strident debates over the interpretation of the Constitution arose not from legislative attempts to stretch the powers of the document (as most of the framers had initially feared) but from the branch that was supposed to protect the Constitution, the Supreme Court. Beginning with the *McCulloch v. Maryland* decision in 1819, the Marshall Court made a series of rulings that many feared were undermining the federal principles of the Constitution, creating a truly national government that dwarfed the state governments.

Faced with a rising tide of disgust within his home state at these rulings, Madison struggled to defend the Constitution against the attacks of his fellow Virginians. Jefferson himself repeatedly found reason to challenge Madison's handiwork. He questioned the wisdom of placing the power of constitutional and legislative interpretation in the judiciary, which he thought made the judiciary "a despotic branch."[85] Madison reminded him that the Supreme Court remained the proper "Constitutional resort for determining the line between the federal and State jurisdictions" and that "the abuse of a trust does not disprove its existence." Arguing against Jefferson's proposed remedy of frequent constitutional amendments (reminiscent of his words in the *Federalist Papers*), he warned Jefferson in 1823 that a recourse to amendments to adjudicate every constitutional dispute would have a "tendency to lessen salutary veneration for an Instrument so often calling for such explanatory interpositions."[86]

Even as Madison continued to call for veneration and respect for the Constitution, though, the difficulties inherent in language and the problems they posed for constitutional interpretation were never far from his mind. Noting that America's political system was "emphatically *sui generis*," he repeatedly emphasized the importance of using language in a careful fashion. Linguistic indeterminacy was not a license for linguistic incompetence.[87] Properly defining the terms in an argument was "the only effectual precaution against fruitless and endless discussion."[88] Madison considered this even more essential for constitutional questions, "to which, for want of more appropriate words, such are often applied as lead to error and confusion."[89] America's political experimentation made it susceptible to linguistic misrepresentation, according to this logic. "Known words express known ideas; and new ideas, such as are presented by our novel and unique political system, must be expressed either by new words, or by old words with new definitions," he wrote.[90] America's political situation was so novel, though, that it defied easy linguistic resolution: "The actual system of Government for the United States is so unexampled in its origin, so complex in its structure, and so peculiar in some of its features," Madison noted, "that in describing it the political vocabulary does not furnish terms sufficiently distinctive and appropriate, without a detailed resort to the facts of the case."[91] Given this problem, a certain amount of disagreement over constitutional interpretation was inevitable. Madison wrote in 1819, "It could not but happen, and was foreseen at the birth of the Constitution, that difficulties and differences of opinion might occasionally arise in expounding terms & phrases necessarily used in such a charter . . . and that it might require a regular course of practice to liquidate and settle the meaning of some of them."[92]

Madison realized, though, that even a regular course of practice would offer only a partial solution, for meaning never could be fixed irrevocably.

He wrote in 1827 about "The change which the meaning of words inadvertently undergoes, examples of which are already furnished by the Constitution of the U. States."[93] Again in 1830 he noted to a correspondent "the silent innovations of time on the meaning of words and phrases."[94] In expounding the meaning of a constitutional phrase, he argued, politicians must be guided by the intentions of those who adopted the Constitution and "must decide that intention by the meaning attached to the terms by the *'usus'* which is the *arbitrium*, the *jus* and the *norma loquendi*, a rule as applicable to phrases as to single words." He feared the variety of constructions that later generations could give to phrases based on changes in the language. "It need scarcely to be observed that, according to this rule, the intention, if ascertained by contemporaneous interpretation and continued practice," he wrote, "could not be overruled by any latter meaning put on the phrase, however warranted by the grammatical rules of construction were these at variance with it."[95] Madison feared that the protean quality of language would render the Constitution open to any interpretation. In approving of a national philological academy to provide for "the stability of language," he wrote worriedly:

> The language of our Constitution [was] already undergoing interpretations unknown to its founders' will. . . . If the meaning of the text be sought in the changeable meaning of the words composing it, it is evident that the shape and attributes of the government must partake of the changes to which the words and phrases of all living languages are constantly subject. What a metamorphosis would be produced in the code of law if all its ancient phraseology were to be taken in its modern sense![96]

As he recognized, though, "a perfect remedy for the evil must, therefore, be unattainable."[97] Language itself would simply never offer a perfect means of resolving interpretive ambiguity or of keeping private interests from invading public deliberations.

For Madison, this difficulty became not a license for constitutional reinterpretation but a limitation on it. He argued that the inherent ambiguity in language should forestall, rather than encourage, later attempts to reinterpret the document. In the midst of the South Carolina nullification crisis, the Virginian warned, "It is but too common to read the expressions of a remote period through the modern meaning of them."[98] After decades spent trying to protect the Constitution from misinterpretation, he still found himself battling to preserve the document as the source of an unbiased and just government. He warned: "But, in expounding it now, is the danger of bias less from the influence of local interests, of popular currents, and even from an estimate of national utility?"[99] Local interests, popular feeling, even national goals—all were inappropriate grounds for interpreting the Constitution, according to Madison. Although he had hoped the Constitution would create a government of impartial legislators, he recognized that language would always be susceptible to the "more frequent and formidable . . . spirit of party or the temptations of interest." Even the republican mainstay, the public good, would occasionally betray "honest minds into misconstructions of the Constitutional text."[100] Echoing Adams's mistrust, he warned, "The purest motives can be no security against innovations materially changing the features of the government."[101] And he certainly did not trust representatives to interpret the document. Instead of the Constitution providing the parameters of political life, too often political life had attempted to alter the parameters of the Constitution. Madison decried the tendency of politicians to use the Constitution to prop up their own programs, "all admitting that to be the paramount authority, and claiming it for themselves in its true meaning."[102]

Madison hoped to achieve a just government through the careful construction of a written constitutional order, which would limit the ability of private interests to influence the public councils. As Francis Bacon had warned, though, "Although we think we govern our words, certain it is that words, as Tartar's bow, do shoot back upon the understanding of the wisest, and mightily entangle and pervert the judgment."[103]

Figure 14. *George Washington*, painted by Gilbert Stuart, 1795. Courtesy of the National Gallery of Art.

CONCLUSION

Veneration

IN THE CLOSING MONTHS of the 1790s, the Federalist party's popular support was dwindling, the result of the draconian Alien and Sedition Acts and high taxes, passed in preparation for a war with France that never came. Instead, party leaders found themselves with peace and unpopularity on their hands. Some Federalists hoped to revive the party's fortunes by turning once again to George Washington, who seemed the perfect solution for a Federalist party desperate to regain its popular appeal. But Washington refused to seek a third term as president. By way of explanation, he called attention to a profound shift in the early republic from a politics of character to a politics of party allegiance:[1]

> Let that party set up a broomstick and call it a true son of Liberty; a Democrat, or give it any other epithet that will suit their purpose, and it will command their votes in toto! as an analysis of this position, look to the pending Election of Governor in Pennsylvania. Will not the Federalists meet them or rather defend their cause, on the opposite ground? Surely they must, or they will discover a want of Policy, indicative of weakness, and pregnant of mischief which cannot be admitted. Wherein then would lye the difference between the present Gentleman in Office [John Adams], and myself?[2]

The undefined political world of the revolutionary and early national periods had relied on that which Washington so abundantly had—character. All the founders had engaged in attempts to fashion a character for themselves, but none had been more successful than George Washington. The very titles he was known by—father to his country, Cincinnatus—attested to his success, revealing how thoroughly he managed to embody those roles.[3] The success of his own self-construction made it largely invisible, so that Abigail Adams could claim, "Simple truth is his best, his greatest eulogy."[4] Although exacerbating the ambiguous and problematic divide between public and private, the politics of character had bestowed tremendous power on some individuals, but that world had come to an end.[5] According to Washington, even a character as esteemed as his own no longer carried weight.

With Washington's death in 1799, though, others would become the custodians of his character, and new opportunities would be found for

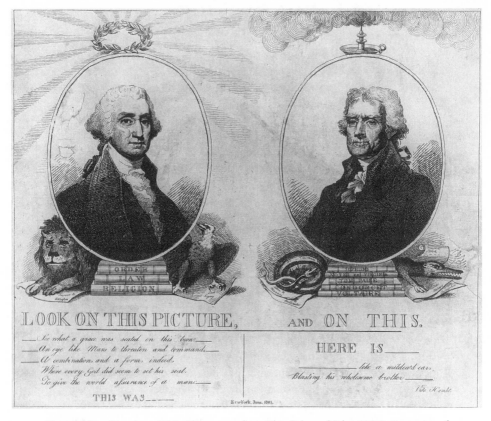

Figure 15. "Look on This Picture, and on This," broadside, 1807. Courtesy of the New-York Historical Society. Even after his death, Washington remained a potent political symbol as shown in this 1807 anti-Jefferson broadside.

its use.[6] While alive, Washington had unavoidably become entangled in the nation's political divisions, but Washington as symbol offered consensus in a way that Washington as president never could. No one would play a more important role in refashioning his character to fit the new political realities than Mason Locke Weems, an itinerant preacher and bookseller, who wrote the astoundingly popular *Life of Washington*.[7] Madison had hoped that the Constitution would come to inspire the veneration and reverence of Americans, but Weems's Washington proved to be the first and, for many years, the most powerful object of veneration in the new nation. Henry Knox claimed, "It is the President's character, and not the written constitution, which keeps [the nation] together."[8] The quintessential eighteenth-century man of character, Washington had built that character through his public actions. Weems offered a far different conception of character, though, one that was first and foremost based on private life and that revealed the emerging nineteenth-century ideas about character.

"Washington below the clouds"
The Changing Nature of Character

Weems proved to be a keen interpreter of Washington. He crafted a capacious understanding of him and, by extension, America that transcended party battles. His book cast the Revolution as a history to be cherished, rather than an object of contention. Adeptly refashioning Washington's image, Weems presented the Virginian as a national model to all citizens, whether Federalists or Republicans.

Weems's checkered revolutionary credentials made him an unlikely candidate to fashion a national myth. He had chosen not to serve in America's revolutionary armies and had spent much of the war in Great Britain. He had also taken orders in the Church of England while in Britain, a choice that probably marked him for a time with the taint of Loyalist sympathies, given that Anglican clergymen were notorious Loyalists.[9] Even his biography of Washington emerged from mixed, although in his mind not irreconcilable, motives. For Weems, the book presented the possibility to promote both personal gain and national union. Although he told his publisher that he wanted "to show that [Washington's] unparalleled rise and elevation were owing to his Great Virtues," he also emphasized the commercial possibilities of the project. In fact, the two went hand in hand for Weems, who wrote to his publisher, "O what might not be the results in Good to the Country, & in Gold and Glory to Ourselves."[10] Weems also displayed an intellectual flexibility that bordered on impropriety. When confronted by a minister for selling Thomas Paine's supposedly blasphemous *Age of Reason* along with religious tracts, Weems held up the Bible and responded, "Behold the antidote. The bane and the antidote are both for you."[11] In writing his *Life of Washington*, Weems turned his ambiguous status to good use. Coupled with a desire to please that was stronger than any doctrinal commitments, it made him particularly sensitive to the often unspoken but deeply felt hopes and fears of the nation.[12]

In biography, Weems found ample generic resources for his project. During the first few decades of the nineteenth century, the genre became firmly linked with building the nation's character. Patriotic and didactic, biographies presented the founders as public figures to be emulated. Alongside this language of national assertion, another approach to biography was also developing. Reflecting changing ideas about character, biographers increasingly emphasized private life as the true measure of a man's

character in contrast to the eighteenth-century conceptions based on public life.[13] Weems melded these two strands in his *Life of Washington*.

Many questioned the need for a biography of Washington, whose life
already seemed so well known. Weems himself raised this issue: "But is
not his history *already* known? Have not a thousand orators spread his
fame abroad?"[14] He dismissed this argument, claiming that people knew
little of Washington's private life:

> But this is not *half* his fame. . . . True, he is there seen in *greatness*,
> but it is only the greatness of public character, which is no evidence
> of *true greatness*; for a public character is often an artificial one. At
> the head of an army or nation, where gold and glory are at stake,
> and where a man feels himself the *burning focus* of unnumbered eyes;
> he must be a paltry fellow indeed, who does not play his part pretty
> handsomely . . . even the common passions of pride, avarice, or ambi-
> tion, will put him up to his metal, and call forth his best and bravest
> doings. (1–2)

Washington had labored to build a public character that carried weight,
but Weems embraced a different notion of character. In his *Life*, the word
no longer referred primarily to one's public reputation but instead to one's
private life. Only private actions, according to Weems, provided a real sense
of a man's character. He explained:

> It is not in the glare of *public*, but in the shade of *private life*, that we
> are to look for the man. Private life is always *real* life. Behind the cur-
> tain, where the eyes of the million are not upon him, and where a man
> can have no motive but *inclination*, no excitement but *honest nature*,
> there he will always be sure to act *himself*; consequently, if he act
> greatly, he must be great indeed. Hence it has been justly said, that,
> "our *private deeds*, if *noble*, are noblest of our lives." (2)

Weems promised to show his readers this private Washington. Citizens had
seen "nothing of Washington below *the clouds*. . . . 'tis only Washington
the HERO, and the Demigod," according to Weems (2). This elevated view
of Washington failed to acknowledge his true greatness by treating his
private virtues like "good old *aunts* and *grandmothers*, huddling them
together in the *back rooms*, there to wheeze and cough by themselves"
(3). Weems's views echoed Adams's own distrust of public life, but unlike
Adams, whose corrosive skepticism undermined his confidence in finding
even private virtue, Weems confidently presented a Washington whose
private virtue was beyond reproach.

Scottish rhetorician Hugh Blair offered support for Weems's conception
of his task. Although not qualifying as history according to Blair's criteria
of "impartiality, fidelity, gravity, and dignity," *The Life of Washington* did

fall under what Blair called "inferior kinds of historical composition."
"Biography, or the writing of lives" was a genre "less formal and stately"
than history but "no less instructive." Showing an understanding of the
enterprise similar to Weems, Blair wrote that a biography should "give the
private, as well as the public life." He argued that "it is from private life,
from familiar, domestic, and seemingly trivial occurrences, that we often
receive the most light into the real character."[15]

Weems intuitively grasped the sea change in how one's character was
evaluated, a new world where private life had become the true measure
of an individual's worth. He called his expanded edition of the biography
the "private life" of Washington.[16] This emphasis on private life as the true
basis for public esteem represented a new development, the beginning of
the end of the postrevolutionary political realm with its commingling of
public and private, political and personal, and the beginning of a new world
in which public and private were distinctly different, if related, realms.[17]
His rhetoric anticipated a political world largely freed from the confusion
created by the intermingling of public and private life. In the nineteenth
century, the meaning of character would be altered from a quality one consciously constructed for public purposes to a private quality. Character
would be based on inner morality rather than outward reputation. The
rise of the term "personality" revealed this shift. The word first came into
use in the 1790s, a harbinger of a world where one was less worried about
having a character and more worried about being one.[18]

Translating the Virginian's distinctly upper-class and eighteenth-century
concerns with character into a democratic and domestic idiom, Weems
refashioned Washington according to this emerging conception. In
Weems's hands, Washington's efforts to build a public character became
a different tale of private triumphs on the path to personal virtue. Private
life was now supposed to provide the true measure of a man, free from
the kind of conscious performance so crucial to the politics of character
in late-eighteenth-century America. This shift signaled the end of America's
political infancy, in which eighteenth-century notions of character served as
the grounds, shifting and unstable as they were, for creating the new polity.

"An exemplification of the American character"

Washington as a Self-Made Man

Weems realized that his Washington needed to be a representative hero,
an illustration not of eighteenth-century conceptions of character that
were used to differentiate elite men from others but of a more private character that could serve as a model for all Americans to emulate. Washington
was the one man who could become the symbol for the entire nation, a

symbol in which all citizens found agreement. Although intensely devoted throughout his life to constructing his character, Washington would have to be recast by Weems as entirely free from such artifice, a "natural" expression of America's greatness.[19] Recognizing this, Weems firmly tied Washington's greatness to America, which allowed him to encompass the other strand of biography, the patriotic and didactic project of building the nation's character. Dismissing some skeptics' view that "*so great a man could never have been born in America,*" Weems saw the nation and the man's greatness as thoroughly intertwined. "Where shall we look for Washington, the greatest among men, but in *America?*" Weems wrote. "That greatest Continent. . . . so far superior to any thing of the kind in other continents, that we may fairly conclude that great men and great deeds are designed for America" (5). This Washington allowed Americans to have a kind of greatness by proxy, naturalizing in the process a certain national character as the birthright of all citizens.[20] Turning Adams's pessimism about American virtue on its head, Weems confidently asserted native virtue not on the grounds of the kind of austere self-discipline that Adams desired but as the natural outgrowth of being born American.

As part of the project of Washington as national exemplar, Weems remade the Virginian as a common man who achieved greatness through his own efforts. By focusing on Washington's private life, Weems freed himself, at least for Washington's early years, from offering an account that remained true to well-known facts. He could invent his own Washington, which he freely did (most famously with the story of Washington chopping down the cherry tree), and remake him along lines that proved remarkably appealing to the nation as a whole. It was not important to provide an accurate representation of Washington's early life. It was important only to provide a Washington who accurately represented what Americans wanted to believe about him and about themselves.[21] Raised in a "modest" house, Weems's Washington called his father "Pa" and ran around barefoot (*"with his little naked toes he scratched in the soft ground"* [8]). He spent his early manhood in the "laborious life of a woodsman" (10). Throughout, Weems emphasized Washington's common beginnings, writing of how "from such low beginnings" and as a "poor young man" who "from a sheep-cot ascended the throne of his country's affections," Washington advanced "to such unparalleled usefulness and glory among men!" (134). Modest beginnings were not simply a sign of what Washington had overcome; they were the very source of his greatness and a sign of the opportunities that the new nation had created for all. "HAPPILY for America, George Washington was not born with a "silver spoon in his

Figure 16.   Lansdowne Portrait of George Washington, painted by Gilbert Stuart, 1796. Courtesy of the National Portrait Gallery, Smithsonian Institution. This

portrait shows Washington in a vastly different light than the homespun image
Weems attempted to create—and is much closer to how Washington saw himself.

mouth" and was forced to make his way in the world "by his own merit," according to Weems (19). No longer the product of an elite gentry culture, Weems's Washington was a self-made man. By recasting Washington in this fashion, Weems extricated him from the elitism that had proved crippling for Hamilton. Stripped of the qualities that Washington himself had carefully cultivated to distinguish himself, Washington's new character became an empowering example to a rapidly expanding populace and an increasingly democratized polity.[22]

"Every countenance was swollen with sentiment"

Venerating Washington

Embracing the didactic strand of biography, Weems intended to instruct the new nation in Washington's virtues, much as Madison had attempted to instruct American citizens through the *Federalist Papers*. For instance, the opening chapters of Weems's biography read like a child-rearing manual.[23] After describing in careful and famous detail how Washington's upbringing had created his character, Weems offered Washington as a role model to his countrymen. In many ways, the bulk of the *Life* attempted to accomplish for Washington the task that Madison had set for himself with the Constitution—to make him an object of veneration.

Americans revered Washington long before Weems wrote his biography, but the battles of the 1790s had threatened to make Washington into a partisan figure, a Federalist propaganda tool, rather than a nationwide force for unity.[24] Weems was able to extricate Washington from such overt politicization and to make him a unifying symbol for the nation by creating a number of tableaus of Washington to instruct readers in the proper method of honoring him. Washington's resignation of his army commission was perhaps his most famous and admired gesture. Weems used the opportunity not simply to recall the scene but to re-create the powerful feelings of reverence that the moment had called forth, offering his own lesson on the proper spirit with which to approach Washington. He wrote:

> The sight of their great countryman, already so beloved, and now acting so generous, so godlike a part, produced an effect beyond the power of words to express. Their feelings of admiration and affection were too delicious, too big, *for utterance*. Every countenance was swollen with sentiment, and a flood of tears gushed from every eye, which, though a silent, was perhaps the richest offering of veneration and esteem ever paid to a human being. (102)

Such adoration solved the problem of language that had so bedeviled Madison. According to Weems's account, Washington had called forth emotions of such power that they were literally beyond words. Since words themselves were frequently the problem, creating not resolution but further text for interpretation, the silent veneration of Washington provided the perfect medium for understanding and clarity. Embodying the character of the nation while the silent tears of others attested to the transparent meaning of that character, Washington became the consensual symbol of nationhood.[25] Weems projected a similar reaction when Washington entered Congress shortly before Adams's inauguration. In this tableau, Washington's appearance managed to reconstitute the fractured national family, if only for a moment, by calling forth universal adoration. "Instantly, the joy of filial love sprung up in all hearts, glowed in each face, and bursted forth in plaudits *involuntary* from every tongue," Weems wrote; "the father of his country was in the presence of his children, and perhaps for the last time" (128–29). Through Washington, Weems reimagined the nation along familial lines, rhetorically achieving Jefferson's imagined sentimental union.[26]

Weems projected similar reactions across the nation. While riding from Mount Vernon to New York after being unanimously elected president of the United States, Washington was greeted with tributes by every town that he passed, according to Weems:

> If it was only said, "General Washington is coming," it was enough. . . .
> In eager throngs, men, women, and children pressed upon his steps, as waves in crowding ridges pursue the course of a ship through the ocean. And as a new succession of waves is ever ready to take the place of those which had just ended their chase in playful foam, so it was with the ever-gathering crowds that followed their Washington. (106)

The celebration of Washington, in Weems's account, seems to take on aspects of almost religious significance. For instance, as Washington rode through Trenton, Weems recounted the "long rows of young virgins" (107). By treating the reaction to Washington in such detail, Weems helped to solidify that which he purported simply to represent.

Weems also devoted great attention to Washington's actual words and made those a source of veneration as well.[27] Including Washington's Farewell Address in its entirety, Weems screened it from political controversy by presenting it as a father's advice to his children. "Feeling towards his countrymen the solicitude of a father for his children, over whom he had long watched, but was about to leave to themselves," Weems wrote, "and fearing, on the *one hand*, that they might go astray, and, hoping, on the other, that from his long labours of love, he might be permitted to impart the counsels of his long experience, he drew up for them a *farewell address*, which the filial piety of the nation has since called '*his Legacy*'"

(113). Weems made Washington's words, like the man himself, an object of admiration. Weems claimed that the address, "about the length of an ordinary sermon, may do as much good to the people of America as any sermon ever preached, that DIVINE ONE on the mount excepted" (113). He even instructed his readers on the proper way to read the address, "with the feelings of children reading the last letter of a once-loved father now in his grave" (113).

Throughout the final pages, Weems returned to the importance of the Union repeatedly and insistently. Making Washington and the Union virtually synonymous, he moved them beyond the reach of politics.[28] Weems's Washington both fostered and represented the success of the project of nation making, symbol of a more stable union. In his *Life of Washington*, Weems combined various elements from each of the founders to create what he called in one of his political pamphlets, *A Good Twenty-Five Cents Worth of Political Love Powder For Honest Adamites and Jeffersonians.*[29] The Weemsian solution came at a cost, though. The founders' struggles with their "characters" represented profound attempts to rethink themselves and their nation in the wake of the Revolution. Draining Washington of any political specificity, Weems threatened to make both Washington's character and the nation's meaningless by creating a symbolic realm in which the people passively venerated an empty icon.

Although Weems's antiseptic answer found avid readers, the founders, most of them many years from their own posthumous re-creations, continued to struggle to secure their understanding of the Revolution and the nation. They surveyed the post-1790s landscape with increasing misgivings about the fate of the republic that they had worked so hard to create, and they often feared that they had labored in vain.

Despite his electoral success, Jefferson became increasingly pessimistic in his final years about the course of his country. In particular, the Missouri crisis shook to the core his faith in the nation. Establishing special admission criteria for Missouri threatened the revolutionary premise of the nation, replacing Jefferson's affective union, a bond among states roughly akin to friendship, with one based on inequality among states that seemed to re-capitulate the tyranny that Americans had escaped with the Revolution. It was nothing less, he wrote in 1820, than "treason against the hopes of the world."[30] Jefferson preferred to see the Union broken. He thought that if the "schism be pushed to separation, it will be for a short term only" and that "two or three years' trial will bring them back, like quarreling lovers to renewed embraces, and increased affections."[31] The bonds of friendship with which Jefferson had so laboriously struggled to tie his nation together threatened to be torn asunder. He could take refuge from this terrifying vision only by imagining his own death, writing "that my only consolation is to be, that I live not to weep over it."[32]

Hamilton never recovered politically from his open letter attacking the character of Adams. He did successfully exert himself one final time on the national stage, persuading and cajoling his reluctant Federalist allies in the House to vote for Jefferson, rather than Burr, in the stalemated election of 1800. As usual, when working among his peers, he was successful. He would die in the duel with Burr only a few years later, and in the final years of his short life, he could do nothing but lament his increasingly irrelevant place in the nation. "Mine is an odd destiny," he wrote in 1802. Despite his efforts "to prop the frail and worthless fabric" of the Constitution, he found himself a political outcast. "I have the murmurs of its friends no less than the curses of its foes for my reward," Hamilton wrote. "What can I do better than withdraw from the Scene? Every day proves to me more and more that this American world was not made for me."[33]

Adams withdrew from politics after his defeat in 1800. Although he could comfort himself with the thought that his unpopularity confirmed his virtue, it was small consolation in the face of what looked to him like the betrayal of both his friends and his party. But Adams's occasional eruptions obscure the serenity he achieved in his later years. In his renewed correspondence with his onetime political nemesis Jefferson, he wrote in 1812, "I am not weary of Living. Whatever a peevish Patriarch might say, I have never yet seen the day in which I could say I have had no pleasure; or that I have had more Pain that Pleasure."[34] He was even able to extricate their friendship from their politics. In 1818, he claimed, "He is the last & oldest of my confidential bosom friends, let party faction & politics say what they will."[35] Through John Quincy Adams, Adams even achieved political reconciliation of a sort, as his son left the Federalist party and became a National Republican, heir to both his father's beliefs and to the political legacy of Jefferson. Perhaps Adams's death can be seen as a final reconciliation. Adams would have found the date of his death, on 4 July 1826, fitting. The end of his life coincided with the celebration of his nation's beginning (even if the celebration was not on the day Adams thought it should be), a circumstantial reconciliation with the history and legacy of the Revolution that he had done so much to shape. He did not know that Jefferson had passed away earlier in the day, and his final words were, "Thomas Jefferson survives."[36] In his final moments, Adams rested his hopes for a nation that continued to cherish and safeguard its revolutionary heritage on Jefferson, an acceptance both personal and political of a world in which Adams had been only partially understood, despite all his efforts to help others see behind "the Scenery of the Business."

Madison struggled to the end of his life to safeguard the Constitution. The nation threatened to leave Madison in its wake, though. His subtle understanding of constitutional legitimacy was lost on the South Carolinians in their rush to nullification, and more than one writer accused him of senility.[37] The nullification crisis forced Madison to recognize the precariousness not simply of his own personal authority but of the authority of the Constitution. As he lay dying, he warned his countrymen one final time against casual tampering with the nation. In a statement titled, "Advice to My Country," he called for "the Union of the States to be cherished and perpetuated. Let the open enemy to it be regarded as a Pandora with her box opened, and the disguised one as the serpent creeping with deadly wiles into Paradise."[38] As he himself recognized, though, union depended on faithful interpretation of the Constitution, which in turn depended on "that cloudy medium," language. The serpent was already in the garden.

In 1831, Madison found himself the last surviving founding father. He noted to one correspondent that he was "the only living signer of the Const. of the U.S." as well as "the sole survivor of those who were members of the Revol. Cong. prior to the close of the war; as I have been for some years, of the members of the Convention in 1776 which formed the first Const. for Virg." The last direct link back to those momentous times, Madison realized that his generation's moment had passed, even as he lingered and labored on. "Having outlived so many of my contemporaries," he wrote, "I ought not to forget that I may be thought to have outlived myself."[39]

NOTES

ABBREVIATIONS

Adams-Jefferson Letters   *The Adams-Jefferson Letters: The Complete Correspondence between Thomas Jefferson and Abigail and John Adams.* 2 vols. Ed. Lester J. Cappon. Chapel Hill, N.C.: University of North Carolina Press, 1959.

Correspondence between John Adams and Mercy Warren   *Correspondence between John Adams and Mercy Warren Relating to Her "History of the American Revolution."* Ed. Charles F. Adams. New York: Arno Press, 1972.

Diary of John Adams   *Diary and Autobiography of John Adams.* 4 vols. of *The Adams Papers*, ed. L. H. Butterfield et al. Cambridge, Mass.: Belknap Press of Harvard University Press, 1961.

PAH   *The Papers of Alexander Hamilton.* 27 vols. Ed. Harold C. Syrett et al. New York: Columbia University Press, 1961–81.

PJA   *The Papers of John Adams.* 10 vols. to date, Ed. Robert J. Taylor et al. Cambridge, Mass.: Belknap Press of Harvard University Press, 1977–.

PJM   *The Papers of James Madison.* Series I, *Papers*, 17 vols. Ed. William T. Hutchinson et al. Chicago: University of Chicago Press, 1962–.

PTJ   *The Papers of Thomas Jefferson.* 29 vols. to date. Ed. Julian P. Boyd et al. Princeton, N.J.: Princeton University Press, 1950–.

Republic of Letters   *The Republic of Letters: The Correspondence between Thomas Jefferson and James Madison, 1776–1826.* 3 vols. Ed. James Morton Smith. New York: W. W. Norton and Company, 1995.

Warren-Adams Letters   *Warren-Adams Letters: Being Chiefly a Correspondence among John Adams, Samuel Adams, and James Warren.* Collections of the Massachusetts Historical Society series, vols. LXXII and LXXIII. Boston: Massachusetts Historical Society, 1925.

WGW   *The Writings of George Washington.* 39 vols. Ed. John C. Fitzpatrick. Washington, D.C.: U.S. Government Printing Office, 1931–44.

WJA   *The Works of John Adams, Second President of the United States.* 10 vols. Ed. Charles Francis Adams. Boston: Little, Brown and Company, 1850–56.

WJM   *Letters and Other Writings of James Madison.* 4 vols. New York: Worthington, 1884.

Writings   Thomas Jefferson. *Writings.* Ed. Merrill Peterson. New York: Library of America, 1984.

WTJ   *The Works of Thomas Jefferson.* 12 vols. Ed. Paul L. Ford. New York: G. P. Putnam's Sons, 1892–98 (reprint 1905).

PREFACE

1. George Washington to John Augustine Washington, 15 June 1783, in *The Writings of George Washington*, 39 vols. ed. John C. Fitzpatrick, (Washington, D.C.: U.S. Government Printing Office, 1931–44), XXVII, 13. Hereafter *WGW*.

2. John Adams to Benjamin Rush, 11 November 1807, in *The Spur of Fame: Dialogues of John Adams and Benjamin Rush, 1805–1813* (San Marino, Calif.: Huntington Library, 1966), 97–98.

INTRODUCTION

1. George Washington (hereafter GW), Circular Letter of Farewell to the Army, 8 June 1783, *WGW*, XXVII, 8.

2. For a brief but suggestive account of the "unexpected, impromptu, artificial" nature of American identity, see John Murrin, "A Roof without Walls: The Dilemma of American National Identity," in *Beyond Confederation: Origins of the Constitution and American National Identity*, ed. Richard Beeman et al. (Chapel Hill: University of North Carolina Press, 1987), 333–48. The founders attempted to disguise this problem through textual dexterity. For the literary artifice used to create the fiction of union, see Robert Ferguson, "'We Do Ordain and Establish': The Constitution as Literary Text," *William and Mary Law Review* 29.1 (1987): 3–25. For American mastery of what Ferguson calls "consensual literature," see Ferguson, *The American Enlightenment, 1750–1820* (Cambridge, Mass.: Harvard University Press, 1997), 80–149. For the invention of the "people," see Edmund Morgan, *Inventing the People: The Rise of Popular Sovereignty in England and America* (New York: Norton, 1988).

3. See T. H. Breen, "Ideology and Nationalism on the Eve of the American Revolution: Revisions Once More in Need of Revising," *Journal of American History* 84 (1997): 13–39. British national identity also began with negative referents. See Linda Colley, *Britons: Forging the Nation, 1707–1837* (New Haven, Conn.: Yale University Press, 1992).

4. Alexander Hamilton (hereafter AH), *Federalist #11*, 24 November 1787, in *The Papers of Alexander Hamilton*, 27 vols., ed. Harold C. Syrett et al. (New York: Columbia University Press, 1961–87), IV, 342. Hereafter *PAH*.

5. According to a 1775 *Essay Upon Government*: "For every division in any degree, is in a Political, what we call a disease in a Natural Body, which as it weakens its strength, so it tends to its destruction." *An Essay Upon Government, Adopted by the Americans* (Philadelphia, 1775), 38, as cited in Gordon Wood, *The Creation of the American Republic, 1776–1787* (Chapel Hill, N.C.: University of North Carolina Press, 1969 reprint, New York: Norton, 1993), 59 n. 25. Ralph Ketcham writes, "Perhaps the most commonplace theme in eighteenth-century political discourse was the condemnation of faction or party." Ketcham, *Presidents above Party: The First American Presidency, 1789–1829* (Chapel Hill: University of North Carolina Press, 1984), vii. For English attitudes toward political parties, see Caroline Robbins, "'Discordant Parties': A Study of the Acceptance of Party by Englishmen," *Political Science Quarterly* 73.4 (December 1958): 505–29.

6. See Richard Hofstadter, *The Idea of a Party System: The Rise of Legitimate Opposition in the United States, 1780–1840* (Berkeley: University of California Press, 1970).

7. See Stanley Elkins and Eric McKitrick, *The Age of Federalism* (New York: Oxford University Press, 1993), 31–75, and Joanne Freeman, *Affairs of Honor: National Politics in the New Republic* (New Haven, Conn.: Yale University Press, 2001). For the anxiety of navigating a political world without established rules, see Andy Trees, "The Diary of William Maclay and Political Manners in the First Congress," *Pennsylvania Magazine of History and Biography: A Journal of Mid-Atlantic Studies* 69.2 (spring 2002): 210–29.

8. A number of historians have explored the self-conscious construction of character during this period. See, for example, Jay Fliegelman, *Declaring Independence: Jefferson, Natural Language, and the Culture of Performance* (Stanford, Calif.: Stanford University Press, 1993); Alan Taylor, *William Cooper's Town: Power and Persuasion on the Frontier of the Early American Republic* (New York: Knopf, 1995); Richard Bushman, *The Refinement of America: Persons, Houses, Cities* (New York: Knopf, 1992); Freeman, *Affairs of Honor*; Elizabeth M. Renker, "'Declaration-Men' and the Rhetoric of Self-Presentation," *Early American Literature* 24.2 (1989): 120–34; and Jack P. Greene, "Character, Persona, and Authority: A Study of Alternative Styles of Political Leadership in Revolutionary Virginia," in *The Revolutionary War in the South: Power, Conflict, and Leadership*, ed. W. Robert Higgins (Durham, N.C.: Duke University Press, 1979), 3–42. Greene writes that political persona as much as ideology or institutions "gives coherence to the ragged world of politics" (5).

9. For the intertwining of personal and national character, see Robert Wiebe, *The Opening of American Society: From the Adoption of the Constitution to the Eve of Disunion* (New York: Knopf, 1984); Richard Helgerson, *Forms of Nationhood: The Writing of Elizabethan England* (Chicago: University of Chicago Press, 1992), 107–91; and Lauren Berlant, *The Anatomy of National Fantasy: Hawthorne, Utopia, and Everyday Life* (Chicago: University of Chicago Press, 1991), 3, 20–24. David Waldstreicher writes, "The nation was theorized and discussed in terms of the individual: that is, the very language used to discuss the national polity involved personifying tropes like 'national character.'" Waldstreicher, *In the Midst of Perpetual Fetes: The Making of American Nationalism, 1776–1820* (Chapel Hill: University of North Carolina Press, 1997), 125.

10. As Washington wrote of one officer during the war, "From the Character he seems justly to have acquired, I should suppose he will act with caution and prudence, and do nothing that will not be promotive of [his character]." George Washington to Daniel Brodhead, 18 October 1779, *WFW*, XVI, 987. For eighteenth-century notions of character, see Elkins and McKitrick, *Age of Federalism*, 37.

11. As Dena Goodman writes, "The eighteenth century was a historical moment in which public and private spheres were in the process of articulation, such that no stable distinction can or could be made between them—a moment in which individuals needed to negotiate their actions, discursive and otherwise, across constantly shifting boundaries between ambiguously defined realms of experience." Goodman, "Public Sphere and Private Life: Toward a Synthesis of Current Historiographical Approaches to the Old Regime," *History and Theory* 31.1

(1992): 14. The distinction remains elusive. According to the *Oxford English Dictionary*, "The varieties of sense [of public] are numerous and pass into each other by many intermediate shades of meaning. The exact shade often depends upon the substantive qualified, and in some expressions more than one sense is vaguely present; in others the usage is traditional, and it is difficult to determine in what sense precisely the thing in question was originally called 'public.'" *Oxford English Dictionary*, 2d ed. (on-line) See also Richard Sennett, *The Fall of Public Man* (Cambridge: Cambridge University Press, 1977).

This study does not use the term "public sphere" in the sense that Jurgen Habermas has defined in *The Structural Transformation of the Public Sphere: An Inquiry into a Category of Bourgeois Society*, trans. Thomas Burger (Cambridge, Mass.: MIT Press, 1991). Many studies have made excellent use of Habermas's work to provide insight into the political culture of revolutionary and early national America. Instead, this study focuses on the invention and structuring of public and private in the founders' own writings and is informed more by Keith Baker's analysis of the emergence in France of "public opinion" as a political invention, rather than a sociological function. See Keith Baker, *Inventing the French Revolution: Essays on French Political Culture in the Eighteenth Century* (Cambridge: Cambridge University Press, 1990), 167–99. Habermas's model offers a better description of European monarchies than American colonies and states. Given the weak presence of royal officials in America as well as widespread political participation among white males, Habermas's vision of the public sphere emerging to mediate the tension between the state and civil society does not have as much relevance for America. For a systematic discussion of the various forms that the public/private distinction can take, see Jeff Weintraub, "The Theory and Politics of the Public/Private Distinction," *Public and Private in Thought and Practice*, ed. Jeff Weintraub and Krishan Kumar (Chicago: University of Chicago Press, 1997), 1–42. This study relies on what he calls the republican-virtue model, which sees the public sphere as a political community rather than a community associated with the administrative state or the market.

12. For brief introduction to the voluminous literature on this subject, see Linda Kerber et al., "Beyond Roles, Beyond Spheres: Thinking about Gender in the Early Republic" (forum), *William and Mary Quarterly* 46.3 (1989): 565–85, and Linda Kerber, "Separate Spheres, Female Worlds, Woman's Place: The Rhetoric of Women's History," *Journal of American History* 75.1 (1988): 9–39. For public and private as interrelated, rather than opposition, see Goodman, "Public Sphere and Private Life," and Fredrika Teute, "Roman Matron on the Banks of Tiber Creek: Margaret Bayard Smith and the Politicization of Spheres in the Nation's Capital," in *A Republic for the Ages: The United States Capitol and the Political Culture of the Early Republic*, ed. Donald Kennon (Charlottesville: University of Virginia Press, 1999): 89–111.

13. For studies that have recognized the centrality of this distinction to early American political life, see Jan Lewis, "'The Blessings of Domestic Society': Thomas Jefferson's Family and the Transformation of American Politics," in *Jeffersonian Legacies*, ed. Peter Onuf (Charlottesville: University of Virginia Press, 1993) 109–46; Fliegelman, *Declaring Independence*; Joanne Freeman, *Affairs of Honor*; and Michael Warner, *The Letters of the Republic: Publication and the*

Public Sphere in Eighteenth-Century America (Cambridge, Mass.: Harvard University Press, 1990).

14. Paine, "Common Sense," in *Collected Writings*, ed. Eric Foner (New York: Library of America, 1995), 6.

15. Benjamin Rush, "On the Defects of the Confederation," in *Selected Writings*, ed. Dagobert Runes (New York: Philosophical Library, 1947), 31. As Rush's quote makes clear with its republican conception of sacrifice for the public good, the debates about the distinction between public and private are related to the long-running debate among scholars of the early republic over the importance of republicanism versus liberalism. The consensus among historians now is that republicanism and liberalism overlapped in a variety of ways and that there was no sharp distinction between them in the minds of early Americans. For a discussion of the mixing of various discourses during this period, see Isaac Kramnick, "The 'Great National Discussion': The Discourse of Politics in 1787," *William and Mary Quarterly* 45 (1988): 3–32. Although related in important ways, the debates over public and private life do not map neatly onto the distinction between republicanism and liberalism. In addition, by focusing attention on the distinction between public and private, we can avoid the scholarly conundrum that has given us a republican Jefferson, Hamilton, Adams, and Madison, and a liberal Jefferson, Hamilton, Adams, and Madison.

16. Their efforts were certainly not the only efforts. Although confidence men are rarely, if ever, compared to the founders, the story of Stephen Burroughs, a notorious confidence man in the early republic, reveals how the issue of character was a pervasive problem and not simply a matter for the elite. In his *Memoirs*, Burroughs attempted to remake himself from rogue to revolutionary hero. See Daniel Williams, "In Defense of Self: Author and Authority in the *Memoirs of Stephen Burroughs*," *Early American Literature* 25.2 (1990): 96–122. An impostor and a counterfeiter, he called himself a "republican" and spoke of his jailers as "petty tyrants." Burroughs, *Memoirs of Stephen Burroughs*, ed. Philip Gura (Boston: Northeastern University Press, 1988; reprint of 1798 edition), 6 and 118. Although an extreme case, Burroughs was not so much an aberration as a symptom, an example of a new world in which many Americans were busy improvising and inventing new identities, often based on the lessons of the Revolution. See Robert Gross, "The Impudent Historian: Challenging Deference in Early America," *Journal of American History* 85.1 (June 1998): 92–108. What truly differentiated the founders from men such as Burroughs was audacity—and not the audacity of Burroughs but the audacity of the founders. The scope of the founders' ambitions reveals Burroughs as the paltry fellow he was, for the founders were inventing an identity not simply for themselves but for the nation. For the contributions to national identity from more popular and broad-based movements, see Simon Newman, *Parades and the Politics of the Street: Festive Culture in the Early American Republic* (Philadelphia: University of Pennsylvania Press, 1997); Len Travers, *Celebrating the Fourth: Independence Day and the Rites of Nationalism in the Early Republic* (Amherst: University of Massachusetts Press, 1997); and Waldstreicher, *In the Midst of Perpetual Fetes*.

17. For a study of the creation of identity through writing, see Albert Furtwangler, *American Silhouettes: Rhetorical Identities of the Founders* (New Haven, Conn.: Yale

University Press, 1987). The founders' efforts to create a new identity through writing were mired in larger questions about the nature of representation itself, questions foregrounded and exacerbated by the American Revolution. See Warner, *Letters of the Republic*; Waldstreicher, *In the Midst of Perpetual Fetes*; and Thomas Gustafson, *Representative Words: Politics, Literature, and the American Language* (New York: Cambridge University Press, 1992).

18. David Ramsay, *The History of the American Revolution* (1789), as cited in Ferguson, *American Enlightenment*, 80.

19. For the creation of the nation through writing, see Mark Patterson, *Authority, Autonomy, and Representation in American Literature, 1776–1865* (Princeton, N.J.: Princeton University Press, 1988); Robert Ferguson, "'We Hold These Truths': Strategies of Control in the Literature of the Founders," in *Reconstructing American Literary History*, ed. Sacvan Bercovitch (Cambridge, Mass.: Harvard University Press, 1986), 1–28; and Ferguson, "'We Do Ordain and Establish.'" For print culture during the early national period, see Richard Brown, *Knowledge Is Power: The Diffusion of Information in Early America, 1700–1865* (New York: Oxford University Press, 1989; and Warner, *Letters of the Republic*.

20. Washington Irving, *Washington Irving*, ed. James Tuttleton (New York: Library of America, 1983), 144.

21. Historians have tended to overlook the generic differences in various political writings. For historians who have recognized the importance of genre, see Freeman, *Affairs of Honor*; Emory Elliott, Myra Jehlen, and David Shields, *The Cambridge History of American Literature, 1590–1820*, vol. 1 (Cambridge: Cambridge University Press, 1994), particularly the section by Robert Ferguson; Andrew Burstein, *The Inner Jefferson: Portrait of a Grieving Optimist* (Charlottesville: University of Virginia Press, 1995); and Donald Lutz, *The Origins of American Constitutionalism* (Baton Rouge: Louisiana State University Press, 1988). For an examination of genre as a shared form of understanding, see Carol Berkenkotter and Thomas Huckin, *Genre Knowledge in Disciplinary Communication: Cognition, Culture, Power* (Hillsdale, N.J.: L. Erlbaum Associates, 1995).

22. The politics of character did not disappear and, indeed, remains with us today, but it no longer played the preeminent role; it was displaced by party politics and by a society that offered the opportunity of establishing a character to a much broader array of citizens.

23. TJ to Maria Cosway, October 12, 1786, in Thomas Jefferson, *Writings*, ed. Merrill Peterson (New York: Library of America, 1984), 875. Hereafter *Writings*.

24. Stephen Conrad writes, "From his earliest entry into political life, Jefferson argued that fraternal love and harmony should be the basis of imperial relations." Conrad, "Putting Rights Talk in Its Place: *The Summary View* Revisited," in *Jeffersonian Legacies*, ed. Onuf, 259. See also Peter Onuf, *Jefferson's Empire: The Language of American Nationhood* (Charlottesville: University of Virginia Press, 2000).

25. Thomas Jefferson (hereafter TJ), original version of the Declaration of Independence, *Writings*, 23. As he wrote to Ducoigne, the Kashaskia chief, the

war had begun "as a family quarrel between us and the English, who were then our brothers." TJ to Jean Baptiste Ducoigne, June 1781, *The Papers of Thomas Jefferson*, ed. Julian P. Boyd et al. (Princeton, N.J.: Princeton University Press, 1950–), VI, 60. Hereafter *PTJ*. For Jefferson, such an understanding of the Revolution was not simply a personal but a national one. In later years, he claimed that the Declaration "was intended to be an expression of the American mind." TJ to Henry Lee, 8 May 1825, *The Works of Thomas Jefferson*, ed. Paul L. Ford (1892–98; reprint, 12 vols., New York, 1905), X, 343. Hereafter *WTJ*.

26. AH to Edward Stevens, 11 November 1769, *PAH*, I, 4.

27. AH to ———, December 1779–March 1780, *PAH*, II, 241.

28. AH to John Laurens, 30 June 1780, *PAH*, II, 347.

29. For example, Jefferson complained of his service in the Continental Congress and wanted to return to Virginia, where he felt the real work of the Revolution, the revision of state constitutions, was being done.

30. AH to George Clinton, 13 February 1778, *PAH*, I, 425–28.

31. AH to John Laurens, 12 September 1780, *PAH*, II, 428.

32. AH to George Clinton, 13 February 1778, *PAH*, I, 425–28. Jerald Combs writes, "He transmuted personal goals into national goals. His private life, his domestic political system, and his foreign policy were thoroughly intertwined." Jerald Combs, *The Jay Treaty: Political Battleground of the Founding Fathers* (Berkeley: University of California Press, 1970), 33.

33. AH to John Laurens, 30 June 1780, *PAH*, II, 347.

34. AH to George Clinton, 12 March 1778, *PAH*, I, 439–40.

35. AH to GW, 30 September 1783, *PAH*, III, 461.

36. John Adams (hereafter JA) to Hezekiah Niles, 3 January 1817, Adams Papers, reel 123, microfilm, Library of Congress. Like Washington, Adams also felt that the meaning of the Revolution was still to be established. He called the Revolution "a memorable epoch in the annals of the human race" but noted that his country was still "destined in future history to form the brightest or the blackest page, according to the use or the abuse of those political institutions by which they shall in time come to be shaped by the *human mind*." JA to John Whitney, 7 June 1826, *The Works of John Adams, Second President of the United States*, 10 vols., ed. Charles Francis Adams (Boston: Little, Brown and Company, 1854), X, 416–17. Hereafter *WJA*.

37. JA to TJ and Thomas McKean, 30 July 1815, *The Adams-Jefferson Letters: The Complete Correspondence between Thomas Jefferson and Abigail and John Adams*, 2 vols., ed. Lester J. Cappon (Chapel Hill, N.C.: University of North Carolina Press, 1959), II, 451. Hereafter, *Adams-Jefferson Letters*.

38. JA, "Novanglus," *WJA*, IV, 18.

39. JA to Benjamin Rush, 30 September 1805, in *Spur of Fame*, 42–43.

40. JA to Benjamin Rush, 4 April 1790, *Old Family Letters: Copied from the Original for Alexander Biddle*, 2 vols. (Philadelphia: J. B. Lippincott Company, 1892), I, 55.

41. JA, "On Self-Delusion," for the *Boston Gazette*, 29 August 1763, *WJA*, III, 433.

42. JA, "On Self-Delusion," for the *Boston Gazette*, 29 August 1763, *WJA*, III, 434–35.

43. James Madison (hereafter JM), "Vices of the Political System," April 1787, in *The Papers of James Madison*, series I, *Papers*, 17 vols., ed. William T. Hutchinson et al. (Chicago: University of Chicago Press, 1962), IX, 348–57. Hereafter *PJM*. All quotes in this section are from this source unless otherwise noted.

44. The best account of state constitutionalism remains Wood, *Creation of the American Republic*.

45. He noted, "However strong this motive may be in individuals, it is considered as very insufficient to restrain them from injustice. In a multitude its efficacy is diminished in proportion to the number which is to share the praise or the blame."

46. Anthony Ashley Cooper, Earl of Shaftesbury, *Miscellaneous Reflections*, as cited in David Marshall, *The Figure of Theater: Shaftesbury, Defoe, Adam Smith, and George Eliot* (New York: Columbia University Press, 1986), 7. For the unpredictable nature of a reader's response, see Carlo Ginzburg, *The Cheese and the Worms: The Cosmos of a Sixteenth-Century Miller* (Baltimore: Johns Hopkins University Press, 1980), and Stanley Fish, *Is There a Text in This Class? The Authority of Interpretive Communities* (Cambridge, Mass.: Harvard University Press, 1980).

47. On the ability of texts to create their ideal readers, see James Boyd White, *When Words Lose Their Meaning: Constitutions and Reconstitutions of Language, Character, and Community* (Chicago: University of Chicago Press, 1984).

CHAPTER ONE
Friendship

1. Elbridge Gerry (henceforth EG) to TJ, 12 November 1798, Jefferson Papers, microfilm, Library of Congress.

2. Dumas Malone, *Jefferson and His Time*, 6 vols. (Boston: Little, Brown, 1948–81), III, 386 ff. Although not used as extensively as Jefferson feared, the Sedition Act did result in some extremely questionable prosecutions, including the imprisonment of a Republican congressman for comments made in a private letter and the jailing of a drunkard for refusing to stand as the president rode by. As president, Jefferson himself does not have a spotless record as a defender of civil liberties. See Leonard Levy, *Jefferson and Civil Liberties: The Darker Side* (Cambridge, Mass.: Belknap Press of Harvard University Press, 1963).

Even before the Sedition Act, the vulnerability of political opposition was made abundantly clear in the case of Samuel Cabell, a member of the House of Representatives from Virginia. Cabell had criticized the government in a circular letter to his constituents and had subsequently been charged in the federal circuit court in Richmond with disseminating "unfounded calumnies against the happy government of the United States." See Adrienne Koch and Harry Ammon, "The Virginia and Kentucky Resolutions: An Episode in Jefferson's and Madison's Defense of Civil Liberties," *William and Mary Quarterly* 5:2 (1948), 152–53.

As for his office, Jefferson believed that the vice president had only a limited role. Shortly before taking office, Jefferson wrote, "The constitution will know me only as the member of a legislative body." TJ to Madison, 22 January 1797, *WTJ*, VII, 108. Such a view proved congenial to Jefferson, since he would come to oppose vehemently the direction of Adams's administration. According to Dumas Malone, as vice president, Jefferson did not think of himself as part of the administration and felt free to criticize it but only through private channels. Malone, *Jefferson and His Time*, III, 319 and 323.

3. Gideon Granger was perhaps the only other significant New England figure whom Jefferson pursued. In fact, Jefferson often wrote letters to the two men at similar times, but Granger did not become a significant figure in Jefferson's correspondence until after the election of 1800 had been decided.

4. Jefferson's reliance on what could be called a politics of personality differs from the public sphere theorized by Michael Warner in *Letters of the Republic*. Drawing on Jurgen Habermas's notion of the public sphere, Warner's historicized treatment ties the emancipatory character of the emergent print culture to its impersonality. While persuasive for certain strands of American political culture, his account neglects the intensely personal nature of much of the writing throughout this period. The stance of anonymous and disinterested author that was supposed to embody Enlightenment ideals was only one rhetorical pose among many. Anonymity itself was often attacked as the refuge of a writer too cowardly to stand behind his accusations. See also Fliegelman, *Declaring Independence*, 128–29.

5. Peter Onuf writes, "By thinking of the republic 'in familial terms,' and not in terms of self-promotion and partisan interests, he could sustain an apolitical conception of republican leadership." Onuf, "The Scholar's Jefferson," *William and Mary Quarterly* 50 (1981): 691. Joanne Freeman also notes, "A politics of friendship was a politics of deniability, where the most political of actions seemed personal in nature, it was easy to deny one's political ambitions, even to oneself." Freeman, *Affairs of Honor*, 319.

6. Henry Adams wrote, in what has become a well-known characterization of Thomas Jefferson, "Almost every other American statesman might be described in a parenthesis. A few broad strokes of the brush would paint the portraits of all the early Presidents with this exception . . . Jefferson could be painted only touch by touch, with a fine pencil, and the perfection of the likeness depended upon the shifting and uncertain flicker of its semi-transcendent shadows." Henry Adams, *History of the United States during the Administrations of Thomas Jefferson*, 9 vols. (New York: C. Scribner's Sons, 1889–91), 1:188. After decades spent studying Jefferson, Merrill Peterson wrote, "Jefferson remains for me, finally, an impenetrable man." Merrill Peterson, *Thomas Jefferson and the New Nation: A Biography* (New York: Oxford University Press, 1970), viii. Historians of Thomas Jefferson have continued to find him an enigmatic figure. Sympathetic historians usually cite Jefferson's careful protection of his private life. Detractors take a harsher line, accusing the former president of hypocrisy and duplicity. For example, see Paul Finkelman, "Jefferson and Slavery: 'Treason against the Hopes of the World,'" in *Jeffersonian Legacies*, ed. Onuf, 181–224. Recently, a new literature has attempted to offer us a more intimate picture of Jefferson's time and of Jefferson himself. Historians such as Jan Lewis and Jay Fliegelman have revealed a late-eighteenth-century world where sharing private emotions became central to one's identity, and Andrew Burstein has offered a portrait of Jefferson as a man thoroughly enmeshed in this sentimental world. See Jan Lewis, *The Pursuit of Happiness: Family and Values in Jefferson's Virginia* (Cambridge: Cambridge

University Press, 1983); Fliegelman, *Declaring Independence*; and Burstein, *Inner Jefferson*. For an earlier account of the sentimental Jefferson, see Garry Wills, *Inventing America: Jefferson's Declaration of Independence* (Garden City, N.Y.: Doubleday and Company, 1978). This chapter bridges the gap between the impenetrable and the "inner" Jefferson, offering an account that reveals how the sentimental Jefferson's commitment to a polity based on emotional ties enmeshed him in political and cultural problems that undermined his own sincerity and that helped create the opaque Jefferson who confronts us today.

On sincerity as a larger cultural problem, particularly during the eighteenth century, see Fliegelman, *Declaring Independence*; Claude Rawson, *Satire and Sentiment, 1660–1830* (Cambridge: Cambridge University Press, 1994). See also Karen Halttunen, *Confidence Men and Painted Women: A Study of Middle-Class Culture in America, 1830–1870* (New Haven, Conn.: Yale University Press, 1982); John Martin, "Inventing Sincerity, Refashioning Prudence: The Discovery of the Individual in Renaissance Europe," *American Historical Review* 102.5 (December 1997): 1309–42; Marjorie Morgan, *Manners, Morals, and Class in England, 1774–1858* (New York: St. Martin's Press, 1994); Efrat Tseelon, "Is the Presented Self Sincere? Goffman, Impression Management, and the Postmodern Self," *Theory, Culture, and Society* 9.2 (May 1992): 115–28; Paul Parnell, "The Sentimental Mask," *PMLA* 78.5 (December 1963): 529–35; and Lionel Trilling, *Sincerity and Authenticity* (New York: Harcourt Brace Jovanovich, 1972).

7. Although there certainly were letters of mutual confidence, they sprang from entirely different motives. Gerry wrote to Jefferson in the spirit of an antiparty republican, calling on Jefferson to renounce party difference and to work with Adams. Jefferson, on the other hand, expressed confidence in Gerry precisely because of the exigencies of party difference. When Gerry was nominated for the mission to France, Jefferson immediately wrote to Gerry begging him to take the post because Gerry was the only non-Federalist on the commission. Jefferson wrote, "My reliance for our preservation is in your acceptance of the mission." TJ to EG, 21 June 1797, *WTJ*, VIII, 314.

8. TJ to EG, 26 January 1799, *WTJ*, IX, 15–16.

9. Peter Onuf notes that the letter "is both means and end for Jefferson, the practical embodiment of the republican idea." Onuf, "The Scholar's Jefferson," 690.

10. Madison bore the brunt of these requests. During 1798 and 1799 alone, Jefferson asked him to write a number of newspaper articles, publish his notes on the Constitutional Convention debates, and put together a simplified version of the XYZ correspondence to help people see past the Federalist lies. See TJ to JM, 3 August 1797, *WTJ*, VIII, 334; TJ to Wilson C. Nichols, 5 September 1799, *WTJ*, IX, 81; TJ to James Thomson Callender, 6 October 1799, *WTJ*, IX, 84; and TJ to Philip Norborne Nicholas, 7 April 1800, *WTJ*, IX, 128. For Jefferson's hesitation to write for a public audience, see Douglas L. Wilson, "Jefferson and the Republic of Letters," in *Jeffersonian Legacies*, ed. Onuf, 50–76.

11. For examinations of the familiar letter, see Howard Anderson, Philip Daghlian, and Irvin Ehrenpreis, eds., *The Familiar Letter in the Eighteenth Century* (Lawrence: University of Kansas Press, 1968); Frank Stewart, *Honor* (Chicago: University of Chicago Press, 1994); Robert Adams Day, *Told in Letters: Epistolary Fiction before Richardson* (Ann Arbor: University of Michigan

Press, 1966); Elizabeth Heckendorn Cook, *Epistolary Bodies: Gender and Genre in the Eighteenth-Century Republic of Letters* (Stanford, Calif.: Stanford University Press, 1996); Bruce Redford, *The Converse of the Pen: Acts of Intimacy in the Eighteenth-Century Familiar Letter* (Chicago: University of Chicago Press, 1986); Elizabeth Drew, *The Literature of Gossip: Nine English Letterwriters* (New York: Norton, 1964); William Henry Irving, *The Providence of Wit in the English Letter Writers* (Durham, N.C.: Duke University Press, 1955); and Janet Gurkin Altman, *Epistolarity: Approaches to a Form* (Columbus: Ohio State University Press, 1982). For an exploration of Jefferson's use of the familiar letter, see Burstein, *Inner Jefferson*, 116–49.

12. Samuel Johnson to Mrs. Thrale, 11 April 1780, *The Letters of Samuel Johnson*, ed. R. W. Chapman (Oxford: Clarendon Press, 1952), 657; William Cowper to Mrs. Cowper, 4 April 1766, *The Correspondence of William Cowper*, ed. Thomas Wright (New York: Haskell House, 1969), I, 66.

13. Samuel Johnson, "The Rambler #152," in *The Rambler*, ed. Donald Eddy (New York: Garland Publishing, 1978), 908.

14. Hugh Blair, *Lectures on Rhetoric and Belles Lettres* (Philadelphia: Hayes and Zell, 1854), 414.

15. *The Critical Review*, as cited in Keith Stewart, "Towards Defining an Aesthetic for the Familiar Letter in Eighteenth-Century England," *Prose Studies* 5.2 (1982): 179–92, quote on 184.

16. Blair, *Lectures*, 414.

17. Samuel Johnson, *Life of Pope*, as cited in Anderson et al., *Familiar Letter*, 2. Redford has characterized this aspect of letter writing as "artful spontaneity" in which the "truest letter was also the most feigning." Redford, *Converse of the Pen*, 4.

18. See Howard Anderson and Irvin Ehrenpreis, "The Familiar Letter in the Eighteenth Century: Some Generalizations," in Anderson et al., *Familiar Letter*, 282. Fliegelman has called this phenomenon "natural theatricality." See Fliegelman, *Declaring Independence*. This was a widespread cultural problem. For example, Daniel Defoe in his writing emphasized that proper behavior needed to be learned but also that it needed to appear natural. See Carol Houlihan Flynn, "Defoe's Idea of Conduct: Ideological Fictions and the Fictional Reality," in *The Ideology of Conduct: Essays in Literature and the History of Sexuality*, ed. Nancy Armstrong and Leonard Tennenhouse (New York: Methuen and Co., 1987), 74.

19. Cook, *Epistolary Bodies*.

20. For one of the most famous examples of private correspondence passing into public view, see Dena Goodman, "The Hume-Rousseau Affair: From Private Querelle to Public Procès," *Eighteenth-Century Studies* 25.2 (winter 1991–92): 171–202.

21. For fuller exploration of the chronic worries about letters and the intricacies of epistolary correspondence, see Freeman, *Affairs of Honor*, chapter 2.

22. Patricia Meyer Spacks, *Imagining a Self: Autobiography and Novel in Eighteenth-Century England* (Cambridge, Mass.: Harvard University Press, 1976), 69. Some worried that this rash of publication would ruin the "artless" nature of correspondence. One contemporary claimed that the very fact of publishing letters

would change the way letters were written by tending "to restrain that unsuspicious openness, which is the principal delight of writing to our friends." John Boyle, Earl of Orrery, *Remarks on the Life and Writings of Dr. Jonathan Swift* (London, 1752), 156.

23. TJ to Tench Coxe, 21 May 1799, *WTJ*, IX, 69.

24. TJ to JM, 22 November 1799, *WTJ*, IX, 89, and TJ to Mary Jefferson Eppes, 17 January 1800, *WTJ*, IX, 95.

25. TJ to JM, 1 February 1801, *WTJ*, IX, 173.

26. See Malone, *Jefferson and His Time*, III, 267 and 302.

27. As many critics have pointed out, the unpredictable response of the reader is "the crucial element in letter writing." Anderson and Ehrenpreis, "The Familiar Letter in the Eighteenth Century," 278. Jefferson's favorite novelist, Laurence Sterne, repeatedly emphasized the difficulty of reaching one's reader. See Burstein, *Inner Jefferson*.

28. TJ to EG, 26 January 1799, *WTJ*, IX, 16.

29. TJ to EG, 26 January 1799, *WTJ*, IX, 16.

30. Dr. George Logan sailed for France in June 1798 on a personal peace mission. Although Jefferson did provide some letters of introduction, he was not involved in Logan's scheme. That a private citizen would make an unauthorized attempt to conduct diplomacy only further highlights not just the undeveloped nature of the national government but the ambiguity between private and public life. Logan's efforts brought him only ridicule and resulted in the Logan Act of 1799, which prohibited private diplomacy. See Malone, *Jefferson and His Time*, III, 432.

31. Quoted in George Billias, *Elbridge Gerry, Founding Father and Republican Statesman* (New York: McGraw-Hill, 1976), 292.

32. Jefferson himself was well aware of this. As he recorded after a vote in Congress, "Gerry changed sides." Quoted in S. E. Morison, "Elbridge Gerry, Gentleman-Democrat," *New England Quarterly* 2 (1929): 6.

33. For a brief overview of Gerry's peculiarity, see Morison, "Elbridge Gerry, Gentleman-Democrat." See also Billias, *Elbridge Gerry*. Historians have proposed a number of theories to explain Gerry's career. Morison argues that Gerry was both a gentleman and a democrat, who was never able to reconcile those two sides of his personality. George Billias claims that Gerry's republicanism is the key and that Gerry was not interested in creating a systematic political theory. Billias, *Elbridge Gerry*, xiv.

34. By the summer of 1792, Gerry owned thirty shares of bank stock worth $12,000. See Billias, *Elbridge Gerry*, 242.

35. Jefferson, *PTJ*, XXV, 433. The list was part of an effort by Republicans to document how Hamilton's financial system had corrupted Congress.

36. The term "antiparty" is somewhat inappropriate because all politicians at this time declared themselves to be antiparty. Unlike most, though, Gerry refused to align himself consistently with either the Republicans or the Federalists and tried to unify the two parties, so the term is an accurate description of his position. He did eventually become a Republican, propelled by his lifelong fear of standing armies. Billias, *Elbridge Gerry*, 289. Yet, he maintained his inconstant ways. While accepting the Republican nomination for governor of Massachusetts in 1800, he voted for Adams for president. His first term as governor of

Massachusetts in 1810 was marked by moderation; his second became infamous for its partisan character. He acquired lasting political infamy through his association with the political reshaping of a district to help a political party or, as it is commonly known, gerrymandering. As Billias points out, this practice had been used since colonial times, and according to Gerry's son-in-law, Gerry even argued against the 1812 attempt by Republicans to reshape the senatorial districts along partisan lines. Elkanah Tisdale, an obscure Federalist artist, drew a map of one of the new districts, and someone remarked that it looked like a salamander. No, another wit proclaimed, it looked more like a "gerrymander." A new word was born, and an old politician was borne away. See Billias, *Elbridge Gerry*, 317.

37. Even his family was harassed. Neighborhood ruffians hung figures in the trees around the house, burned torches, and yelled obscenities. On more than one occasion, the family awoke to find a guillotine smeared with blood in their front yard bearing the effigy of a decapitated man. James T. Austin, *The Life of Elbridge Gerry*, 2 vols. (Boston, 1829), II, 267. Timothy Pickering, Adams's secretary of state, wrote if the French "would . . . guillotine Mr. Gerry they would do a favor to this country." Pickering to Rufus King, 12 June 1798, in Charles King, ed., *The Life and Correspondence of Rufus King*, 6 vols (New York, 1894–1900), II, 347.

38. The literature on friendship and patronage (and its combination of private and public) is voluminous. For a sampling, see Allan Silver, "Friendship in Commercial Society: Eighteenth-Century Social Theory and Modern Sociology," *American Journal of Sociology* 95.6 (May 1990): 1474–504, and Sharon Kettering, "Patronage in Early Modern France," *French Historical Studies* 17.4 (fall 1992): 839–62. For friendship in the early republic, see Jay Fliegelman, *Prodigals and Pilgrims* (Cambridge: Cambridge University Press, 1982); Gordon Wood, *The Radicalism of the American Revolution* (New York: Random House, 1991); Lewis, *Pursuit of Happiness*; Jan Lewis, "The Republican Wife: Virtue and Seduction in the Early Republic," *William and Mary Quarterly* 44.4 (October 1987): 689–721; Fliegelman, *Declaring Independence*; Alan Taylor, "The Art of Hook and Snivey: Political Culture in Upstate New York in the 1790s," *Journal of American History* 79 (March 1993): 1371–96; and Joanne Freeman, *Affairs of Honor*, chapter 1.

39. Samuel Johnson, *A Dictionary of the English Language on CD-ROM*, ed. Anne McDermott. These were not the only available modes of friendship, but they help establish a spectrum of possibilities.

40. Many feared that any sort of "interest" imperiled true friendship. See David Shields, *Civil Tongues and Polite Letters in British America* (Chapel Hill: University of North Carolina Press, 1997), 137; Taylor, "The Art of Hook and Snivey"; and T. H. Breen, *Tobacco Culture: The Mentality of the Great Tidewater Planters on the Eve of the Revolution* (Princeton, N.J.: Princeton University Press, 1985), 104–5.

41. This was also part of a larger, transatlantic shift from vertical ties to more horizontal ones. See Leonore Davidoff and Catherine Hall, *Family Fortunes: Men and Women of the English Middle Class, 1780–1850* (Chicago: University of Chicago Press, 1993); Jan Lewis, "'Those Scenes for Which Alone My Heart Was

Made': Affection and Politics in the Age of Jefferson and Hamilton," in *An Emotional History of the United States*, ed. Peter Stearns and Jan Lewis (New York: New York University Press, 1998), 52–65.

42. Wood, *Radicalism*, 342. Before widespread acceptance of political parties, the use of instrumental friendships for political purposes was a fairly common practice. See James Sterling Young, *The Washington Community, 1800–1828* (New York: Columbia University Press, 1966), 128–31; Taylor, "The Art of Hook and Snivey."

43. TJ, entry 149, quoting from Euripides, *Hippolytus*, in *Jefferson's Literary Commonplace Book*, ed. Douglas Wilson (Princeton, N.J.: Princeton University Press, 1989), 77. For Jefferson, the true test of friendship was adversity, as shown by a number of passages he commonplaced. See entries 105, 109, and 112, *Literary Commonplace Book*, 68–69. Jefferson's commonplace book provides a good picture of his reading and thinking about friendship during his formative years. Gilbert Chinard argues that it could be retitled "Jefferson Self-revealed." Commonplace books also reveal different notions of authorship in the eighteenth century, centering not on originality but on the author's ability to arrange materials in a pleasing and instructive manner. In this sense, the commonplace book provided training for Jefferson's greatest intellectual talent—the ability to synthesize material and express the essence in a pleasing style.

44. TJ, entry 133, quoting from Euripides, *Medea*, in *Literary Commonplace Book*, 73.

45. TJ to Maria Cosway, 12 October 1786, *Writings*, 872–73.

46. TJ to Catherine Church Cruger, 15 December 1808, Church Papers, as cited in Jan Lewis, "'Those Scenes for Which Alone My Heart Was Made,'" 60–61.

47. He also eventually promised to give him inside news of foreign affairs, to help him land some of the lucrative public printing contracts and to aid his subscription efforts. See Elkins and McKitrick, *Age of Federalism*, 240.

48. Jefferson's circular letter about his relationship with President Madison, March 1809, in *The Republic of Letters: The Correspondence between Thomas Jefferson and James Madison, 1776–1826*, 3 vols., ed. James Morton Smith (New York: W. W. Norton and Company, 1995), III, 1574. Hereafter *Republic of Letters*. Madison wrote a similar letter when he left office.

49. TJ to GW, 9 September 1792, *Writings*, 994.

50. TJ to Francis Hopkinson, 13 March 1789, *Writings*, 941.

51. TJ to William Duane, 28 March 1811, *WTJ*, XI, 193.

52. TJ to Edward Rutledge, 24 June 1797, *WTJ*, VIII, 318–19. Jefferson complained that "party animosities here have raised a wall . . . between those who differ in political sentiments." TJ to Angelica Schuyler Church, 11 January 1798, Special Collections, Alderman Library, University of Virginia.

53. TJ to Thomas Jefferson Randolph, 24 November 1808, *The Family Letters of Thomas Jefferson*, ed. Edwin Morris Betts and James A. Bear (Columbia: University of Missouri Press, 1966), 362–65.

54. TJ to Anne Cary, Thomas Jefferson, and Ellen Wayles Randolph, 2 March 1802, *Writings*, 1102.

55. TJ to Edward Rutledge, 24 June 1797, *WTJ*, VIII, 319.

56. Jefferson's heightened sense of the significance of political differences was characteristic of the period. Given the beliefs about the fragility of republican

governments, the 1790s became a period of violent rhetoric, as every decision seemed to forebode potential disaster. See John R. Howe, Jr., "Republican Thought and the Political Violence of the 1790s," *American Quarterly* 19.2 (summer 1967): 147–65; Marshall Smelser, "The Federalist Period as an Age of Passion," *American Quarterly* 10 (1958): 391–419; and Richard Buel, Jr., *Securing the Revolution: Ideology in American Politics* (Ithaca, N.Y.: Cornell University Press, 1972).

57. Jan Lewis has extensively explored the reshaping of the late-eighteenth- and early-nineteenth-century emotional landscape, particularly within the family. See Lewis, *Pursuit of Happiness*. She has also examined with great perception Jefferson's views on both domestic and political society. For example, see Lewis, "'The Blessings of Domestic Society,'" 109–46. She argues that Jefferson sought to separate political arguments from private life. Although Jefferson certainly voices these sentiments at times, his political vision for the nation precluded any easy separation.

58. TJ to EG, 26 January 1799, *WTJ*, IX, 17.

59. For example, Jefferson wrote an appeal to Aaron Burr (see TJ to Burr, 17 June 1797, *WTJ*, VIII, 309) and to Gideon Granger (see TJ to Granger, 13 August 1800, *WTJ*, IX, 138), but both men were more clearly in the Republican camp, freeing Jefferson from many of the problems that he faced in his letter to Gerry.

60. *Letters of Laurence Sterne*, ed. Lewis Curtis (Oxford: Clarendon Press, 1935), 212.

61. Different etiquettes underlay different epistolary exchanges. To confuse or combine those different etiquettes risked undermining the purpose of the letter. For a French example of this, see Goodman, "Public Sphere and Private Life," 18–19 n. 69.

62. As someone anxiously insecure about his own presentation, Jefferson was ruthless in "unmasking" others' insincerity based on their formality. In his *Anas*, a collection of political gossip, Jefferson recorded a 1791 conversation that he had with Alexander Hamilton in which Hamilton made his own profession. Hamilton claimed that despite misgivings about the current form of government, he was "for giving it a fair course, whatever [Hamilton's] expectations may be." In his analysis of the conversation, Jefferson wrote that Hamilton's declaration "seemed to be more formal than usual, for a private conversation between two, and as if intended to qualify some less guarded expressions which had been dropped on former occasions." Franklin Sawvel, ed., *The Complete Anas of Thomas Jefferson* (New York: Round Table Press, 1903), 44. Jefferson mistrusted Hamilton's words because Hamilton seemed more formal than a private conversation warranted. In other words, Jefferson feared that Hamilton was not displaying his private, "natural" self. Jefferson now faced a similar problem with Gerry.

63. TJ to EG, 26 January 1799, *WTJ*, IX, 17–18. For discussions of republicanism as a central discourse of the Revolution and early national periods, see Wood, *Creation of the American Republic*, and J.G.A. Pocock, *The Machiavellian Moment: Florentine Political Thought and the Atlantic Republican Tradition* (Princeton: Princeton University Press, 1975). For an overview of the ensuing debates about the significance of republicanism, see Robert E. Shalhope, "Toward a Republican Synthesis: The Emergence of an Understanding of Republicanism in American Historiography, *William and Mary Quarterly* 29 (1972): 49–80;

Shalhope, "Republicanism and Early American Historiography," *William and Mary Quarterly* 39 (1982): 334–56; and Daniel T. Rodgers, "Republicanism: The Career of a Concept," *Journal of American History* 79 (1992): 11–38.

64. TJ to EG, 26 January 1799, *WTJ*, IX, 19.

65. Both Jefferson and Madison would occasionally remark on their affection for one another, but neither ever held forth at any length on their friendship. Seen in this light, Jefferson's strong protestations of friendship for various people take on a far more ambiguous meaning. As in the case with Gerry, they were usually attempts to make someone his friend by the rhetorical assumption that the person already was one. Unfortunately for Jefferson, in the politics of friendship, less was usually more, and attempts to prove friendship often only undermined it.

66. As Onuf writes, "Political life could be seen as a conversation among friends, recognizing diverse perspectives and interests while seeking a common ground and a common good." Onuf, "The Scholar's Jefferson," 697. Freeman notes the difficulty of distinguishing between friendships and political alliances. See Freeman, *Affairs of Honor*, particularly chapter 2.

67. TJ to James Lewis, Junior, 9 May 1798, *WTJ*, VIII, 417. Of course, with Gerry, Jefferson was willing to allow pragmatic political considerations to soften his views. "In truth," Jefferson wrote to Gerry, "we never differed but on one ground, the funding system." According to Jefferson, that difference had ceased to exist because, after adoption of Hamilton's financial plans, Jefferson became "religiously principled in the sacred discharge of it." Political differences ceased to matter, according to this logic, as soon as policies were in place addressing the issue.

68. TJ to Pinckney, 29 May 1797, *WTJ*, VIII, 292.

69. In fact, Jefferson posited an inbred political character in the "different constitutions of the mind." If one was not born a republican, there appeared to be little hope.

70. The difficulty Jefferson faced is revealed in his letters to men he attempted to draw into the Republican circle, such as Gerry. Malone notes his discomfort with such appeals, writing, "Jefferson's cultivation of men whom he thought moderate was rather too obvious, his language too cajoling." Malone, *Jefferson and His Time*, III, 316. Emphasizing feeling rather than practical political considerations, Jefferson faced the risk of insincerity, of undermining the affective bonds that he proposed to make the basis for political union.

71. TJ to Archibald Stuart, 4 January 1797, Library of Congress, as cited by Freeman, *Affairs of Honor*, 277. Many others also thought that Adams could perhaps be persuaded to join with the Republicans.

72. TJ to JA, 28 December 1796 (unsent), *WTJ*, VII, 95–96.

73. TJ to Madison, 1 January 1797, *WTJ*, VIII, 262–63. TJ to EG, 13 May 1797, *Writings*, 1042.

74. JM to TJ, 15 January 1797, *PJM*, XVI, 455–57.

75. William Cunningham to John Adams, 9 August 1809, in *A Review of the Correspondence between Hon. John Adams, late President of the United States, and the late William Cunningham* (Salem, Mass.: Cushing and Appleton, 1824), 153–54. Others, including historians, have criticized Jefferson in similar terms. Fliegelman writes that sincerity proved to be an "exhausting ruler," demanding at

all times "that private and public character cohere in a single externalized self" — that one's character be "self-evident." Fliegelman, *Declaring Independence*, 131 and 200. Usually, the more one proclaims one's sincerity, the less sincere one sounds.

76. JA to Abigail Adams, 1 and 3 January 1797, as cited in *PJM*, XVI, 457n.

77. The use of private information for public purposes was a tricky business, though. Alexander Hamilton found himself defensively justifying himself to his friend James McHenry after he had published information with McHenry's name attached to give it credence. In large part, Hamilton argued that the information was already public and that his use of it was therefore unexceptionable: "Extracts from [a public document of McHenry's] . . . have been in free circulation and have been seen by many. . . . Thus circumstanced the thing is in possession of the public & in no wise to be regarded as a confidential communication to me. I am therefore at liberty to use it." AH to James McHenry, 22 November 1800, *PAH*, XXV, 246.

78. Jefferson's relationship to Adams remained deeply problematic, though, because of their political differences. Jefferson struggled to maintain their personal relationship, to keep it from becoming caught up in the larger political conflict, but his solution failed to recognize Jefferson's own unfolding hopes for an affectionate union as well as the crucial place that "friendship" played in that vision. Eventually, their differences caused a rupture. Neither man would write or speak to the other for almost a decade after the election of 1800. Letters between Jefferson and Abigail Adams shortly after the election of 1800 once again revealed the complex intermingling of the personal and the political in the early republic. From Abigail's point of view, Jefferson had acted ignobly not because of any political disagreement but because he had countenanced personal attacks on her husband. She wrote, "I have never felt any enmity towards you Sir for being elected president of the United States. But the instrument made use of, and the means which were practised to effect a change, have my utter abhorrence and detestation, for they were the blackest calumny, and foulest falsehoods." Her enmity arose from "a personal injury. This was the Sword that cut asunder the Gordian knot, which could not be untied by all the efforts of party Spirit, by rivalship by Jealousy or any other malignant fiend." Abigail Adams to TJ, 1 July 1804, *Adams-Jefferson Letters*, I, 272.

79. TJ to EG, 26 January 1799, *WTJ*, IX, 20.

80. To share political gossip was to share political alliance in the young republic. For an elaboration of this idea as well as the "rules" governing political gossip, see Joanne Freeman, "Slander Poison, Whispers, and Fame: Jefferson's 'Anas' and Political Gossip in the Early Republic," *Journal of the Early Republic* 15.1 (1995): 25–57.

81. France had begun raiding American shipping in response to the Jay Treaty, widely seen as overly favorable to England. America and France were soon engaged in an undeclared "quasi war" on the high seas and seemed to be on the verge of a declared war.

82. TJ to EG, 26 January 1799, *WTJ*, IX, 21–22. Jefferson apparently did not know that the XYZ affair was not only known to Talleyrand but had been instigated by him. In his most questionable conduct, Gerry allowed Talleyrand to mislead the French Directory into thinking that Talleyrand had no knowledge of

X,Y, and Z. What Jefferson and nearly everyone on the American side also failed to realize was the utter insignificance of the United States of America to France during this period. Talleyrand himself claimed that America was "not of greater consequence . . . than Geneva or Genoa," and the proceedings of the Directory during the months that the American commission was in Paris contain virtually no mention of America. William Stinchome, *The XYZ Affair* (Westport, Conn.: Greenwood Press, 1981), 35. Because of their unimportance, the Americans were probably doomed to fail until French leaders saw increasing tensions with America as a more significant problem. Ironically, Republican efforts to block President John Adams's military measures probably undermined negotiations with France, convincing French officials that they did not need to take American threats of war seriously.

83. In terms of foreign policy, Jefferson pinned his hopes on delay and inaction, hoping that time would allow France to emerge triumphant over the British and optimistically believing that the French nation would then spread republicanism across the European continent.

84. In the end, Jefferson eschewed the idea of using force, calling, instead, for what he called "passive firmness." TJ to JM, 30 January 1799, *WTJ*, VII, 341. Later, Madison claimed that the Kentucky Resolutions were really just an appeal to public opinion.

85. A number of leading Republicans did expect Gerry to negotiate a treaty. Henry Tazewell wrote, "I confess I have strong expectations that Gerry will make a Treaty, which altho. subsequent circumstances may prevent its ratification, will have the effect of procuring time for cooler reflection on both sides." Tazewell to Madison, 28 June 1798, *PJM*, XVII, 159.

86. TJ to EG, 26 January 1799, *WTJ*, IX, 22–23.

87. TJ to EG, 26 January 1799, *WTJ*, IX, 24. They did, at first, yield to these unofficial conferences, which provided Talleyrand with his chance to ask for a bribe through X,Y, and Z.

88. Jefferson did not know that Gerry himself wanted to publish a defense of his conduct, particularly after Thomas Pickering wrote an inflammatory letter that was widely publicized in an effort to discredit Gerry before he returned from France. In the letter, Pickering insinuated that Gerry had collaborated with Talleyrand. See Pickering's 29 September 1798 letter to the freeholders of Prince Edward County, in Charles Upham, *The Life of Thomas Pickering*, 3 vols. (Boston, 1873), III, 471–78. Gerry bridled at Pickering's high-handed tactics. He wrote a defense of his conduct and asked Adams to let him print it in the newspapers. Adams thought this was a reasonable request, but Pickering was outraged and threatened to expose Gerry's "*duplicity* and *treachery*." Billias, *Elbridge Gerry*, 294. To avoid a pamphlet fight that would only worsen the situation, Adams prevailed on Gerry not to publish his defense.

89. TJ to EG, 26 January 1799, *WTJ*, IX, 24–25.

90. TJ to Mary Jefferson Eppes, 17 January 1800, *WTJ*, IX, 94. See Lewis, "'The Blessings of Domestic Society.'" Even with his own death, Jefferson attempted to distance himself from the contamination of politics and to seek refuge and reputation on higher ground. He asked that his tombstone refer only to his authorship of the Declaration of Independence and the Virginia Statute of

Religious Freedom and his role in founding the University of Virginia, leaving unmentioned a lifetime of political office holding.

91. TJ to Martha Jefferson Randolph, 15 January 1792, *Family Letters of Thomas Jefferson*, ed. Betts and Bear, 93.

92. TJ to Martha Jefferson Randolph, 17 May 1798, *Family Letters of Thomas Jefferson*, ed. Betts and Bear, 162.

93. TJ to Martha Jefferson Randolph, 8 June 1797, *Writings*, 1047. As Lewis notes, "The two terms, family and politics, were so closely linked in his mind that he could barely mention one without invoking the other." Lewis, "'The Blessings of Domestic Society,'" 114.

94. According to his grandson, "In speaking of the calumnies which his enemies had uttered against his public and private character with such unmitigated and untiring bitterness, he said that he had not considered them as abusing him; they had never known *him*. They had created an imaginary being clothed with odious attributes, to whom they had given his name." Sarah Randolph, *The Domestic Life of Thomas Jefferson* (1871; reprint Charlottesville: University of Virginia Press, 1978), 369.

95. The power of republics, according to George Mason, came from "the love, the affection, the attachment of the citizens to their laws, to their freedom, and to their country." Mason, in *The Records of the Federal Convention of 1787*, 4 vols., ed. Max Farrand (New Haven, Conn.: Yale University Press, 1966), I, 112. As Jan Lewis writes, "In the republic envisioned by American writers, citizens were to be bound together not by patriarch's duty or liberalism's self-interest, but by affection." Lewis, "The Republican Wife," 689. See also Caleb Crain, *American Sympathy: Men, Friendship, and Citizenship in the New Nation* (New Haven, Conn.: Yale University Press, 2001); Wills, *Inventing America*; and Fliegelman, *Declaring Independence*.

96. Lewis, "The Republican Wife."

97. TJ to Hugh Williamson, 11 February 1798, *WTJ*, VIII, 368. He also spoke of his cabinet as his family. See Catherine Allgor, *Parlor Politics: In Which the Ladies of Washington Help Build a City and a Government* (Charlottesville: University of Virginia Press, 2000), 30.

98. TJ to Benjamin Rush, 21 April 1803, *Writings*, 1125.

99. TJ to John Henry, 31 December 1797, *PTJ*, XXIX, 603.

100. TJ to William Short, 3 January 1793, *Writings*, 1004.

101. TJ to Martha Jefferson Randolph, 4 April 1790, *Family Letters of Thomas Jefferson*, ed. Betts and Bear, 51. See Lewis, "'Blessings of Domestic Society,'" 132–38.

102. TJ to Anne Willing Bingham, 11 May 1788, *Writings*, 923. As president, when faced with a woman's request for a position as postmistress, he refused not just her request but even the possibility of a woman in office—even the Post Office, claiming that neither he nor the public were ready for that. He also claimed to have given little thought to the issue of female education. For Jefferson's attempt to keep women from wielding political influence, see Allgor, *Parlor Politics*, 4–47. Even in his attempt to relegate women to a purely domestic role, Jefferson illustrated Joan Wallach Scott's dictum that "gender constructs politics." Scott, *Gender and the Politics of History* (New York: Columbia University Press, 1999), 46. Her remark is equally relevant to the other founders

discussed here, all of whom struggled with notions of gender, a concept very much in flux during this period, as they attempt to draw a line between public and private life. For the use of gender to construct identity, see Kathleen Brown, "Brave New Worlds: Women's and Gender History," *William and Mary Quarterly* 50.2 (April 1993); Lewis, "'The Blessings of Domestic Society'"; Toby Ditz, "Shipwrecked; or, Masculinity Imperiled: Mercantile Representations of Failure and the Gendered Self in Eighteenth-Century Philadelphia," *Journal of American History* 81.1 (June 1994): 51–80; Carol Smith-Rosenberg, "Domesticating "Virtue": Coquettes and Revolutionaries in Young America," in *Literature and the Body*, ed. Elaine Scarry (Baltimore: Johns Hopkins University Press, 1988) 160–84; and C. Dallett Hemphill, "Class, Gender, and the Regulation of Emotional Expression in Revolutionary-Era Conduct Literature," in *An Emotional History of the United States*, ed. Stearns and Lewis, 33–51.

103. See Rosemarie Zagarri, "Gender and the First Party System," in *Federalists Reconsidered*, ed. Doron Ben-Atar and Barbara B. Oberg (Charlottesville: University of Virginia Press, 1998), 118–34.

104. See Peter Onuf, "'To Declare Them a Free and Independent People': Race, Slavery, and National Identity in Jefferson's Thought," *Journal of the Early Republic* 18.1 (spring 1998): 1–46.

105. Thomas Jefferson, *Notes on the State of Virginia*, ed. William Peden (Chapel Hill: University of North Carolina Press, 1982), 138.

106. See Fliegelman, *Declaring Independence*, 193–95. For Jefferson's inability to imagine blacks as part of the nation, see Peter Onuf, *Jefferson's Empire: The Language of American Nationhood* (Charlottesville: University of Virginia Press, 2000), chapter 5. Such reasoning was part of a larger cultural transformation. David Waldstreicher writes, "In this new body politic, having the right nerves demonstrated social worth. Interior and organic yet transparently visible, sentimental signs and their language were the perfect vehicle for a patriotism that aspired simultaneously to include and to exclude more people, according to natural principles." Waldstreicher, *In the Midst of Perpetual Fetes*, 79. For an exploration of how race, class, and gender were essential to constituting new American citizens, see Carroll Smith-Rosenberg, "Dis-Covering the Subject of the 'Great Constitutional Discussion,' 1786–1789," *Journal of American History* 79.3 (1992): 841–73. For the body itself as a source of contestation, see Bruce Burgett, *Sentimental Bodies: Sex, Gender, and Citizenship in the Early Republic* (Princeton, N.J.: Princeton University Press, 1998).

107. Jefferson's public declarations of faith are justly famous. And in a way, they are just as exceptional as his private professions. As Jeffrey Tulis notes, "the early president known most for his democratic views, spoke the least to the public directly." Tulis, *The Rhetorical Presidency* (Princeton, N.J.: Princeton University Press, 1987), 70–71. He delivered his first inaugural address in such a whisper that most in the audience did not hear a word he said. He also chose to give his state of the union addresses in writing to Congress, overturning precedent, since both Adams and Washington had addressed Congress in person. See Alf J. Mapp, *Thomas Jefferson: A Strange Case of Mistaken Identity* (New York: Madison Books, 1987), 397.

108. TJ, second inaugural, 4 March 1805, *Writings*, 518–23.

109. TJ, first inaugural, 4 March 1801, *Writings*, 492–96. When newspapers printed his speech, he appeared even more conciliatory. In the sentence "We are all republicans, we are all federalists," "Republicans" and "Federalists" were mistakenly capitalized, so that Jefferson seemed to embrace the legitimacy of both parties, instead of simply affirming his belief in republicanism and federalism as governing principles.

110. TJ to Horatio Gates, 8 March 1801, *WTJ*, VIII, 11–12. To another correspondent, he wrote that he intended to "sink federalism into an abyss from which there shall be no resurrection for it." TJ to Levi Lincoln, 25 October 1802, *WTJ*, VIII, 175–76.

111. TJ to William B. Giles, 31 December 1795, *WTJ*, IX, 317.

112. TJ to William Duane, 28 March 1811, *WTJ*, XI, 193.

113. TJ to Taylor, 1 June 1798, *WTJ*, VIII, 430; TJ to Nathaniel Niles, 22 March 1801, *WTJ*, IX, 221; TJ to Archibald Stuart, 14 March 1799, *WTJ*, IX, 67; and TJ to Stephen Thompson Mason, 27 October 1799, *WTJ*, IX, 86.

114. TJ to Samuel Smith, 22 August 1798, *WTJ*, VIII, 444. The problem with the people of Massachusetts, according to Jefferson, was that they were hearing only "the Federalist line." TJ to Thomas Mann Randolph, Jr., 16 November 1792, *PTJ*, XXIV, 623. All they needed were "faithful reports of what's going on." TJ to Thomas Mann Randolph, Jr., 3 March 1793, *PTJ*, XXIV, 314. In no small part, Jefferson blamed the hold of established religion on New England. Of Vermont and Connecticut, he wrote, "they are so priest-ridden, that nothing is expected from them, but the most bigoted passive obedience." TJ to JM, 2 March 1798, *WTJ*, VIII, 380. One crucial aspect of Jefferson's political project was the discovery and cultivation of "natural" Republican leaders in New England, such as Gerry, who could potentially "rally the people back," to bring them to their senses (and, pragmatically, to provide needed votes outside the South and West).

115. TJ to Rutledge, 24 June 1797, *WTJ*, VIII, 317. Jefferson employed a highly selective ideological system in which only the good could be incorporated, while the bad was never part of the people's "true selves." See Robert E. Shalhope, "Thomas Jefferson's Republicanism and Antebellum Southern Thought," *Journal of Southern History* 42 (1976): 529–56. He even imagined war breaking out so that the Federalists could be destroyed and the Union purified. See Onuf, *Jefferson's Empire*, 109–46. Such harsh visions could be justified, according to Richard Hofstadter, for "if one imagined that no less fundamental a principle than monarchy versus republicanism was at stake, one could of course waive all scruples about a strong partisan allegiance." Hofstadter, *Idea of a Party System*, 124.

116. TJ to Martha Jefferson Randolph, 16 January 1801, *Family Letters of Thomas Jefferson*, ed. Betts and Bear, 191.

117. Not surprisingly, these foreign states were generally found in New England. See TJ to Samuel Kerchival, 5 September 1816, in Andrew A. Lipscomb and Albert Ellery Bergh, eds., *The Writings of Thomas Jefferson*, vols. 20 (Washington, D.C., 1903), XV, 72. Hereafter Lipscomb and Bergh, *Writings of Thomas Jefferson*.

118. TJ to Horatio Gates, 30 May 1797, *WTJ*, VIII, 295.

119. TJ to EG, 21 June 1797, *WTJ*, VIII, 314, and TJ to EG, 13 May 1797, *WTJ*, VIII, 287. In his commonplace book, he quoted from Euripides, "Better far, . . . prize equality that ever linketh friend to friend, city to city, and allies to

each other; for equality is man's natural law." TJ, entry 122, quoting from Euripides, *Phoenissae*, in *Literary Commonplace Book*, 71. For Euripides and Jefferson, equality was best embodied in the relationship of friendship, offering a framework to achieve the sentimental union Jefferson sought on personal, national, and international levels. As president, he called for "honest friendship with all nations—entangling alliances with none." Although historians have repeatedly faulted Jefferson for his disastrous embargo policy, his actions made perfect sense in light of his views on friendship. To choose either side in the war between France and Britain may have helped American trade, but it would have been a tacit admission of America's dependence on a foreign country. By refusing to involve the country in the war or even trade, however, Jefferson at least vindicated his belief that any true relationship must be based on equality and independence. To achieve the proper family model of affective union, though, Jefferson was willing to resort to force. Jefferson thought that France would provide the solution to the English problem: "Nothing can establish firmly the republican principles of our government but an establishment of them in England. France will be an apostle for this." TJ to Edmund Randolph, 27 June 1797, *WTJ*, VIII, 320. He had no trouble justifying a perhaps coercive apostleship: "Never was any event so important to this country since it's revolution, as the issue of the invasion of England." TJ to JM, 7 June 1798, *WTJ*, VIII, 436. Jefferson disclaimed a desire for force, but not very convincingly: "I do not indeed wish to see any nation have a form of government forced on them; but if it is to be done, I should rejoice at it's being a freer one." TJ to Peregrine Fitzhugh, 23 February 1798, *WTJ*, VIII, 378.

120. TJ to EG, 26 January 1799, *WTJ*, IX, 25.

121. TJ to EG, 26 January 1799, *WTJ*, IX, 26.

122. TJ to EG, 26 January 1799, *WTJ*, IX, 25–26.

123. Billias writes that Gerry "successfully resisted the blandishments of the Virginian." Billias, *Elbridge Gerry*, 247. Malone concurs, saying that Gerry feared being disloyal to Adams and being revealed as an intriguer. Malone, *Jefferson and His Time*, III, 433.

124. TJ to EG, 29 March 1801, *WTJ*, IX, 241.

125. TJ to EG, 29 March 1801, *WTJ*, IX, 241.

126. Jefferson's memory proved unreliable. His first visit to New York had been in 1766.

127. Roughly translated, the passage means, "To want the same, and not to want the same, that is, finally, what friendship is."

128. TJ to EG, 11 June 1812, in Lipscomb and Bergh, *Writings of Thomas Jefferson*, IX, 359–61.

CHAPTER TWO
Honor

1. Hamilton's "character" has often been at the center of scholarly treatments of him, but historians usually dismiss his sense of honor as the posturing of an insecure upstart. Three recent books have relied on vague psychological explanations of his "affairs of honor," seeing these as an outgrowth of various flaws in

his character. See Roger Kennedy, *Burr, Hamilton, and Jefferson: A Study in Character* (New York: Oxford University Press, 2000); Thomas Fleming, *Duel: Alexander Hamilton, Aaron Burr, and the Future of America* (New York: Basic Books, 1999); and Arnold Rogow, *A Fatal Friendship: Alexander Hamilton and Aaron Burr* (New York: Hill and Wang, 1998). For a review of the shortcomings of these approaches, see Joanne Freeman, "Grappling with the Character Issue," *Reviews in American History* 28.4 (2000): 518–22. Although at times Hamilton's actions clearly bordered on the irrational, this study explores Hamilton's use of honor not primarily as compensation for psychological shortcomings but as the foundation of Hamilton's vision for himself, the polity, and the nation.

2. Hamilton constantly found himself embroiled in defenses of his honor. Freeman counts eleven affairs of honor for Hamilton. See Joanne Freeman, "Dueling as Politics: Reinterpreting the Burr-Hamilton Duel," *William and Mary Quarterly* 53 (1996): 294. When his duels, near duels, and pamphlets (which one historian has likened to a ritual duel), are considered together, it can be argued that Hamilton was continually involved in affairs of honor throughout the 1790s. For an exploration of the role of honor in early American politics, see Freeman, *Affairs of Honor*. For a more general exploration of honor, see Julian Pitt-Rivers, "Honour and Social Status," in *Honour and Shame: The Values of Mediterranean Society*, ed. J. G. Peristiany (Chicago: University of Chicago Press, 1966), 21–73. Pitt-Rivers describes honor as a mechanism that distributes power and roles, a clearinghouse for conflicts in the social structure between the individual and society. Also see J. K. Campbell, *Honour, Family, and Patronage: A Study of Institutions and Moral Values in a Greek Mountain Community* (Oxford: Oxford University Press, 1964); Hans van Wees, *Status Warriors: War, Violence, and Society in Homer and History* (Amsterdam: J. C. Gieben, 1992); Stewart, *Honor*; Bertram Wyatt-Brown, *Southern Honor: Ethics and Behavior in the Old South* (Oxford: Oxford University Press, 1982); Kenneth, Greenberg, *Honor and Slavery* (Princeton, N.J.: Princeton University Press, 1996); and *Honour and Shame*, ed. J. G. Peristiany. Honor and dueling were not confined to the South. See Joanne Freeman, "Aristocratic Murder and Democratic Fury: Honor and Politics in Early National New England," presented at the American Historical Association, January 1997. For the duel as a form of deep play, see Clifford Geertz, "Deep Play: Notes on the Balinese Cockfight," in *The Inter pretation of Cultures* (New York: Harper Collins, 1973), 412–54.

3. Lewis, "'The Blessings of Domestic Society,'" 129.

4. JM, Commonplace book (from Montesquieu), 1759–72, *PJM*, I, 17.

5. JA to Greene, 9 March 1777, *WJA*, V, 108.

6. JA, *Boston Patriot*, 1809, *WJA*, IX, 295.

7. Most commentators do not find any great changes within the honor code during this time. For example, see Wyatt-Brown, *Southern Honor*.

8. On the decline of deference, see Michael Zuckerman, "Tocqueville, Turner, and Turds: Four Stories of Manners in Early America," *Journal of American History* 85.1 (June 1998): 13–42; Taylor, *William Cooper's Town*; Melvin Yazawa, *From Colonies to Commonwealth: Familial Ideology and the Beginnings of American Politics* (Baltimore: Johns Hopkins University Press, 1985); Fliegelman, *Prodigals and Pilgrims*; Edwin Burrows and Michael Wallace, "The

American Revolution: The Ideology and Psychology of National Liberation," *Perspectives in American History* 6 (1972); Winthrop Jordan, "Familial Politics: Thomas Paine and the Killing of the King, 1776," *Journal of American History* 60 (September 1973): 294–308; Richard Beeman, "Deference, Republicanism, and the Emergence of Popular Politics in Eighteenth-Century America," *William and Mary Quarterly* 49 (July 1992): 401–30; and Robert Weir, "Who Shall Rule at Home: The American Revolution as a Crisis in Legitimacy for the Colonial Elite," *Journal of Interdisciplinary History* 6 (spring 1976): 679–700.

9. For the increasingly democratic nature of American politics, see Wood, *Radicalism*; Wood, *Creation of the American Republic*; and Taylor, *William Cooper's Town*. For the growth in print culture, see Brown, *Knowledge Is Power*; Warner, *Letters of the Republic*; and Larzer Ziff, *Writing in the New Nation: Prose, Print, and Politics in the Early United States* (New Haven, Conn.: Yale University Press, 1991). For the role of printers, see Jeffrey L. Pasley, *"The Tyranny of Printers": Newspaper Politics in the Early American Republic* (Charlottesville: University of Virginia Press, 2001).

10. See Newman, *Parades and the Politics of the Street*; Travers, *Celebrating the Fourth*; Waldstreicher, *Perpetual Fetes*.

11. J. G. Peristiany writes, "Honour and shame are the constant preoccupation of individuals in small scale, exclusive societies where face to face personal, as opposed to anonymous, relations are of paramount importance and where the social personality of the actor is as significant as his office. . . . In this insecure, individualist, world where nothing is accepted on credit, the individual is constantly forced to strive and assert himself." See Peristiany, "Introduction," in *Honour and Shame*, ed. Peristiany, 11.

12. Wolcott to AH, 3 July 1797, *PAH*, XXI, 145.

13. William Jackson to AH, 24 July 1797, *PAH*, XXI, 182–83. He later changed his mind when Monroe refused to confirm publicly Hamilton's innocence: "It appears to me that your publication must go on, as Mr. M did not seem willing to grant the certificate, and I confess I should be unwilling to recommend any compromise short of that." Jackson to AH, 31 July 1797, *PAH*, XXI, 192.

14. Printed version of the "Reynolds pamphlet," August 1797, *PAH*, XXI, 243. All future page references are included in the text.

15. Even as he wrote his own pamphlet in defense of his conduct, Hamilton complained of political pamphlets: "A measure new in this country has lately been adopted to give greater efficacy to the system of defamation—periodical pamphlets."

16. For an in-depth exploration of political pamphlets, see Ferguson, *American Enlightenment*, 80–123. The polemical, topical, and even contrapuntal nature of pamphlets that Ferguson notes made them a perfect medium for personal defense.

17. TJ to JM, 7 July 1793, *WTJ*, VI, 338. William Maclay, *The Diary of William Maclay and Other Notes on Senate Debates*, ed. Kenneth Bowling and Helen Veit, volume IX of the *Documentary History of the First Federal Congress of the United States of America* (Baltimore: Johns Hopkins University Press, 1988), 252. Robert Wiebe has suggested that pamphlets in the early republic were akin to "ritual duels." Wiebe, *Opening of American Society*, 101.

18. On another occasion, an ally warned him, "The throat of your political reputation is to be cut, *in Whispers.*" William Willcocks to AH, 5 September

1793, *PAH*, XV, 324. In the lead-up to the Burr-Hamilton duel, Burr made similar complaints about Hamilton. Burr's second in the negotiations argued, "secret whispers traducing his fame and empeaching his honor, are at least equally injurious, with slanders publickly uttered." Van Ness to Pendleton, 27 June 1804, *PAH*, XXVI, 272.

19. Freeman writes, "In written statements, identifiable politicians virtually stood before the reader in person, contradicting a rumor with evidence and with their status, offering an alternate way of seeing the world." Freeman, "Dueling as Politics," 51. Freeman offers an overview of the kind of written defenses available to politicians. According to her, the least dignified was a handbill or broadside. Private letters were more impressive but were restricted to a few readers. Newspaper essays reached a wide audience but could not be used when strong proof of wrongdoing had been provided by someone with national stature. See Freeman, *Affairs of Honor*, chapter 4. David Cohen argues that in situations in which men transact their socially significant selves, their rhetorical practices are public, discursive, and performative constructions of their character, quintessential public acts by which individuals invite judgment through attempts to establish a particular social biography. Cohen, *Law, Violence, and Community in Classical Athens* (Cambridge: Cambridge University Press, 1995), 63–83. The increasing use in the postrevolutionary period of defense pamphlets to defend one's reputation further complicates Warner's argument in *The Republic of Letters* about impersonality as the source of print's power. In contrast to Warner's emphasis on anonymity, defense pamphlets were tied to the individual and his reputation.

20. See Ferguson, *American Enlightenment*, 86–87. The unpredictability of readers is one of the recurrent subthemes of this work. As Goodman shows in her exposition of a quarrel between David Hume and Jean Jacques Rousseau, the reading public had its own standards for determining truth and could choose to ignore documentary evidence (upon which Hume relied) in favor of a well-crafted emotional appeal (upon which Rousseau relied). See Goodman, "The Hume-Rousseau Affair."

21. In exploring French *mémoires judiciare* before the French Revolution, Sarah Maza has argued that the pamphlets appealed to readers in a similar fashion and transformed the reading public from a passive recipient of spectacle to an active judge of events. See Maza, *Private Lives and Public Affairs: The Causes Celebres of Prerevolutionary France* (Berkeley: University of California Press, 1993).

22. TJ to James Callender, 6 October 1799, in Freeman, *Affairs of Honor*, 210.

23. Monroe wrote: "You know I presume that Beckley published the papers in question." Monroe to Burr, 1 December 1797, *PAH*, XXI, 133 n. 39. Oliver Wolcott also attributed it to Beckley. See Oliver Wolcott to AH, 3 July 1797, *PAH*, XXI, 145.

24. Monroe to Burr, 1 December 1797, *PAH*, XXI, 133 n. 39.

25. See Charles Royster, *A Revolutionary People at War: The Continental Army and American Character, 1775–1783* (New York: Norton, 1979).

26. See AH, "Account of a Duel Between Major General Charles Lee and Lieutenant Colonel John Laurens," 24 December 1778, *PAH*, I, 602–4.

27. It was important to show mastery over one's feelings, including the fear of death. See Greenberg, *Honor and Slavery*. The point of a duel was not killing the

other man. When a mortal wound was given, observers sometimes saw that in itself as dishonorable. In fact, showing any bloodthirsty tendencies or personal animosity during the duel could result in dishonor. This point of etiquette arose in the duel between Laurens and Lee. Laurens wounded Lee with his first shot, and although Lee wanted to continue, Hamilton and Lee's seconds both argued against another shot, "unless the General was influenced by motives of personal enmity." Lee accepted their argument, and the affair ended. When Lee was talked out of firing a second shot, he was being asked to display liberality, to show that he was not motivated by personal enmity and was willing to offer reconciliation when the demands of honor had been satisfied. This exchange showed one of the central paradoxes of honor: a gentleman should be motivated strictly by his desire to defend his honor, not by animosity toward another man. A gentleman's feelings toward other men did not materially affect his own honor. The crucial element was the estimation of other men.

28. Wyatt-Brown writes that conferring or denying honor becomes a form of dramatization, a staging before a responsive audience. Wyatt-Brown, *Southern Honor*, 2–3. To have honor and to be honored were virtually the same thing. See David Chaney, "The Spectacle of Honour: The Changing Dramatization of Status," *Theory, Culture, and Society* 12.3 (August 1995): 147–68. See also Julian Pitt-Rivers "Honor," in *International Encyclopedia of Social Sciences* (New York: Macmillan, 1968), VII, 503–10, and Pitt-Rivers, "Honour and Social Status."

29. John Brooks to AH, 4 July 1779, *PAH*, II, 91.

30. Wiebe notes "how intimately the code entwined with a gentleman's qualifications for public leadership." Wiebe, *Opening of American Society*, 99. Joanne Freeman calls it a "subtle blend" of the political and the personal. Freeman, "Dueling as Politics," 295.

31. As Royster points out, gentlemen were expected to cultivate sensibility, and it was even thought to improve one's martial qualities, inspiring an officer "to occupy his highly visible, vulnerable station without discrediting himself." Royster, *Revolutionary People*, 90. For eighteenth-century notions of sensibility, see Janet Todd, *Sensibility: An Introduction* (London: Methuen, 1986); Wills, *Inventing America*; R. S. Crane, "Suggestions Toward a Genealogy of the 'Man of Feeling,'" *A Journal of English Literary History* 1.3 (1934); G. J. Barker-Benfield, *The Culture of Sensibility: Sex and Society in Eighteenth-Century Britain* (Chicago: University of Chicago Press, 1992); Bushman, *Refinement of America*.

32. Jacob Black-Michaud sees honor as a synonym for effective political power, but he argues that prescribed norms rarely exist, leaving each case to be judged on its own merit. Similarly, David Cohen argues that honor is intensely interactive, rather than a rigid code. See Jacob Black-Michaud, *Cohesive Force: Feud in the Mediterranean and the Middle East* (Oxford: Oxford University Press, 1975), 181, and Cohen, *Law, Violence, and Community*, 63–83. One reason for the volatility was the type of honor code that men in the early republic followed. It was both horizontal (emphasizing equality between all participants) and reflexive (demanding a response when attacked).

33. AH to Monroe, 5 July 1797, with a "Memorandum of substance of declaration of Messrs. Monroe Mughlenburgh & Venable concerning the affair of James Reynolds," *PAH*, XXI, 147–48.

34. Abraham Venable to AH, 9 July 1797, *PAH*, XXV, 154.

35. AH to Muhlenberg and Monroe, 17 July 1797, *PAH*, XXV, 170, 172.

36. AH to John Fenno, 17–22 July 1797, *PAH*, XXI, 167.

37. Monroe to AH, 21 July 1797, *PAH*, XXI, 179. Ironically, Callender's attack was inspired in part by attacks on Monroe, attacks that had led Monroe to write his own defense pamphlet.

38. Monroe to AH, 21 July 1797, *PAH*, XXV, 179.

39. William Jackson to AH, 7 August 1797, *PAH*, XXI, 207.

40. Jackson to AH, 7 August 1797, *PAH*, XXV, 205.

41. Monroe to AH, 25 July 1797, *PAH*, XXV, 184.

42. AH to Monroe, 4 August 1797, *PAH*, XXV, 200.

43. Monroe to AH, 6 August 1797, *PAH*, XXV, 205.

44. William Plumer to Jeremiah Smith, 10 December 1791, William Plumer Papers, Library of Congress, Washington, D.C., as cited in Freeman, "Slanders, Whispers, Poison, and Fame," 32.

45. AH, "Reynolds pamphlet," August 1797, *PAH*, XXI, 240. Freeman writes that "a politician's private identity and his public office were thus inseparably linked." Freeman, "Dueling as Politics," 296.

46. Monroe to TJ, 11 July 1797, *PAH*, XXI, 137 editor's note.

47. Benjamin Moore to William Coleman, 12 July 1804, *PAH*, XXVI, 316.

48. AH's statement on his impending duel with Burr, 28 June–10 July 1804, *PAH*, XXVI, 279–80. For an in-depth treatment of this duel and of the political use of honor, see Freeman, "Dueling as Politics." For the political uses of honor, see also Pitt-Rivers, "Honour and Social Status", and J. E. Lendon, *Empire of Honour: The Art of Government in the Roman World* (Oxford: Clarendon Press, 1997).

49. AH to Monroe, 28 July 1797, *PAH*, XXV, 186. In a process similar to Hamilton's case, Dena Goodman has explored how a private quarrel became public and how the participants then appealed to public opinion through pamphlets. Goodman, "The Hume-Rousseau Affair."

50. Defending himself in this manner was not unknown. In other countries, politicians had made use of similar strategies. See Maza, *Private Lives and Public Affairs*, and Roy Porter, "Mixed Feelings: The Enlightenment and Sexuality in Eighteenth-Century Britain," in *Sexuality in Eighteenth-Century Britain*, ed. Paul-Gabriel Boucé (Totawa, N.J., Manchester University Press, 1982).

51. When he learned that Jefferson had convinced Philip Freneau to open an antiadministration newspaper and then hired Freneau as a translator at the State Department to help support him financially, Hamilton castigated Jefferson in a series of anonymous newspaper articles. Hamilton repeatedly hammered at the point that Jefferson had misused a public office and public funds. See AH, "An American No. 1," 4 August 1792, *PAH*, XII, 159. Just as Jefferson had unmasked Hamilton for being overly formal on a private occasion, Hamilton unmasked Jefferson for abusing a public trust.

52. The story that framed the facts and gave them meaning was crucial. As Harold Syrett has commented, "The pamphlets by Callender and Hamilton are more akin to trial briefs than factual reports, and at several points they present evidence that is flatly contradictory." Syrett, *PAH*, XXI, 123. See also Maza, *Private Lives and Public Affairs*, 16.

53. Others seemed to concur. One gentleman, who abused Hamilton in 1797, later recanted on learning more about Maria Reynolds: "I have represented that woman as an amiable and virtuous wife, seduced from the affections of her husband by artifice and intrigue. That woman, however, I have been informed from the best authority, from the authority of her own acquaintances, to have been one of those unfortunates, who, destitute of every regard for virtue or honor, traffic with the follies of youth, and lay their snares to entrap the feeling heart and benevolent mind; such was the origin of her acquaintance with Mr. Hamilton, whose unsuspecting generosity became the victim of her art and duplicity." John Wood, *A Correct Statement of the Various Sources from which the History of the Administration of John Adams was Compiled and the Motives for its Suppression by Col. Burr* (New York, 1802), 9, as cited in Jacob Cogan, "The Reynolds Affair and the Politics of Character," *Journal of the Early Republic* 16.3 (1966): 389–417, quote on 399. As Cogan points out, part of Hamilton's problem was a society that increasingly saw women as the repository of virtue, rather than corruption. Republicans tried to capitalize on Hamilton's indiscretion by telling a story that depended on Maria's status as an innocent woman victimized by a corrupt aristocrat. See Cogan, "The Reynolds Affair." On the shifting view of women, see Nancy Cott, "Passionlessness: An Interpretation of Victorian Sexual Ideology, 1790–1850," *Signs* 4 (winter 1978): 219–36, and Paula Baker, "The Domestication of Politics: Women and American Political Society, 1780–1920," *American Historical Review* 89 (June 1984): 620–47.

54. Cited in Todd, *Sensibility*, 79.

55. For sensibility as an avenue of female power, see Barker-Benfield, *Culture of Sensibility*, 37–103. See also Teute, "Roman Matron on the Banks of Tiber Creek." Teute also argues that Federalists were more accepting of this kind of female influence. The ill-defined boundary between public and private also provided some space for women to influence the public world. See Goodman, "Public Sphere and Private Life."

56. AH to Susanna Livingston, 18 March 1779, *PAH*, II, 22–23.

57. AH to Edward Carrington, 26 May 1792, *PAH*, XI, 439. For the greater willingness of Federalists to consider some role for women in the political sphere, see Zagarri, "Gender and the First Party System." For the social spaces in which women could exert influence, see David Shields and Fredrika Teute, "The Republican Court and the Historiography of a Woman's Domain in the Public Sphere," paper delivered at the annual meeting of the Society for Early American Historians, 16 July 1994. On gender and political culture in the early republic, see Norma Basch, "Marriage, Morals, and Politics in the Election of 1828," *Journal of American History* 80 (1993): 890–918; Anne M. Boylan, "Women and Politics in the Era before Seneca Falls," *Journal of Early Republic* 10 (1990): 363–82; Lewis, "The Republican Wife"; Linda K. Kerber, *Women of the Republic: Intellect and Ideology in Revolutionary America* (Chapel Hill: University of North Carolina Press, 1980); Mary P. Ryan, *Women in Public: Between Banners and Ballots, 1825–1880* (Baltimore: Johns Hopkins University Press, 1990); Kirsten E. Wood, "'One Woman So Dangerous to Public Morals': Gender and Power in the Eaton Affair," *Journal of the Early Republic* 17 (1997): 237–75. Gender as a primary way of signifying relationships of power was also crucial to conceptions of

national identity. See Shirley Samuels, *Romances of the Republic: Women, the Family, and Violence in the Literature of the Early American Nation* (Oxford: Oxford University Press, 1996).

58. This was particularly true of honor's key attribute, sensibility. For the use of sensibility and sentiment to define citizenship in the new nation, see Julia Stern, *The Plight of Feeling: Sympathy and Dissent in the Early American Novel* (Chicago: University of Chicago Press, 1997); Burgett, *Sentimental Bodies*; Julie Ellison, "Cato's Tears," *ELH* 63 (1996): 571–601; and Andy Trees, "Benedict Arnold, John André, and his Three Yeoman Captors: A Sentimental Journey or American Virtue Defined," *Early American Literature* 35.3 (2002): 246–73. Burgett writes that sentiment was "the dividing line between citizenship and subjection in the early republic." Burgett, *Sentimental Bodies*, 21.

59. *Oxford English Dictionary*, 2d ed. (on-line).

60. Thomas Monroe, *Olla Podrida* (23 June 1787), 15, as cited in Todd, *Sensibility*, 13.

61. AH, speech to the Constitutional Convention, *Records of the Federal Convention of 1787*, ed. Farrand, I, 381.

62. AH, *Federalist #6*, 14 November 1787, *PAH*, IV, 310.

63. AH, "The Farmer Refuted," 23 February 1775, *PAH*, I, 95.

64. AH to Robert Morris, 13 August 1782, *PAH*, III, 135.

65. AH, speech at the Constitutional Convention (as recorded by James Madison), June 1787, *PAH*, IV, 193.

66. See Douglass Adair, "A Note on Certain of Hamilton's Pseudonyms," in *Fame and the Founding Fathers*, ed. Trevor Colbourn (New York: W. W. Norton, 1974), 272–85. Adair notes how the characters, real or fictional, that we identify with offer a window into our secret fears and hopes for ourselves.

67. Hamilton's views contrasted starkly with those of Adams, who feared the aristocracy as the greatest danger to republican government.

68. AH, speech at the Constitutional Convention (as recorded by Robert Yates), 22 June 1787, *PAH*, IV, 216.

69. AH, "The Continentalist" I and II, *PAH*, II, 649, 656. As Jerald Combs notes, Hamilton did make brilliant use of Washington's popularity to win approval for his policies, despite their unpopularity. See Combs, *Jay Treaty*, 37–38.

70. AH, "The Examination," *New York Evening Post*, 8 April 1802, *PAH*, XXV, 597. The Federalists also courted popular favor but did so with what David Waldstreicher has called "a stylized antistyle." See Waldstreicher, "Federalism, the Style of Politics, and the Politics of Style," in *Federalists Reconsidered*, ed. Ben-Atar and Oberg, 99–117.

71. AH, *Federalist #63*, *PAH*, IV, 407–8. Hamilton was following the arguments of David Hume, quoting him to the effect that "honour is a great check upon mankind. But, where a considerable body of men act together, this check is in a great measure removed." AH, "The Farmer Refuted," 23 February 1775, *PAH*, I, 94–95.

72. AH, *Federalist #70*, 15 March 1788, *PAH*, IV, 605.

73. AH to GW, 2 August 1794, *PAH*, XVII, 18.

74. AH to James McHenry, 18 March 1799, *PAH*, XXII, 552–53. His elitism and his understanding of the lessons of the Revolution can be seen in the army he

tried to create in the late 1790s, a professional force that revealed his disgust with state militias and with the nature of the armed forces during the Revolution. The state militias represented to him all the problems of the government under the Articles of Confederation. Besides failing to meet Hamilton's standards of efficiency and order, they fostered state over national loyalties and were politically unreliable. Not surprisingly, Jefferson took the opposite view, seeing the state militias as a sign of America's strength, its ability to rely on virtuous citizens to protect the nation, rather than a professional army.

75. AH, "Tully" No. 1, 23 August 1794, *American Daily Advertiser*, *PAH*, XVII, 135.

76. AH, "An American" No. 1, 4 August 1792, *Gazette of the United States*, *PAH*, XII, 161.

77. For Hamilton's statecraft, see Karl-Friedrich Walling, *Republican Empire: Alexander Hamilton on War and Free Government* (Lawrence: University Press of Kansas, 1999). On the importance of national honor, Wiebe writes, "Although the meaning of independence defied a precise definition, it either existed or it did not. It never came in hues. Either the United Sates stood honorably before the world or it lay in a shambles of disgrace." Wiebe, *Opening of American Society*, 107.

78. AH, *Federalist #15*, 1 December 1787, *PAH*, IV, 357.

79. AH, *Federalist #15*, 1 December 1787, *PAH*, IV, 357. As he noted in *Federalist #85*, "A nation without a national government is, in my view, a sad spectacle."

80. AH, *Federalist #15*, 1 December 1787, *PAH*, IV, 358.

81. AH, *Federalist #11*, 24 November 1787, *PAH*, IV, 342.

82. AH to GW (enclosure), 15 September 1790, *PAH*, VII, 55, 49.

83. AH, "Report Relative to a Provision for the Support of Public Credit", 9 January 1790, *PAH*, VI, 68. For Hamilton's overly ambitious vision to establish public credit, see Herbert E. Sloan, "Hamilton's Second Thoughts: Federalist Finance Revisited," in *Federalists Reconsidered*, ed. Ben-Atar and Oberg, 61–76. For a discussion of credit and reputation, see Mary Beth Norton, *Founding Mothers and Fathers: Gendered Power and the Forming of American Society* (New York: Knopf, 1966), chapter 4.

84. Private credit was equally a matter of honor. On the eve of his duel with Burr, he felt compelled to explain his own indebtedness and his potential inability to repay those debts if killed. He wrote, "It is perhaps due to my reputation to explain why I have made so considerable an establishment in the country." He hoped that "the opinion of candid men will be, that there has been no impropriety in my conduct." AH's explanation of his financial situation, 1 July 1804, *PAH*, XXVI, 288–89.

85. Hamilton was one of many leaders to be left behind by these developments. See Taylor, *William Cooper's Town*.

86. AH to Fenno, 17–22 July 1797, *PAH*, XXI, 167–68.

87. Troup to King, 3 June 1798, in King, ed., *Life and Correspondence of Rufus King*, II, 330.

88. John Barnes to TJ, 3 October 1797, *PAH*, XXI, 139n.

89. JM to TJ, 20 October 1797, *PAH* XXI, 139n.

90. Callender to TJ, 28 September 1797, *PAH*, XXI, 140n.

91. His essays as Camillus defending the Jay Treaty drove Jefferson to such despair that he wrote to Madison, "Hamilton is really a colossus to the anti-republican party—without numbers, he is an host within himself. . . . We have had only middling performances to oppose to him—in truth, when he comes forward there is nobody but yourself who can meet him." TJ to JM, 21 September 1795, Lipscomb and Bergh *Writings of Thomas Jefferson*, IX, 309, 311.

92. Wiebe notes, "The pursuit of women, like the pursuit of wealth, never by itself disqualified a public leader." Wiebe, *Opening of American Society*, 13. Janet Todd writes, "In the eighteenth century sexual continence became a predominantly female virtue." Todd, *Sensibility*, 17. In his exploration of Andalusia, Pitt-Rivers notes that the male offender was simply seen as following his nature, while the cuckold had clearly failed as a man, damaging his honor. Pitt-Rivers, "Honour and Social Status." Reynolds was the one to resent the injury to his honor, and if a man of honor, he should have challenged Hamilton to a duel. But he refused to do that, except in "vague" terms, leaving Hamilton to conclude: "It was easy to understand that he wanted money." When Reynolds finally named his price, Hamilton wrote dismissively, "He was willing to take a thousand dollars as the plaister for his wounded honor" (253). Filing a criminal action or seeking money damages were both seen as unsuitable for a man of honor. Violence was the proper response. See Wyatt-Brown, *Southern Honor*, chapter 12.

93. Daniel Defoe, *The Complete English Tradesman in Familiar Letters: Directing Him in All the Several Parts and Progressions of Trade* (London, 1727), 187. Norton writes, "If one was male, it was more damaging to be accused of theft than to be charged with sexual misconduct." Norton, *Founding Mothers*, 16. On the legal codification of the double standard, see Cornelia Hughes Dayton, *Women before the Bar: Gender, Law, and Society in Connecticut, 1639–1789* (Chapel Hill: University of North Carolina Press, 1995), chapter 6.

94. David Cobb to Henry Knox, 1 October 1797, as cited in Cogan, "The Reynolds Affair," 411.

95. John Pintard, Reading Diary in Newark Prison, 4 October 1797, as cited in Cogan, "The Reynolds Affair," 411.

96. Freeman notes that the letter was actually a "posting," a ritualistic public declaration that Adams was a liar after Adams refused to respond to Hamilton's inquiry. Freeman, *Affairs of Honor*, 149.

97. McHenry to John McHenry, Jr., 20 May 1800, *PAH*, XXIV, 507–12.

98. One Hamilton ally wrote, "He every where denounces the man, and almost all of the men in whom he confided, at the beginning of his administration, as an oligarchish faction, who are combined to drive him from office, because they cannot govern him, and to appoint Pinckney, by whose agency, under the controul of this faction & particularly of Hamilton its head, the country is to be driven into a war." Sedgewick to King, 26 September 1800, *PAH*, XXV, 198 n. 107. Wolcott wrote Ames, "His resentments against General Hamilton are excessive; he declares his belief of the existence of a British faction in the United States." Wolcott to Fisher Ames, 29 December 1800, *PAH*, XXV, 5 n. 5.

99. Cabot wrote Wolcott, "The P denies that he ever called us 'British Faction' or any of the hard names of which he has been accused—he does not recollect

these intemperances & thinks himself grossly misunderstood or misrepresented." Cabot to Wolcott, September 1800, *PAH*, XXV, 5 n. 5.

100. AH to James McHenry, 27 August 1800, *PAH*, XXV, 97.

101. George Cabot to AH, 23 August 1800, *PAH*, XXV, 77.

102. AH to Wolcott, 1 July 1800, *PAH*, XXV, 5.

103. AH to JA, 1 August 1800, *PAH*, XXV, 51.

104. AH to JA, 1 October 1800, *PAH*, XXV, 125–26.

105. Monroe faced a similar dilemma after Adams publicly censured his conduct as minister to France in 1798. Although feeling that he had to respond, he also thought a duel was not an option "as [Adams] is an old man & the Presidt." And he believed he could not resort to a pamphlet, because he had already written one in defense of his conduct. James Monroe to JM, 8 June 1798, *PJM*, XVII, 146.

106. AH to Wolcott, 1 July 1800, *PAH*, XXV, 4–5. Many commentators have struggled to understand the peculiar logic behind his public missive, since it seemed to counter the objectives he hoped to bolster (i.e., vindicating his character and promoting Pinckney over Adams). See Syrett, *PAH*, XXV, 172.

107. Cabot to AH, 21 August 1800, *PAH*, XXV, 74–75.

108. Fisher Ames to AH, 26 August 1800, *PAH*, XXV, 86–88. Wolcott argued that the president was his own worst enemy and needed no help from Hamilton to discredit himself: "To return to the point in which we are interested—namely whether a *formal defense* against Mr. Adams's observations is expedient—permit me to say, that the poor old Man is sufficiently successful in undermining his own Credit and influence. . . . the people believe that their President is Crazy. This is the honest truth & what more can be said on the subject." Wolcott to AH, 3 September 1800, *PAH*, XXV, 104–8.

109. AH, "Letter from Alexander Hamilton, concerning the public conduct and character of John Adams, Esq. President of the United States," 24 October 1800, *PAH*, XXV, 190. All future references included in the text.

110. As we will see in the next chapter, for Adams, a man of virtue, consistency of plan was not particularly important. Prickly and contrarian, Adams often felt compelled to change course precisely because he had no support. In his mind, lack of popularity confirmed his virtue.

111. AH to Wolcott, 1 July 1800, *PAH*, XXV, 4–5. Syrett argues that his intentions about how extensively he wanted the letter circulated are not clear. See Syrett, *PAH*, XXV, 178.

112. Beckley possibly played a role in the publication of the letter. See Shaw to William Smith, 8 November 1800, PAH, *XXV*, 177. Hamilton could not simply disavow the letter. As a man of honor, he believed in standing behind his words, not in shaping his views to fit his audience (a stark contrast to Jefferson's approach with Gerry). Gouverneur Morris claimed Hamilton's greatest fault was an inability to trim his opinions to his audience: "One marked trait of the General's character was the pertinacious adherence to opinions he had formed. . . . [He] was of all men the most indiscreet. He knew that a limited monarchy, even if established, could not preserve itself in this country. . . . And he very well knew that no monarchy whatever could be established but by the mob. But although general Hamilton knew these things . . . he never failed on every occasion to advocate the excellence of, and avow his attachment to, monarchical government.

By this course he not only cut off all chance of rising into office, but singularly promoted the views of his opponents, who with the fondness and love of power which he had not, affected a love of the people, which he had and they had not." Morris to Robert Walsh, 15 February 1811, in Jared Sparks, *The Life of Gouverneur Morris*, 3 vols. (Boston: Gray and Bowen, 1832), II, 260–62. Fisher Ames agreed, calling Hamilton "the most frank of men." Ames to Rufus King, 15 July 1800, in King, ed., *Life and Correspondence of Rufus King*, III, 275–76. When Hamilton had made his opinion on a subject clear, he felt bound to maintain it. When discussing his position toward Great Britain, he wrote, "I recommended one definitive effort to terminate differences by negociation, to be followed, if unsuccessful, by a declaration of war. . . . I became so firmly pledged to the friends and enemies of the Administration, and especially to the President of the United States, in writing as well as verbally, that I could not afterwards have retracted without a glaring and disgraceful inconsistency." AH, "Letter . . . concerning the public conduct and character of John Adams," 24 October 1800, *PAH*, XXV, 230.

113. How to create a broad, democratic context for honor was unclear. Some would have argued that even seeking such a context for honor was misguided. Bacon noted that praise depended on where it came from. "If it be from the common people, it is commonly false and naught. . . . If persons of quality and judgment concur," it "is like unto a sweet ointment . . . and will not easily away." Sir Francis Bacon, "Of Praise,"in *The Essays or Counsels, Civil and Moral* (New York: A. L. Burt, 1883), 252.

114. Beckley to Ephraim Kirby, 25 October 1800, *PAH*, XXV, 181.

115. JM to TJ, 1–3 November 1800, *PAH*, XXV, 181.

116. Most expected Adams to respond immediately with a defense pamphlet, but as usual, he had little interest in what popular opinion seemed to demand of him. He did not respond publicly to the letter for nine years. In a private letter, he wrote: "He has talents, if he would correct himself, which might be useful. There is more burnish however on the outside than standing silver in the substance." JA to Uzal Ogden, 3 December 1800, *PAH*, XXV, 183.

117. Morse to Wolcott, 27 October 1800, *PAH*, XXV, 178n.

118. Troup to Rufus King, 9 November 1800, *PAH*, XXV, 178–79n.

119. Troup to King, 31 December 1800, *PAH*, XXV, 170 n. 1.

120. Noah Webster, "A Letter to General Hamilton Occasioned by his Letter to President Adams", September 1800, *Letters of Noah Webster*, ed. Harry Warfel (New York: Library Publishers, 1953), 223–26.

121. Troup to King, 8 August 1801, in King, ed., *Life and Correspondence of Rufus King*, III, 496.

CHAPTER THREE
Virtue

1. John Adams, *Diary and Autobiography of John Adams*, 4 vols. of *The Adams Papers*, ed. L. H. Butterfield et al. (Cambridge, Mass.: Belknap Press of Harvard University Press, 1961), I, 13–14. Hereafter *Diary of John Adams*. See Steven Kagle, *American Diary Literature, 1620–1799* (Boston: Twayne Publishers, 1979), for Adams's tendency to see people as types.

2. JA, entry, *Diary of John Adams*, I, 14.

3. For gentility as a project of inner, as well as outer, refinement, see Bushman, *Refinement of America*. Adams himself exhibited a profound ambivalence toward the outward trappings of gentility. See Bushman, *Refinement of America*, 97 ff.

4. JA, as cited in Zoltan Haraszti, *John Adams and the Prophets of Progress* (New York: Grosset and Dunlap, 1964), 76.

5. JA, as cited in Haraszti, *John Adams and the Prophets of Progress*, 147.

6. JA, *Discourses on Davila*, WJA, VI, 249. John Adams does not fit comfortably in the historiographical landscape of the founding. Some scholars have seen him as a backward-looking republican, out of touch with the emerging democratic polity. For example, see Wood, *Creation of the American Republic*, chapter 14. Others have cast him as a more liberal political thinker. See Robert Webking, *The American Revolution and the Politics of Liberty* (Baton Rouge: Louisiana State University Press, 1988), and John Patrick Diggins, *The Lost Soul of American Politics: Virtue, Self-Interest, and the Foundations of Liberalism* (New York: Basic Books, 1984). Historians are also not in agreement about whether Adams's central views changed over time. For a discussion of this, see Peter Shaw, *The Character of John Adams* (Chapel Hill: University of North Carolina Press, 1976), 214n. 40. The debate largely hinges on the meaning of virtue in Adams's political thought. The role of virtue in his life and his political beliefs is complicated and multilayered, a complexity that explains the radically contrasting opinions about Adams. To make sense of Adams's views, this chapter considers his thinking on a variety of different levels. For example, on the personal level, he remained committed throughout his life to virtue as a fundamental prerequisite of the good life. But he also prided himself as a shrewd student of human nature and nearly always rejected the notion that American citizens would freely choose the virtuous path, unless guided by the proper form of government. Politically, he showed a pragmatic flexibility, recognizing the right of people to choose their own government and adapting his own principles to fit the various situations in which he found himself.

7. Given the intense identification between diarist and diary, Robert Fothergill calls the diary "the book of self." Fothergill, *Private Chronicles: A Study of English Diaries* (London: Oxford University Press, 1974), 217. For the importance of the diary to Adams, see Shaw, *Character of John Adams*; Steven Kagle, "The Diary of John Adams and the Motive of 'Achievement,'" *Hartford Studies in Literature* 3.2 (1971): 93–107; Kagle, *American Diary Literature*; and Edmund Morgan, "John Adams and the Puritan Tradition," *New England Quarterly* 34.4 (December 1961): 518–29. For broader considerations of the genre of the diary, see Rhys Isaac, "Stories and Constructions of Identity: Folk Tellings and Diary Inscriptions in Revolutionary Virginia," in *Through a Glass Darkly: Reflections on Personal Identity in Early America*, ed. Mechal Sobel and Fredrika Teute (Chapel Hill: University of North Carolina Press, 1997), 206–37, and Fothergill, *Private Chronicles*.

His diary keeping owed a debt to the Puritans, who frequently kept diaries to measure the gap between God's demands and their performances. Many commentators have noted Adams's Puritan mind-set. See Morgan, "John Adams and the Puritan Tradition," 523; Shaw, *Character of John Adams*, 23; and Joseph

Ellis, *Passionate Sage: The character and legacy of John Adams* (New York: W. W. Norton and Company, 1993), 52. For a contrasting view, see C. Bradley Thompson, *John Adams and the Spirit of Liberty* (Lawrence: University of Kansas Press, 1998).

8. In his reading, Adams invariably scribbled in the margins of the book, unable even in someone else's work to remain silent.

9. In fact, to see the diary as solely a private genre would be to impose our understanding on it. Although intended primarily for self-examination, a diary frequently served more public purposes, particularly for well-known figures. It could be a reference guide and justification for past behavior, as well as a resource to defend or attack another's character. It could also serve as a future justification for fame and public recognition. Despite the largely private nature of the genre, the public still appeared at the dim and murky edges of it. The diary was a slippery, ill-defined genre. Rachael Langford and Russell West write, "The diary, as an uncertain genre uneasily balanced between literary and historical writing, between the spontaneity of reportage and the reflectiveness of the crafted text, between selfhood and events, between subjectivity and objectivity, between the private and the public, constantly disturbs attempts to summarise its characteristics within formalised boundaries." Rachael Langford and Russell West, "Introduction: Diaries and Margins," in *Marginal Voices, Marginal Forms: Diaries in European Literature and History*, ed. Langford and West (Amsterdam: Rodopi, 1999), 8. For the diary as both a private and a public document, see Trees, "The Diary of William Maclay and Political Manners in the First Congress." For an example of diaries written explicitly for others to read, see Crain, *American Sympathy*, 16–52.

10. Because of the lack of outside readers, the diary lay open to the danger of solipsism. As Langford and West have noted, "The diary advertises its link with subjectivity by virtue of the prominence it accords to the speaking 'I.'" Langford and West, "Introduction: Diaries and Margins," 7.

11. JA, "On Self-Delusion," for the *Boston Gazette*, 29 August 1763, *WJA*, III, 433.

12. The genre typically embodied a distrust of all human capabilities. See Jurgen Schlaeger, "Self-Exploration in Early Modern English Diaries," in *Marginal Voices, Marginal Forms*, ed. Langford and West, 29–32.

13. For a brief overview of some of the different strands embedded in the meaning of virtue, see James Kloppenberg, "Virtue," in *The Blackwell Encyclopedia of the American Revolution*, ed. Jack Greene and J. R. Pole (Oxford: Blackwell Publishers, 1991): 688–93. This ambiguity also created a gendered dimension to the meaning of virtue, conceived of primarily in public and masculine terms through most of the eighteenth century. Increasingly, though, virtue was both privatized and feminized. See Ruth Bloch, "The Gendered Meanings of Virtue in Revolutionary America," *Signs* 13.1 (autumn 1987): 37–58. For further considerations of virtue, see Lester Cohen, "Explaining the Revolution: Ideology and Ethic in Mercy Otis Warren's Historical Theory," *William and Mary Quarterly* 37.2 (April 1980): 200–218; Edmund Morgan, "The Puritan Ethic and the American Revolution," in *In Search of Early America: The William and Mary Quarterly, 1943–1993*, ed. Michael McGiffert (Richmond, Va.: William Byrd Press, 1993) 78–108; Lewis, "The Republican Wife"; Ruth Bloch, "American

Feminine Ideals in Transition: The Rise of the Moral Mother, 1785–1815," *Feminist Studies* 4 (June 1978), 101–26; and Kerber, *Women of the Republic*.

14. See JA to Abigail Smith, 20 April 1763, *Adams Family Correspondence*, ed. L. H. Butterfield (Cambridge, Mass.: Harvard University Press, 1963), I, 5. Hereafter *Adams Family Correspondence*. JA, entry, 16 February 1756, *Diary of John Adams*, I, 7.

15. JA, entry, 14 June 1756, *Diary of John Adams*, I, 33.

16. JA, entry, 22 July 1756, *Diary of John Adams*, I, 35.

17. JA, entry, 5 October 1758, *Diary of John Adams*, I, 45.

18. See John Ferling, *John Adams: A Life* (Knoxville: University of Tennessee Press, 1992), 23–27.

19. For an exploration of Adams's desire for fame and for his difficulty in separating civic virtue from personal ambition, see Ferling, *John Adams*.

20. JA, entry, 18 October 1761, *Diary of John Adams*, I, 221.

21. JA, entry, *Diary of John Adams*, I, 217.

22. JA to Abigail Adams, 7 December 1796, Adams Papers, reel 382.

23. JA, entry, 3 May 1756, *Diary of John Adams*, I, 25. For Adams, vanity was a subset of the main motive of all of humanity. He wrote that the "desire of the attention, consideration, and congratulations of our fellow men . . . is the great spring of social activity." JA, 1790, *Discourses on Davila*, WJA, VI, 232–34.

24. See JA, entry, 25 July 1756, *Diary of John Adams*, I, 37.

25. JA, entry, January 1759, *Diary of John Adams*, I, 69. For Adams's oppositional tendencies, see Shaw, *Character of John Adams*, 87, and Ellis, *Passionate Sage*, 167.

26. JA, correspondence originally published in the *Boston Patriot*, WJA, IX, 270. On defending the British soldiers after the Boston Massacre, he wrote in 1773, "One of the most gallant, generous, manly and disinterested Actions of my whole Life, and one of the best Pieces of Service I ever rendered my Country." JA, entry, 5 March 1773, *Diary of John Adams*, II, 79.

27. JA to Abigail Adams, 2 December 1778, *Adams Family Correspondence*, III, 125. See Shaw, *Character of John Adams*, 15, and Ellis, *Passionate Sage*, 42. Lack of approval offered proof, Adams thought, that he retained his independence, a quality that played a crucial role in his sense of himself. To John Quincy Adams in 1815, he wrote simply, "I must think myself independent, as long as I live." JA to John Quincy Adams, 16 May 1815, Adams Papers, reel 122.

28. See Ferling, *John Adams*, 28–30, and Shaw, *Character of John Adams*, 58–59.

29. JA to Mercy Warren, 11 July 1807, *Correspondence between John Adams and Mercy Warren Relating to Her "History of the American Revolution,"* ed. Charles F. Adams (New York: Arno Press, 1972), 326. Hereafter, *Correspondence between John Adams and Mercy Warren*.

30. JA to Mercy Warren, 19 August 1807, *Correspondence between John Adams and Mercy Warren*, 471.

31. JA, entry, *Diary of John Adams*, I, 360.

32. JA to James Warren, 24 October 1775, *Warren-Adams Letters: Being Chiefly a Correspondence among John Adams, Samuel Adams, and James Warren*, Collections of the Massachusetts Historical Society series (Boston: Massachusetts

Historical Society, 1925), LXXII, 160. Hereafter, *Warren-Adams Letters*. His diary has a number of descriptions of men's faces as a way of reading their character. See, for example, JA, entry, *Diary of John Adams*, I, 242.

33. JA to Mercy Warren, 8 January 1776, *Warren-Adams Letters*, LXXII, 201.

34. JA to James Warren, 24 October 1775, *Warren-Adams Letters*, LXXII, 161. This need was not limited to the political world, though. Adams expected even courtship to adhere to standards of openness. When as a young man he was somewhat infatuated with Hannah Quincy, he criticized her practice of "the Art of pleasing," since it meant that "Her face and Hart have no Correspondence." He complained, "She is apparently frank, but really reserved, seemingly pleased, and almost charmed, when she is really laughing with Contempt." JA, entry, *Diary of John Adams*, I, 68. Adams was also anguished by his courtship of her because it ate into his time for legal studies and threatened his lofty goals for himself.

35. JA to James Warren, 24 October 1775, *Warren-Adams Letters*, LXXII, 160–61.

36. Some have argued that Adams was paranoid. For example, see Bernard Bailyn, "Butterfield's Adams: Notes for a Sketch," *William and Mary Quarterly* 19.2 (1962): 238–56. For paranoia as an American phenomenon, see Richard Hofstadter, *The Paranoid Style in American Politics, and Other Essays* (Cambridge, Mass.: Harvard University, Press, 1996). Adams's constant search for conspiracies also represented the influence of the Enlightenment, particularly the belief that all actions were explainable as part of a larger pattern. See Gordon Wood, "Conspiracy and the Paranoid Style," *William and Mary Quarterly* 39 (1982): 401–41.

37. JA, "Novanglus," *WJA*, IV, 13, 18, and 28. Adams was not simply striving for rhetorical effect. He wrote privately to Abigail of "the many Windings of Hutchinsons Heart, and the serpentine Wiles of his Head." JA to Abigail Adams, 6 September 1776, *Diary of John Adams*, II, 121. He judged personal enemies, such as Alexander Hamilton, in a similar light, writing, "Dark and insidious manner did this intriguer [Hamilton] lay schemes against me; and, like the worm at the root of the peach did he labor for twelve years, underground and in darkness." JA to Mercy Warren, 20 July 1807, *Correspondence between John Adams and Mercy Warren*, 334.

38. He criticized even Washington, especially in the late 1790s, when Adams came to believe that Washington was merely Hamilton's puppet. See Ferling, *John Adams*, 424–25.

39. Shaw, *Character of John Adams*, 119.

40. JA, entry, *Diary of John Adams*, II, 367. Adams saw this impulse present throughout American society. He wrote, "Modest merit! Is there such a thing remaining in public life? . . . I am often astonished at the boldness with which persons make their pretensions." JA to James Warren, 5 December 1778, *Warren-Adams Letters*, LXXIII, 71–72.

41. JA to James Warren, 13 April 1783, *Warren-Adams Letters*, LXXIII, 210.

42. JA to Richard Cranch, 23 May 1801, Adams Papers, reel 118.

43. JA to Rush, September 1807, in *Spur of Fame*, 93.

44. JA to William Cunningham, 16 January 1814, in *A Review of the Correspondence between John Adams and William Cunningham*, 10–11.

45. Adams also rejected the Jeffersonian notion of some mystical conception of a completely unified "people." See Ellis, *Passionate Sage*, 129.

46. JA to Mercy Warren, 20 July 1807, *Correspondence between John Adams and Mercy Warren*, 337. In terms of personal sacrifice, Adams would not yield to any man, comparing himself to an animal who has taken "the end of a cord with his teeth, and be drawn slowly up by pullies, through a storm of squibs, crackers, and rockets, flashing and blazing round him every moment; and though the scorching flames made him groan, and mourn, and roar, he would not let go his hold till he had reached the ceiling of a lofty theatre, where he hung some time, still suffering a flight of rockets, and at last descended through another storm of burning powder, and never let go till his four feet were safely landed on the floor." JA, correspondence originally published in the *Boston Patriot*, 10 June 1809, WJA, IX, 310.

47. JA to Mercy Warren, 19 August 1807, *Correspondence between John Adams and Mercy Warren*, 474, 477.

48. JA, diary entry, spring 1772, *Diary of John Adams*, II, 58. Gordon Wood argues in *Creation of the American Republic* that Federalists talked both as if virtue was to be restored and as if it had vanished and needed to be replaced by other things.

49. Jefferson, "The Anas," 2 March 1797, *WTJ*, I, 273.

50. John Adams, unpublished newspaper communication, December 1765, *Diary of John Adams*, I, 282.

51. JA, *Boston Gazette*, 20 January 1766, WJA, III, 475.

52. JA to Abigail Adams, 3 July 1776, *Adams Family Correspondence*, II, 31. He originally thought that Americans would celebrate not the fourth of July but the second, writing Abigail, "The Second Day of July 1776, will be the most memorable Epocha, in the History of America." JA to Abigail Adams, 3 July 1776, *Adams Family Correspondence*, II, 30. He failed to realize at the time the power that the written Declaration would come to exert. Years later, he complained, "The Declaration of Independence I always considered as a theatrical show. Jefferson ran away with all the stage effect of that . . . and all the glory of it." JA to Benjamin Rush, 21 June 1811, in *Spur of Fame*, 181–82. Adams was revealing not simply his fascination with and horror of the power of appearances. He was also revealing his envy and resentment of Jefferson's hallowed place as the author of the Declaration of Independence. In a letter to the Virginian, he wrote that he did not remember the writers of any of the petitions and addresses about which Jefferson inquired. Instead, he downplayed the significance of all such writing: "I was so shallow a politician, that I was not aware of the importance of those compositions. They all appeared to me, in the circumstances of the Country like childrens play at marbles or push pin, or rather like misses in their teens emulating each other in their pearls, their braceletts their Diamond Pins and brussells lace." JA to TJ, 12 November 1813, *Adams-Jefferson Letters*, II, 392. In another letter, though, he felt a need to claim priority over Jefferson, albeit jokingly. Commenting on a letter that he wrote as a boy, he remarked, "It is demonstrative evidence THAT JOHN ADAMS' DECLARATION OF INDEPENDENCE WAS ONE AND TWENTY YEARS OLDER THAN THOMAS JEFFERSON'S." JA to William Cunningham, 27 September 1809, in *A Review of the Correspondence between John Adams and William Cunningham*, 167.

53. JA to General Lincoln, 19 June 1789, Adams Papers, reel 115.

54. JA, "To the Young Men of the City of New York," June 1798, *WJA*, IX, 198–99.

55. JA to Joseph Hawley, 21 August 1776, *WJA*, IX, 434.

56. JA to James Warren, 9 January 1787, *Warren-Adams Letters*, LXXIII, 280.

57. JA to Benjamin Rush, 22 October 1812, reel 118, as cited in Ellis, *Passionate Sage*, 107.

58. He wrote, "Our dear Americans perhaps have as much of it as any Nation now existing, and New England perhaps has more than the rest of America. But I have seen all along my Life Such Selfishness and Littleness even in New England, that I sometimes tremble to think that, altho We are engaged in the best Cause that ever employed the Human Heart yet the Prospect of success is doubtful not for Want of Power or of Wisdom but of Virtue." JA to Mercy Warren, 16 April 1776, *Warren-Adams Letters*, LXXII, 222. Although it is tempting to try to find some pattern to Adams's varied declarations about "the people" (historians who posit a shift in his views often point to a growing pessimism), Adams expressed dejection and even a loss of faith during almost all the difficult periods of his life. For an overview of some of the various "crises" that historians have claimed were turning points, see Shaw, *Character of John Adams*, 96n. 62. Shaw persuasively argues that Adams's views shifted slightly over time, as his pessimism in the American people grew. According to Shaw, he gradually elevated government over the people as a way to foster and renew virtue. Shaw, *Character of John Adams*, 214–17.

59. JA to Abigail Adams, 6 July 1774, *Adams Family Correspondence*, I, 125.

60. For gender and its relation to colonial status, see Susan Juster, "Body and Soul: The Modernist Impulse in American Puritanism," *Reviews in American History* 21 (1993), 19–25.

61. JA to Cunningham, 15 March 1804, in *A Review of the Correspondence between John Adams and William Cunningham*, 19.

62. JA to Abigail Adams, 8 September 1777, *Adams Family Correspondence*, II, 338.

63. JA to Abigail Adams, 6 July 1774, *Adams Family Correspondence*, I, 125.

64. JA to Mercy Warren, 16 April 1776, *Warren-Adams Letters*, LXXII, 223.

65. Abigail Adams to JA, 31 March 1776, *Adams Family Correspondence*, I, 370.

66. JA to Abigail Adams, 14 April 1776, *Adams Family Correspondence*, I, 382.

67. Jan Lewis notes the prevalence of the image of the "republican wife," whose role was to "seduce" her husband to virtue. See Lewis, "The Republican Wife." For the possibilities of a feminine virtue, see also Bloch, "The Gendered Meanings of Virtue."

68. JA to James Sullivan, 26 May 1776, *WJA*, IX, 376.

69. Quoted in Zagarri, "Gender and the First Party System," 121.

70. JA to James Warren, 26 September 1775, *PJA*, III, 168. See Zagarri, "Gender and the First Party System."

71. See Kerber, *Women of the Republic*, and Lewis, "The Republican Wife."

72. JA to Mercy Warren, 16 April 1776, *Warren-Adams Letters*, LXXII, 223.

73. JA to Abigail Adams, 6 July 1774, *Adams Family Correspondence*, I, 125. For Adams, any calamities the country might face would only help decrease this

source of corruption: "And perhaps the Punishment that is inflicted, may work medicinally, and cure the Desease." JA to Abigail Adams, 6 July 1774, *Adams Family Correspondence*, I, 125.

74. JA to Abigail Adams, 3 July 1776, *Adams Family Correspondence*, II, 28. Elevating it to a general principle as early as 1767, he wrote, "Calamities are causticks and catharticks of the body politick. They arouse the soul. They restore original virtues. They reduce a constitution back to its first principles." JA, "Governor Winthrop to Governor Bradford," 26 January 1767, *WJA*, I, 192.

75. JA to Rush, 20 June 1808, in *Spur of Fame*, 110. He complained to Rush another time, "Eternal silence! Impenetrable secrecy! Deep cunning! These are the talents and virtues which are triumphant in these days." JA to Rush, 23 July 1806, in *Spur of Fame*, 59.

76. JA, *Defence of the Constitutions*, *WJA*, VI, 158.

77. He was particularly concerned with radical French theorists and their praise of unicameral legislatures, which gave virtually unlimited power to the people. For Adams's dim view of French Enlightenment thinkers, see Haraszti, *John Adams and the Prophets of Progress*. His worries lagged behind events in America. Forces within Pennsylvania had already begun to mobilize against the state constitution, which was the only one to rely on a unicameral legislature. In his attempt to praise the British Constitution's successful balance among the one, the few, and the many, Adams appeared to be an advocate of a conservative retrenchment and even a return to England's mixed monarchy, even though much of the *Defence* was a direct warning against aristocracy. For a discussion of the European context to which Adams was reacting, see Joyce Appleby, "The New Republican Synthesis and the Changing Political Ideas of John Adams," *American Quarterly* 25.5 (1973): 578–95. See also Thompson, *John Adams and the Spirit of Liberty*, 174–201. The French Revolution, as Appleby notes, revealed the limits of the consensus among Americans about the meaning of the Revolution. By exposing that rift as clearly as anyone with his remarks on the importance of rank, Adams became a symbol to many Americans at the time of retrograde efforts to undo the Revolution. Only in retrospect, according to Appleby, as the fear of institutionalized elites has come to seem illusory, have Adams's ideas appeared irrelevant.

78. In this instance, he seemed to accept this fact with equanimity: "Popularity was never my Mistress, nor was I ever, or shall I ever be a popular Man." JA to James Warren, 9 January 1787, *Warren-Adams Letters*, LXXIII, 281.

79. The *Defence* actually received a number of favorable reviews when first published. But as the political battles of the time escalated and after the publication of his *Discourses on Davila* criticizing many of the innovations of the French Revolution, the book began to be seen by many in a much harsher light. See Thompson, *John Adams and the Spirit of Liberty*, 251–58 and 271–77.

80. JA, *Defence of the Constitutions*, *WJA*, IV, 291–92.

81. JA, *Defence of the Constitutions*, *WJA*, IV, 289.

82. JA, Autobiography, *Diary of John Adams*, III, 411.

83. JA, *Thoughts on Government*, *WJA*, IV, 87.

84. JA, *Defence of the Constitutions*, *WJA*, IV, 284.

85. JA to Rush, 23 July 1806, in *Spur of Fame*, 61.

86. JA to Rush, 27 February 1805, in *Spur of Fame*, 24.

87. Adams's thoughts on the form of government go to the heart of the historical debates over his thinking and are closely related to the debate on Adams's feelings about virtue. Did his principles change as he supposedly grew disenchanted with the American people? Adams himself argued that his principles never changed. But he did propose some significant alterations, for example on the issue of the frequency of elections. In 1776, he had warned, "There is not in all science a maxim more infallible than this, where annual elections end, there slavery begins." JA to John Penn, January 1776, *WJA*, IV, 205. In 1787, though, he wrote to Jefferson, "Elections, my dear sir, Elections to offices which are great objects of ambition, I look at with terror." JA to Jefferson, 9 December 1787, *Adams-Jefferson Letters*, I, 213–14. This difference in sentiment is seen by some as evidence of his growing conservatism. See Appleby, "The New Republican Synthesis." But the two statements can also be seen as pragmatic responses to different dangers. In 1776, as the nation was rebelling against a British government that it felt was deaf to its cries, Adams unsurprisingly viewed elections as a way to make government more responsive. However, by 1787, Adams had become concerned with the problems of overly responsive state governments.

88. JA to Mercy Otis Warren, 8 January 1776, *Warren-Adams Letters*, LXXII, 202.

89. JA, *Defence of the Constitutions*, *WJA*, VI, 209. Adams made the same point earlier in the text, expressing little faith in man's ability to act virtuously without inducement. "There have been examples of self-denial and will be again; but such exalted virtue never yet existed in any large body of men and lasted long." JA, *Defence of the Constitutions* (New York: Da Capo Press, 1971), III, 289.

90. JA, *Defence of the Constitutions* (New York: Da Capo Press, 1971), III, 504–5. Adams wrote, "I am not often satisfied with the opinions of Hume, but in this he seems well founded, that all projects of government founded in the supposition or expectation of extraordinary degrees of virtue are evidently chimerical." JA to Samuel Adams, 18 October 1790, *WJA*, VI, 415.

91. JA to Mercy Warren, 16 April 1776, *Warren-Adams Letters*, LXXII, 222.

92. JA to Mercy Warren, 8 January 1776, *Warren-Adams Letters*, LXXII, 202. Unsurprisingly, Adams assumed that living under such a government would be a sacrifice for himself. He wrote, "Altho it will infallibly beggar me and my Children, will produce Strength, Hardiness Activity, Courage, Fortitude and Enterprise; the manly noble and Sublime Qualities in human Nature, in Abundance." JA to Mercy Warren, 8 January 1776, *Warren-Adams Letters*, I, 201–2.

93. JA, entry, 31 December 1772, *Diary of John Adams*, II, 75. For other references to Hercules, see *Diary of John Adams* I, 72, 102–3. Adams even proposed putting Hercules on the national seal.

94. JA, entry, 19 February 1756, *Diary of John Adams*, I, 8.

95. Adams's skepticism about disinterestedness was shared by others. See Gordon S. Wood, "Interests and Disinterestedness in the Making of the Constitution," in *Beyond Confederation*, ed. Beeman et al., 69–112.

96. Editor's note, *WJA*, IX, 533.

97. JA to John Jebb, 21 August 1785, *WJA*, IX, 533. He expressed the same feeling again later in the letter. Adams's fears centered on the aristocracy, the most dangerous threat, he thought at the time, to republican government.

98. JA to John Jebb, 21 August 1785, *WJA*, IX, 533–34.

99. JA to John Jebb, 25 September 1785, *WJA*, IX, 544.

100. JA to John Jebb, 10 September 1785, *WJA*, IX, 542.

101. JA to John Jebb, 21 August 1785, *WJA*, IX, 535. Adams did believe in the possibility of disinterested service, but he claimed that it existed very rarely: "One in two or three ages; certainly not enough to watch over the rights of mankind, for these have been lost in almost all ages and nations." JA to John Jebb, 10 September 1785, *WJA*, IX, 539.

102. JA to John Jebb, 10 September 1785, *WJA*, IX, 539.

103. Adams criticized even Washington's motives, finding in the Virginian's retirement the spring behind all human action, the passion for distinction: "In wiser and more virtuous times, he would not have had [the ambition of retiring], for that is an ambition." JA to John Jebb, 10 September 1785, *WJA*, IX, 541–42.

104. JA to John Jebb, 10 September 1785, *WJA*, IX, 541–42.

105. In many ways, the entire revolutionary period was a sustained debate on the meaning of words, such as republican, liberty, power, government, and independence, and Adams turned a critical eye on a number of central words in the revolutionary lexicon. When questioned about his adherence to republican principles, Adams's first impulse was to question what exactly republicanism meant: "I confess I never understood it, and I believe no other man ever did or ever will." JA to Mercy Warren, 20 July 1807, *Warren-Adams Letters*, II, 353. According to Adams, the instabilities in language allowed politicians to use words to deceive, creating one more veil that the virtuous man had to tear asunder. See JA, *Defence of the Constitutions* (1971), III, 283. See Thompson, *John Adams and the Spirit of Liberty*, and Diggins, *Lost Soul of American Politics*, chapter 3.

106. JA to Rush, 28 August 1811, *WJA*, IX, 636.

107. JA to John Jebb, 21 August 1785, *WJA*, IX, 535.

108. JA to John Jebb, 10 September 1785, *WJA*, IX, 538–40.

109. JA to John Jebb, 25 September 1785, *WJA*, IX, 543.

110. The lower levels of government service began to be staffed this way earlier than the elite levels. This was particularly evident in the military. See William B. Skelton, *An American Profession of Arms: The Army Officer Corps, 1784–1815* (Lawrence: University Press of Kansas, 1992), and Lawrence Delbert Cress, *Citizens in Arms: The Army and the Militia in American Society to the War of 1812* (Chapel Hill: University of North Carolina Press, 1982).

111. According to Thompson, Adams considered the *Discourses* as the fourth volume of his *Defence*. Thompson, *John Adams and the Spirit of Liberty*, 298.

112. Joyce Appleby argues that Adams shifted decisively in his views on deference and rank after reading Jean Louis De Lolme's *Constitution of England*. See Appleby, "The New Republican Synthesis." Adams did lose touch to some extent with American sensibilities while he was in Europe, but his ideas about human nature, especially man's passion for distinction, were largely formed before he read De Lolme. Adams's differing statements can be read as signs of his ambivalence about rank and status.

113. JA to James Warren, 22 April 1776, *Warren-Adams Letters*, LXXII, 234.

114. For the importance of fame to the founders, see Douglass Adair, "Fame and the Founding Fathers," in *Fame and the Founding Fathers*, ed. Colbourn,

3–26. Adams saw this desire as equal to actual physical needs: "The desire of the esteem of others is as real a want of nature as hunger; and the neglect and contempt of the world as severe a pain as the gout or stone. It sooner and oftener produces despair, and a detestation of existence" (234).

115. Alexander Hamilton represents a striking contrast. See Gerald Stourzh, *Alexander Hamilton and the Idea of Republican Government* (Stanford, Calif.: Stanford University Press, 1970), particularly 95–106.

116. JA to TJ, 6 December 1787, *Adams-Jefferson Letters* I, 213.

117. JA to TJ, 15 November 1813, *Adams-Jefferson Letters*, II, 398.

118. JA, *Defence of the Constitutions*, WJA, IV, 290.

119. JA to TJ, 19 December 1813, *Adams-Jefferson Letters*, II, 409.

120. JA, *Discourses on Davila*, 1790, WJA, VI, 491–92. All future page references included in the text.

121. Adams was decisively influenced in his views by Adams Smith's *Theory of Moral Sentiments*. Smith argued that men were motivated to achieve wealth and honors primarily in order to obtain the approval of their fellow men. A number of essays in Adams's *Discourses on Davila* were drawn, sometimes verbatim, from Smith's work. In fact, at least three-fourths of his two major works, the *Defence* and the *Discourses*, are direct quotations from other authors. See Haraszti, *John Adams and the Prophets of Progress*, 46–47.

122. Adams's views were not the outgrowth of a deepening pessimism about his fellow countrymen. Instead, they were based on a consistent understanding of human nature. Even during the Revolution, Adams wrote, "Ambition in a Republic . . . is but another name for . . . Virtue." JA to [James Warren?], 27 April 1777, Adams Papers, reel 91, as cited in Shaw, *Character of John Adams*, 235. In fact, without the desire for attention, Adams believed man would never excel at anything (246).

123. See Thompson, *John Adams and the Spirit of Liberty*, 222–28.

124. James Hutson writes that Adams saw the main problem with the new federal government as its unattractiveness, and he thought titles would be a way to entice the best people as well as to isolate the aristocracy in the Senate. James Hutson, "John Adams' Title Campaign," *The New England Quarterly* 41.1 (March 1968): 30–39.

125. JA, *Discourses on Davila*, WJA, VI, 105.

126. See Elkins and McKitrick, *Age of Federalism*, 48. Some suggested even more grandiose titles, including "His Elective Majesty" and "His Mightiness." See *The Papers of George Washington: Presidential Series*, 9 vols., ed. W. W. Abbot et al. (Charlottesville: University of Virginia Press, 1987–), II, 249n. Hereafter *PGW*. For a discussion of the debates on titles and other matters of etiquette, see Freeman, *Affairs of Honor*, 11–61.

127. GW to David Stuart, 26 July 1789, *PGW*, III, 323. In the same letter, Washington also remarked that creating a title for the presidency was "contrary to my opinion."

128. William Maclay, *Diary*, 33 and 11.

129. Franklin to Robert Livingston, 22 July 1783, *Writings of Benjamin Franklin*, 10 vols., ed. Albert Henry Smyth (New York: Macmillan Company, 1905–7), IX, 62.

130. Larzer Ziff discusses this in the context of a larger shift from immanence to representation. See Ziff, *Writing in the New Nation*, particularly 71–75.

131. JA, *Defence of the Constitutions*, *WJA*, VI, 219. No less an authority than Alexis de Tocqueville described a Jacksonian America that seemed strikingly similar to the one that Adams envisioned. Tocqueville wrote, "The doctrine of self-interest. . . . If it does not lead the will directly to virtue, it establishes habits which unconsciously turn it that way." Alexis de Tocqueville, *Democracy in America*, ed. J. P. Mayer (Garden City, N.Y.: Anchor Books, 1969), 527.

132. For a discussion of Warren and her *History*, see Lester Cohen, "Explaining the Revolution: Ideology and Ethics in Mercy Otis Warren's Historical Theory," *William and Mary Quarterly* 37.2 (April 1980): 200–18, and Lester Cohen, "Mercy Otis Warren: The Politics of Language and the Aesthetics of Self," *American Quarterly* 35.5 (winter 1983): 481–98.

133. JA to Mercy Warren, 11 July 1807, *Correspondence between John Adams and Mercy Warren*, 321.

134. JA to Mercy Warren, 27 July 1807, *Correspondence between John Adams and Mercy Warren*, 335–54, and JA to Mercy Warren, 20 July 1807, *Correspondence between John Adams and Mercy Warren*, 354.

135. JA to Benjamin Rush, 14 May 1812, in *Spur of Fame*, 216.

CHAPTER FOUR
Justice

1. JM, *Federalist #51*, 6 February 1788, *PJM*, X, 479.

2. Daniel Howe writes, "The interlocking relationships among various disciplines within moral philosophy made it all the easier for Publius to base on his concepts of applied psychology both his ideas about good government and his techniques for persuading men to adopt it." Daniel Howe, "The Political Psychology of the Federalist," *William and Mary Quarterly* 44.3 (July 1987): 489. For a discussion of how strong texts teach and, indeed, create their ideal readers, see White, *When Words Lose Their Meaning*.

3. AH, *Federalist #1*, 27 October 1787, *PAH*, IV, 301–2.

4. Unsurprisingly, Jefferson had a far more optimistic view of how to achieve justice. Whereas Madison saw a need to construct government to ensure justice, Jefferson thought it would emerge naturally from human nature, writing that "it is instinct, and innate, that the moral sense is as much a part of our constitution as that of feeling, seeing, or hearing." TJ to JA, 14 October 1816, *Adams-Jefferson Letters*, II, 492.

5. Irving, *Washington Irving*, 144. Thomas Gustafson writes that the United States was a country "united by a text but divided over its interpretation." Gustafson, *Representative Words*, 10. David Currie writes that the first few congresses were almost like a continuing constitutional convention, charged with giving meaning to the bare text of the Constitution itself. David Currie, *The Constitution in Congress: The Federalist Period, 1789–1801* (Chicago: University of Chicago Press, 1997). For the importance of language to the American political project, see Kenneth Cmiel, *Democratic Eloquence* (New York: W. Morrow,

1990); Gustafson, *Representative Words*; and David Simpson, *The Politics of American English, 1776–1850* (Oxford: Oxford University Press, 1986).

6. JM, *Federalist #37*, 11 January 1788, *PJM*, X, 359. All other quotes from *Federalist #37* are from this source and will be cited in the text.

7. For the definitions, see the *Oxford English Dictionary*. My understanding of candor is drawn from Furtwangler, who argues that Publius was interested in fostering candor almost as an end in itself. See Albert Furtwangler, *The Authority of Publius: A Reading of the Federalist Papers* (Ithaca, N.Y.: Cornell University Press, 1984), 62 ff.

8. This literary context for the *Federalist Papers* is drawn from Furtwangler, *Authority of Publius,* 87–97. For print as a means of creating a public sphere, see Furtwangler, *Authority of Publius,* chapter 2; Warner, *Letters of the Republic*; and Habermas, *Structural Transformation of the Public Sphere.*

9. The essay as a genre began to take shape during the Renaissance. For discussions of the essay as genre, see Michael Hall, "The Emergence of the Essay and the Idea of Discovery," in *Essays on the Essay: Redefining the Genre*, ed. Alexander Butrym (Athens: University of Georgia Press, 1989), 78. The rise of the essay has also been tied to the rise of modern, bourgeois individualism. See Claire de Obaldia, *The Essayistic Spirit: Literature, Modern Criticism, and the Essay* (Oxford: Clarendon Press, 1995). For the essay's use in constructing identity, see Alan de Gooyer, "'Selves by Way of Essay': Apprehensions of the Self in the Early English Essayists" (Ph.D. dissertation, University of Virginia, 1994). In many ways, political essays and pamphlets were the great American art of the late eighteenth century. Complaints about the weakness of literature in the early republic fail to account for the strength of public documents, where Americans showed what Robert Ferguson calls a "precocious intellectual maturity." See Ferguson's section in *The Cambridge History of American Literature*, 473. See also Robert Ferguson, *Law and Letters in American Culture* (Cambridge, Mass.: Harvard University Press, 1984), and William Hedges, "The Myth of the Republic and the Theory of American Literature," *Prospects* 4 (1979): 101–20. The Constitution itself can be seen as the crystallization of an American genre, the masterwork of men who had spent most of their adult lives honing their skills in political writing. See Ferguson, "'We Do Ordain and Establish.'" For a critique of this argument, see Michael Les Benedict, "Our 'Sacred' Constitution—Another View of the Constitution as Literary Text," *William and Mary Law Review* 29.1 (1987): 27–34.

10. Madison unsurprisingly treated legislative writing with similar precision. The federal Constitution created by Madison and his fellow delegates was a model of brevity, so much so that Antifederalists complained of the potential for abuses of power hidden in the Constitution's compressed phrases. Madison realized that legislative ambiguities were not necessarily solved through more legislation. In fact, they were often worsened, because they provided more text for interpretation. In Madison's view, less was definitely more. He noted, "A review of the several Codes will shew that every necessary and useful part of the least voluminous of them might be compressed into one tenth of the compass, and at the same time be rendered ten fold as perspicuous." JM, "Vices of the Political System," April 1787, *PJM*, IX, 355.

11. Blair, *Lectures*, 410–11. Madison's *Notes on the Federal Convention* reveal the gaping difference between the writing and personal styles of Adams and Madison. Adams's diary shows his constant need to express himself. Even in his reading, Adams scribbled in the margins of the book, unable even in someone else's work to remain silent. In stark contrast, Madison's *Notes* hardly reveal who the author is and often understate Madison's own role.

12. Hugh Blair Grigsby, *The Virginia Convention of 1776* (Richmond, 1855), 182.

13. Warner, *Republic of Letters*, 108, 113. Madison's use of the essay illustrates Warner's argument about the importance of impersonality to the emancipatory power of print culture. Warner is persuasive in this context.

14. Garry Wills, *Explaining America: The Federalist* (New York: Penguin Books, 1982), 22.

15. Before beginning the *Federalist* essays, Hamilton's first foray into the debate over ratification was a clumsy personal effort. Suspecting that New York governor George Clinton was organizing opposition to the proposed Constitution, Hamilton wrote a long, unsigned letter attacking Clinton, which was printed in a New York paper. In a second published letter a few weeks later, he admitted his authorship, again attacked Clinton as an enemy of the Constitution, and challenged Clinton to deny the accusation. Hamilton also promised to give proof of his charges. Treating the entire controversy more as an affair of honor than as a broad public debate, Hamilton succeeded only in provoking opposition as well as a number of personal attacks. See Furtwangler, *Authority of Publius*, 46–49. In contrast, Publius strived to achieve the pose of objectivity. Hamilton himself wrote in *Federalist #85*, "It is certain that I have frequently felt a struggle between sensibility and moderation, and if the former has in some instances prevailed, it must be my excuse that it has been neither often nor much." AH, *Federalist #85*, 28 May 1788, *PAH*, IV, 716. Sensibility in this case was something to be apologized for, not encouraged.

16. JM, *Federalist #54*, 12 February 1788, *PJM*, X, 503.

17. Publius refers to specific Antifederalists by name only seven times, although implicitly the essays are often responses to Antifederalist critiques. For example, Emery G. Lee III argues that *Federalist #10* should be read as a response to the first essay of the Antifederalist Brutus. See Lee, "Representation, Virtue, and Political Jealousy in the Brutus-Publius Dialogue," *Journal of Politics* 59 (1997): 1073–95. See also Murray Dry, "Anti-Federalism in *The Federalist*: A Founding Dialogue on the Constitution, Republican Government, and Federalism," in *Saving the Revolution: The Federalist Papers and the American Founding*, ed. Charles Kesler (New York: Free Press, 1987), 40–60.

18. John Locke, *An Essay Concerning Human Understanding*, 2 vols., ed. Alexander Campbell Fraser (Oxford: Clarendon Press, 1894), II, 146.

19. Martha Bland to Mrs. St. George Tucker, 30 March 1781, *Virginia Magazine of History and Biography* 43 (1935): 43.

20. Richard Matthews argues that this kind of control represented Madison's ideal of government: *sine ira et studio*, or formalistic impersonality. Richard Matthews, *If Men Were Angels: James Madison and the Heartless Empire of Reason* (Lawrence: University Press of Kansas, 1995), 188. Forrest McDonald claims that Madison was "so carefully contrived and controlled that in comparison

to him Hamilton, Jefferson, and even Burr were open books." Forrest McDonald, *The Presidency of George Washington* (Lawrence: University Press of Kansas, 1974), 31.

21. Frances Hutcheson, in discussing man's various faculties, wrote, "They form a machine, most accurately subservient to the necessities, convenience, and happiness of a rational system." Frances Hutcheson, *An Essay on the Nature and Conduct of the Passions and Affections* . . . (1742), ed. Paul McReynolds (Gainesville, Fla.: Scholar's, Facsimiles and Reprints, 1969), 183.

22. Benjamin Rush, "Of the Mode of Education Proper in a Republic," 1786, in *Essays Literary, Moral and Philosophical*, ed. Michael Meranze (Schenectady, N.Y.: Union College Press, 1988), 9.

23. Edward Coles to Hugh Blair Grigsby, 23 December 1854, in Rives Papers, Library of Congress, box 85, as cited in Drew McCoy, *The Last of the Fathers: James Madison and the Republican Legacy* (New York: Cambridge University Press, 1989).

24. JM, "James Madison's Autobiography," ed. Douglass Adair, *William and Mary Quarterly* 2.2 (1945): 209.

25. JM to TJ, 17 October 1788, *Republic of Letters*, I, 565.

26. JM, *Federalist #43*, 23 January 1788, *PJM*, X, 416. Jay, Hamilton, and Madison each pointed out in different *Federalist* essays the national government's ability to be an "umpire" of state conflicts. See Jay in #4 and Hamilton in #7.

27. Analysis of the Bill of Rights reveals a similar purpose—not so much a pro-toliberal endorsement of individual rights, but a continued structural concern with government, specifically enacting measures to force the government to conform to his ideal vision of a just government, one that would adjudicate in disinterested fashion. The paradigmatic image underlying the Bill of Rights was the jury, once again recurring to Madison's ideal model of the impartial umpire of disputes. It found its way into Amendments 5, 6, and 7, and its absence influences 1, 4, and 8. See Akhil Reed Amar, "The Bill of Rights as a Constitution," *Yale Law Journal* 100.5 (March 1991): 1131–210. For Madison, the Bill of Rights offered one final opportunity to instruct citizens.

28. JM to TJ, 24 October and 1 November 1787, *Republic of Letters*, I, 502. He argued against Jefferson's remedy of a larger legislative body, asking if "two thousand individuals be less apt to oppress one thousand?" JM to TJ, 24 October and 1 November 1787, *Republic of Letters*, I, 501. He would take a similar stance as Publius, convinced that the dynamics of groups were analogous to those of individuals. See Howe, "The Political Psychology of the Federalist," 495.

29. JM to GW, 16 April 1787, *PJM*, IX, 384. At the convention, he argued strenuously but unsuccessfully for a federal veto of state laws, because it would provide a means for the national government to act as an impartial judge of state law. A federal veto would also solve the vexing constitutional problem of the division of sovereignty between the states and the national government. He wrote, "The impossibility of dividing powers of legislation, in such a manner, as to be free from different constructions by different interests, or even from ambiguity in the judgment of the impartial, requires some such expedient as I contend for." JM to TJ, 24 October 1787, *PJM*, X, 206. See Matthews, *If Men Were Angels*.

30. JM, *Federalist #57*, 19 February 1788, *PJM*, X, 521. For a discussion of Madison's conception of the good republican ruler, see Leonard Sorenson, "Madison on Sympathy, Virtue, and Ambition in the *Federalist Papers*," *Polity* 27 (1995): 431–46.

31. JM, "Speech on the revisionary power of the executive and the judiciary" (recorded by Rufus King), 4 June 1787, *PJM*, X, 25. Such a view had a respectable intellectual pedigree, recalling Bolingbroke's idea of the patriot king, who played a similar role.

32. JM, "Vices of the political system of the United States," April 1787, *PJM*, IX, 356.

33. JM, *Federalist #10*, 22 November 1787, *PJM*, X, 267.

34. See Morgan, "The Puritan Ethic and the American Revolution," 877; Jack Rakove, *Original Meanings: Politics and Ideas in the Making of the Constitution* (New York: Vintage, 1996), 203–43; and Isaac Kramnick, "The 'Great National Discussion'."

35. JM, *Federalist #10*, 22 November 1787, *PJM*, X, 268.

36. JM, *Federalist #54*, 12 February 1788, *PJM*, X, 503.

37. JM to TJ, 24 October and 1 November 1787, *Republic of Letters*, I, 502.

38. For the type of men who served in the early congresses, see Jack Rakove, "The Structure of Politics at the Accession of George Washington," in *Beyond Confederation*, ed. Beeman et al., 261–94.

39. Callender, *Philadelphia Gazette*, 31 May 1794, *PJM*, XV, 157.

40. Wills, *Explaining America*. For a discussion of the benefits of "nonfactious" factions in Madison's thought, see James Yoho, "Madison on the Beneficial Effects of Interest Groups: What Was Left Unsaid in Federalist 10," *Polity* 27 (1995): 587–605.

41. All quotes from JM, *Federalist #10*, 22 November 1787, *PJM*, X, 263–70.

42. Robert Dahl writes of *#10* that it was a "compactly logical, almost mathematical piece of theory." Dahl, *Preface to Democratic Theory* (Chicago: University of Chicago Press, 1956), 5. Wills has attributed Madison's dense logic to classical writing patterns of antithetical particles, with *#10* involving antithesis and correlation in almost every sentence, giving a sense of complex relations properly maintained. Wills, *Explaining America*.

43. In legal terms, parties by definition were excluded from decision making— at the time, the term was mainly used to mean "party to" some transaction, the opposite of impartial. Wills, *Explaining America*, 210.

44. For an attempt to address this flaw, see Stephen Elkin, "Madison and After: The American Model of Political Constitution," *Political Studies* 44 (1996): 592–604.

45. Allgor notes, "Women performed the dirty work of politics to ensure their husbands' political purity." See Allgor, *Parlor Politics*, 48–101 (quotation from 145).

46. McCoy, *Last of the Fathers*, 225–40. Without ever launching a substantive assault on enslavement, many Virginians absolved themselves of the guilt they felt through their written attempts to deal with the issue. Unlike those other Virginians (most notably Jefferson), Madison eventually abandoned any effort to write his way out of the problem.

47. Unlike Adams, Madison was not unduly concerned with the people's virtue. In the *Federalist Papers*, Madison's most extended opportunity to discuss the relationship between government and society, he had little to say about private morality or about the relationship between government and virtue. See Howe, "The Political Psychology of the Federalist," 506, 509.

48. JM to TJ, 9 December 1787, *PJM*, X 313.

49. JM, *Federalist #10*, 22 November 1787, *PJM*, X, 269–70. Wood argues that Madison believed that the people had the right and the virtue to vote responsibly, but he questioned whether they had the requisite abilities to perform the duties of statesmen. Wood, *Creation of the American Republic*, 599, 506, and 61.

50. JM, *Federalist #55*, 13 February 1788, *PJM*, X, 508. At the Virginia ratifying convention, Madison again refused to concede the Antifederalists' bleak vision: "But I go on this great republican principle, that the people will have virtue and wisdom. Is there no virtue among us? If there be not, we are in a wretched situation. No theoretical checks, no form of government, can render us secure." JM in *The Debates in the Several State Conventions on the Adoption of the Federal Constitution*, 5 vols., ed. Jonathan Elliot (Philadelphia: Lippincott, 1876), III, 536–37, cited in Matthews, *If Men Were Angels*, 217.

51. Jack Rakove writes, "A fear of the impulsive and dangerous influence that public opinion could exert over legislation lay at the core of this thinking in 1787 and 1788; indeed, it does not go too far to say that he regarded the neutralization of public opinion, or at least the creation of proper mechanisms for its safe expression, as the great desideratum of republican constitutionalism." Rakove, *Original Meanings*, 139. For a discussion of how Madison and Alexander Hamilton rhetorically shaped the concept of popular sovereignty to win approval of the Constitution, even as they tried to insulate it from the effects of widespread political participation, see Joshua Miller, "The Ghostly Body Politic: The Federalist Papers and Popular Sovereignty," *Political Theory* 16 (1988): 99–119.

52. In his famous letter in which he argued that "the earth belongs in usufruct to the living," Jefferson made the case for throwing off the hand of the past, of letting each new generation create its own laws and institutions, making him a supporter of frequent constitutional conventions. For an extended discussion of Jefferson's ideas on this issue, see Herbert Sloan, "The Earth Belongs in Usufruct to the Living,"" in *Jeffersonian Legacies*, ed. Onuf, 281–315. For an extended treatment of the significant differences between Jefferson and Madison, see Matthews, *If Men Were Angels*.

53. JM to TJ, 17 October 1788, *Republic of Letters*, I, 564. For a discussion of Madison's views of the threat that majority rule posed for republican liberty, see David O'Brien, "The Framers' Muse on Republicanism, the Supreme Court, and Pragmatic Constitutional Interpretivism," *The Review of Politics* 53 (1991): 251–88.

54. In 1788, when asked to comment on Jefferson's proposed constitution for Virginia, published in Jefferson's *Notes on the State of Virginia*, Madison wrote an extended critique. Perhaps the clearest expression of his greater emphasis on stability was in his criticism of Jefferson's suggestion that senators be elected to two-year terms. Madison argued that the Senate needed longer terms to "maintain

that system and steadiness in public affairs without which no Government can prosper or be respectable." JM to John Brown, Observations on the "Draught of a Constitution" [ca. 15 October 1788], *PJM*, XI, 285. He argued in a similar fashion to Caleb Wallace in 1785, advising that a senate should give *"wisdom* and *steadiness* to legislation." JM to Caleb Wallace, 23 August 1785, *PJM*, VIII, 350. He made the same point to Jefferson when defending the proposed federal Constitution. See JM to TJ, 8 October 1788, *Republic of Letters*, I, 555.

55. JM, *Federalist #49*, 2 February 1788, *PJM*, X, 460–64.

56. JM, *Federalist #49*, 2 February 1788, *PJM*, X, 463.

57. JM to Edmund Randolph, 10 January 1788, *PJM*, X, 355.

58. JM, *Federalist #49*, 2 February 1788, *PJM*, X, 461–62.

59. For the battles over the meaning of the Constitution, particularly language disputes, see Gustafson, *Representative Words*, chapter 8.

60. Madison's creative defense is still embraced by some today. Laurence Tribe writes of the Constitution, "Perhaps it speaks in the words of Walt Whitman: 'Do I contradict myself? Very well then, I contradict myself, I am large. I contain multitudes.'" Laurence Tribe, "The Idea of the Constitution: A Metaphor-morphosis," *Journal of Legal Education* 37 (1987): 173.

61. Jefferson also held this view. Following Scottish commonsense philosophy, Jefferson believed that language could be made transparent simply by sharing a desire for mutual understanding, problematically relying on sincerity once again.

62. JM, *Federalist #14*, 30 November 1787, *PJM*, X, 285. Alexander Hamilton, *Federalist #31*, 1 January 1788, *PAH*, IV, 457.

63. Michael Kramer, *Imagining Language in America: From the Revolution to the Civil War* (Princeton, N.J.: Princeton University Press, 1992), 132.

64. For an excellent discussion of *Federalist #37* as the only paper to take a Lockean position emphasizing the problems inherent in language, see Kramer, *Imagining America*, chapter 4. In his *Essay on Human Understanding*, John Locke devoted a whole section to the problem of language, titled "Of Words." In it, he warned that words "interpose themselves so much between our understandings, and the truth . . . that . . . [their] obscurity and disorder do not seldom cast a mist before our eyes, and impose upon our understanding." See John Locke, *An Essay Concerning Human Understanding*, 2 vols., ed. Alexander Campbell Fraser (Oxford: Clarendon Press, 1894), II, 119. According to Perry Miller, "For two or three generations after 1690 practically all theorizing upon language attempted by English or colonial American writers, and much of that on the Continent, was a reworking or reinterpretation of Locke." Perry Miller, *Errand into the Wilderness* (New York: Harper and Row, 1964), 168.

65. Ferguson argues that the point of #37 is that "real agreement becomes impossible without manipulation and design." Ferguson, "'We Do Ordain and Establish,'" 8.

66. JM, Federalist #49, 2 February 1788, *PJM*, X, 462. As David Hume wrote, in an essay that Madison undoubtedly read, "Nothing appears more surprizing to those, who consider human affairs with a philosophical eye, than the easiness with which the many are governed by the few; and the implicit submission, with which men resign their own sentiments and passions to those of their rulers. When we enquire by what means this wonder is effected, we shall find, that, as

FORCE is always on the side of the governed, the governors have nothing to support them but opinion. It is therefore, on opinion only that government is founded." Hume, "Of the First Principles of Government," in *Essays Moral, Political, and Literary*, ed. T. H. Green and T. H. Grose (Ann Arbor: University Microfilms, 1996), 109. For the importance of opinion as the basis of government, see Garry Wills, *Cincinnatus: George Washington and the Enlightenment* (Garden City, N.Y.: Doubleday, 1984), 100–103.

67. JM, *Records of the Federal Convention of 1787*, II, 192.

68. Once again, Jefferson had a far different view of constitutions than his friend, arguing that the nation's republicanism was "in the spirit of our people, not in our constitution certainly." He attacked the veneration that Madison was calling for, noting that "some men look at constitutions with sanctimonious reverence, and deem them like the ark of the covenant, too sacred to be touched. . . . forty years of experience in government is worth a century of book-reading." TJ to Samuel Kercheval, 12 July 1816, *WTJ*, XV, 35, 40. His attitude was not as dismissive as Hamilton's, though. The New Yorker called paper constitutions such as the U.S. Constitution "frail and worthless fabrics," arguing that the crucial matter was organizing the government in such a way as to give it as much power as possible. See Forrest McDonald, *Alexander Hamilton: A Biography* (New York: W. W. Norton and Company, 1982), chapter 5, for an exploration of Hamilton's thinking on this issue. For an excellent exploration of Madison's constitutionalism, see McCoy, *Last of the Fathers*, chapter 3.

69. JM, "Public Opinion," 19 December 1791, *PJM*, XIV, 170.

70. JM to M. L. Hurlbert, May 1830, *Letters and Other Writings of James Madison*, 4 vols. (New York: Worthington, 1984), IV, 75. Hereafter *WJM*.

71. JM to N. P. Trist, December 1831, *WJM*, IV, 211.

72. JM to Judge Spencer Roane, 6 May 1821, *WJM*, III, 221.

73. JM to Martin Hurlbert, May 1830, *WJM*, IX, 372.

74. JM to H. Lee, 25 June 1824, *WJM*, III, 442.

75. McCoy has noted, "Many of his letters—especially those that considered constitutional issues and the nature of the Union—were addressed as much to posterity as to the nominal recipient. We might say, indeed, that Madison's self-conscious effort to preserve an eighteenth-century legacy became the burden of his retirement, which was in effect no retirement from public life at all." McCoy, *Last of the Fathers*, 74.

76. For a discussion of original intent, see Rakove, *Original Meanings*, chapter 11. See also H. Jefferson Powell, "The Original Understanding of Original Intent," *Harvard Law Review* 98.5 (March 1985): 885–948.

77. JM to Thomas Ritchie, 15 September 1821, *WJM*, III, 228.

78. JM to N. P. Trist, December 1831, *WJM*, IV, 211. See also JM to Henry Lee, 25 June 1824, *WJM*, III, 442.

79. JM, *Debates and Proceedings in the Congress of the United States, 1789–1824*, ed. Joseph Gales (Washington, D.C., 1834–56), 4th Congress, 1st session, 776.

80. JM to Thomas Ritchie, 15 September 1821, *WJM*, III, 228.

81. JM to H. Lee, 25 June 1824, *WJM*, III, 442. The Constitution did eventually become an object of veneration, although that veneration was not necessarily a

sign of understanding. See Michael Kammen, *A Machine That Would Go of Itself: The Constitution in American Culture* (New York: Knopf, 1986).

82. JM to N. P. Trist, 2 March 1827, *WJM*, III, 565. Such an attitude toward the document would make it, as Madison called it in his first inaugural, "the cement of the Union." Madison, in James D. Richardson, ed., *A Compilation of the Messages and Papers of the Presidents, 1789–1897* (Washington, D.C., 1896), I, 467–68.

83. JM, *Federalist #14*, 30 November 1787, *PJM*, X, 288.

84. For an excellent account of Madison's final years, see McCoy, *Last of the Fathers.*

85. TJ to Abigail Adams, 11 September 1804. For "judges as ultimate arbiters of all constitutional questions," as a "very dangerous doctrine" that would "place us under the despotism of oligarchy," see TJ to William Jarvis, 28 September 1820, *WTJ*, XV, 277.

86. JM to TJ, 27 June 1823, *WJM*, III, 326–27. See also JM to Edward Everett, August 1830, *WJM*, III, 97–98.

87. JM to Robert Garnett, 11 February 1824, *WJM*, III, 367.

88. JM to Edward Livingston, 17 April 1824, *WJM*, III, 436.

89. JM to Edward Livingston, 17 April 1824, *WJM*, III, 436.

90. JM to Edward Livingston, 17 April 1824, *WJM*, III, 436. What Madison saw as a problem, Jefferson embraced as a strength. Jefferson was a firm proponent of neology, itself a neologism at the time. He called himself a "zealous [friend] to *Neology*," because only then could language express "every shade of idea, distinctly perceived by the mind." TJ to John Waldo, 16 August 1813, *Writings*, 1295, 1299. He argued that attempting to fix language permanently would halt progress: "Had the preposterous idea of fixing the language been adopted by our Saxon ancestors, . . . the progress of ideas must have stopped with that of the language. On the contrary, nothing is more evident than that as we advance in the knowledge of new things, and of new combinations of old ones, we must have new words to express them." TJ to Joseph Milligan, 6 April 1816, *WTJ*, XIV, 463.

91. JM to Daniel Webster, 27 May 1830, *WJM*, IV, 85.

92. JM to Judge Roane, 2 September 1819, in *The Mind of the Founder: Sources of the Political Thought of James Madison*, ed. Marvin Meyers (Indianapolis: Bobbs-Merrill Company, 1973), 361. Madison praised the work of dictionary maker and language fixer Noah Webster. "Whilst few things are more difficult, few are more desirable than a standard work, explaining, and as far as possible fixing, the meaning of words and phrases," he wrote. "How many important errors may be produced by mere innovations in the use of words and phrases, if not controulable by a recurrence to the original and authentic meaning attached to them." JM to Converse Sherman, 10 March 1826, *WJM*, III, 519. Webster saw his dictionary as a means of creating a stable polity as much as a stable language, writing, "Our political harmony is concerned in a uniformity of language." Noah Webster, *Dissertations on the English Language* (Boston: Isaiah Thomas, 1789), 20. The task of creating a stable language was a larger cultural project that engaged many early Americans. Hugh Henry Brackenridge declared in his picaresque novel *Modern Chivalry* that he was going to attempt what "dictionaries" and "Institutes"

had failed to do—"Fix the English language." Adams also hoped to secure a better political world through a more stable linguistic one, calling for an "American Academy for refining, improving, and ascertaining the English language." JA, "To the President of Congress," 5 September 1780, *WJA*, VII, 250.

93. JM to N. P. Trist, 2 March 1827, *WJM*, III, 565.

94. JM to McDuffie, 30 March 1830, *WJM*, IV, 70.

95. JM to Professor Davis (unsent), 1832, *WJM*, IV, 242.

96. JM to H. Lee, 25 June 1824, *WJM*, III, 442.

97. JM to Converse Sherman, 10 March 1826, *WJM*, III, 519.

98. JM, 1833, as cited in Gustafson, *Representative Words*, 283.

99. JM to Edward Livingston, 17 April 1824, *WJM*, III, 436.

100. JM to N. P. Trist, 2 March 1827, *WJM*, III, 565.

101. JM to Andrew Stevenson, 25 March 1826, *WJM*, III, 522.

102. JM to N. P. Trist, 2 March 1827, *WJM*, III, 565.

103. Sir Francis Bacon, *The Advancement of Learning*, ed. G. W. Kitchin (London: J. M. Dent and Sons, 1934), 134.

CONCLUSION
Veneration

1. While party politics would still make ample use of character, it no longer held preeminent place in the political world.

2. GW to Jonathan Trumbull, 21 July 1799, *WGW*, XXXVII, 312–14. For an exploration of how Republicans self-consciously rejected the veneration of individuals, particularly Washington, who had become a Federalist symbol, in favor of principles, see Simon Newman, "Principles or Men? George Washington and the Political Culture of National Leadership, 1776–1801," *Journal of the Early Republic* 12.4 (winter 1992): 477–507. According to Newman, Washington reemerged as a universal figure only after both his death and the electoral success of the Republicans.

3. Many historians have noted this. Garry Wills writes, "More than most men, this man *was* what he meant to his contemporaries. If he played a necessary role at the birth of our republic, it is important for us to assess the expectations of his audience, along with his willingness consciously to meet those expectations." Wills, *Cincinnatus*, xxiv. Paul Longmore writes, "What emerges is a Washington different from the one his biographers have presented; politically shrewd, closely in touch with the beliefs, aspirations, and fears of his countrymen, a consummate political leader and public actor who sought to embody and to be perceived as embodying their highest ideals." Paul Longmore, *The Invention of George Washington* (Berkeley: University of California Press, 1988), x.

4. Abigail Adams, as cited in Bernard Mayo, *Myths and Men: Patrick Henry, George Washington, Thomas Jefferson* (New York: Harper and Row, 1963), 39.

5. For an excellent firsthand example of how a reliance on character blurred the boundaries between public and private, see Maclay, *Diary*. For an exploration of this aspect of Maclay's diary, see Trees, "The Diary of William Maclay and Political Manners in the First Congress."

6. The scholarship on the fashioning of Washington is voluminous. See Longmore, *Invention of George Washington*; Barry Schwartz, *George Washington: The Making of an American Symbol* (New York: The Free Press, 1987); Eugene Miller and Barry Schwartz, "The Icon of the American Republic," *Review of Politics* 47 (1985): 516–43; William Alfred Bryan, *George Washington in American Literature, 1775–1865* (New York: Columbia University Press, 1952); Furtwangler, *American Silhouettes*, chapter 4; Wendy Wick, *George Washington, an American Icon: The Eighteenth-Century Graphic Portraits* (Baltimore: Smithsonian Institution, 1982); Marcus Cunliffe, *George Washington: Man and Monument* (Boston: Little, Brown and Company, 1958); Lawrence Friedman, *Inventors of the Promised Land* (New York: Knopf, 1975) chapter 2; and Fliegelman, *Prodigals and Pilgrims,* chapter 5.

7. Weems's very popularity is a large part of his ongoing significance, revealing the importance of popular sovereignty not simply in politics but in the marketplace. Daniel Boorstin claims that Weems's *Life of Washington* became "perhaps the most widely read, most influential book ever written about American history." Daniel Boorstin, *The Americans*, 3 vols. (New York: Random House, 1965), II, 343. For the history behind Weems's *Life* as well as its subsequent publishing history, see William Bryan, "The Genesis of Weems' 'Life of Washington,'" *Americana* 36.2 (1942): 147–65. Only in the sixth edition of 1808, when Weems vastly expanded his biography, did the *Life of Washington* reach the form that remains with us today. For brief but insightful discussions of Weems, see Steven Watts, *The Republic Reborn: War and the Making of Liberal America, 1790–1820* (Baltimore: Johns Hopkins University Press, 1987), 141–51, and Scott Casper, *Constructing American Lives: Biography and Culture in Nineteenth-Century America* (Chapel Hill: University of North Carolina Press, 1999), 68–76.

8. As reported by TJ, "Anas," in Lipscomb and Bergh, *Writings of Thomas Jefferson*, IX, 344.

9. See Peter Onuf, "Introduction," in Mason Locke Weems, *The Life of Washington* (Armonk, N.Y.: M. E. Sharpe, 1996), xix.

10. Weems to Carey, in Emily Ellsworth Ford Skeel, ed., *Mason Locke Weems, His Work and Ways*, 3 vols. (Norwood, Mass.: Plimpton Press, 1929), III, 122 and 58.

11. Weems, as cited in Harold Kelock, *Parson Weems of the Cherry-Tree* (New York: Century Company, 1928), 104–5. Marcus Cunliffe thinks it unlikely that Weems had any fixed political opinions, citing Weems's remark that a pamphlet that Weems wrote was "my political Placebo, my aristocratico-Democratico political Anodyne." Weems to Carey, 28 September 1801, in Skeel, *Mason Locke Weems,* I, 156.

12. Cunliffe argues that Weems's experiences were crucial to his ability to write a popular biography of Washington: "Traveling widely and continuously, Weems discovered by experiment what Americans wanted to read. . . . What better literary fare than the Weemsian biographies, which satisfied all their wants—religion (or religiosity), romanticism, patriotism—simultaneously?" Marcus Cunliffe, "Introduction," in Mason Locke Weems, *The Life of Washington*, ed. Marcus Cunliffe (Cambridge, Mass.: Belknap Press of Harvard University Press, 1962), xliv. Both he and Onuf suggest that Weems's acute sense of popular appetites arose from his own uncertain circumstances and divided loyalties.

13. These remarks are drawn from Casper, *Constructing American Lives*, 1–67.

14. Mason Locke Weems, *The Life of Washington* (Armonk, N.Y.: M. E. Sharpe, 1996), 1. All future page references included in the text.

15. Blair, *Lectures*, 398, 408, 409.

16. Although more than seven thousand people and institutions purchased copies, John Marshall's five-volume biography of Washington failed to find the kind of popular audience that Weems reached and offered evidence of the shift in character to which Weems called attention. In Marshall's biography, Washington hardly appears until the second volume, and his entire early life is covered in a page and a half. Adams called it "a Mausoleum, 100 feet square at the base and 200 feet high." JA to TJ, July 1813, Lipscomb and Bergh, *Writings of Thomas Jefferson*, XIII, 301. By contrast, Weems dwelled at length on Washington's childhood.

17. For the rise and meaning of separate-spheres rhetoric with its clear distinction between public and private life, as well as recent critiques of the explanatory power of separate spheres, see Brown, "Brave New Worlds"; Kerber, *Women of the Republic*; Norton, *Founding Mothers*; and Kerber, "Beyond Roles, Beyond Spheres." Historians of gender have focused on how the notion of separate spheres shaped the lives of women. Weems's biography foregrounds how that same ideology played an important role in shaping male identities as well.

18. Advice manuals from the nineteenth century lavished concern on the malleability of a young man's character, no longer seeing it as something shaped by his own efforts but as something shaped by outside influences. See Halttunen, *Confidence Men and Painted Women*, 3–5.

19. For Washington as a figure of corporate nationalism, see Burgett, *Sentimental Bodies*, 68–73.

20. Weems was certainly not the first to argue that Washington's greatness was America's own. Even John Adams called him "an exemplification of the American character." JA to John Jebb, 10 September 1785, *WJA*, IX, 541. Historian Wendy Wick writes, "Washington was to become, in his retirement, a national symbol. His accomplishments were no longer seen as the work of a single human being but as the destiny of a new nation. His likeness came to represent the whole country; his career became its history." Wick, *George Washington*, 53. Fliegelman also claims that in exalting Washington, the Americans were glorifying themselves. He writes, "The fact that all natives had a character such that, given the right circumstances, they might grow up to be a second Washington, reaffirmed the ultimate power of nurture to create Crevecoeur's 'new man.'" Fliegelman, *Prodigals and Pilgrims*, 223.

21. As Peter Brown writes, "In studying both the most admired and the most detested figures in any society, we can see, as seldom through other evidence, the nature of the average man's expectations and hopes for himself." Peter Brown, "The Rise and Function of the Holy Man in Late Antiquity," *Journal of Roman Studies* 61 (1971): 81.

22. This was distinctly different from how Washington was perceived during his lifetime, as a contemporary's description makes clear: "Washington got out of his carriage, and slowly crossing the pavement, ascended the steps of the edifice, upon the upper platform of which he paused, and turning half round, looked in the direction of a carriage which had followed the lead of his own. Thus he stood for a minute, distinctly seen by every body. He stood in all his civic dignity and moral

grandeur, erect, serene, majestic. His costume was a full suit of black velvet; his hair, in itself blanched by time, powdered to a snowy whiteness, a dress sword at his side, and his hat held in his hand. Thus he stood in silence; and what moments those were! Throughout the dense crowd a profound stillness reigned. Not a word was heard, not a breath. Palpitations took the place of sounds. It was a feeling infinitely beyond that which vents itself in shouts. Every heart was full. In vain would any tongue have spoken. All were gazing, in mute unutterable admiration. Every eye was riveted on that form—the greatest, purest, most exalted of mortals. It might have seemed as if he stood in that position to gratify the assembled thousands with a full view of the father of their country. Not so. He had paused for his secretary, then, I believe, Mr. Dandridge or Colonel Lear, who got out of the other carriage, a chariot, decorated like his own. The secretary, ascended the steps, handed him a paper—probably a copy of the speech he was to deliver—when both entered the building. Then it was, and not until then, that the crowd sent up huzzahs, loud, long, earnest, enthusiastic." Richard Rush, 1794 or 1795, as cited in Rufus Wilmot Griswold, *The Republican Court; or, American Society in the Days of Washington* (New York, 1868), 311–12. For an exploration of how gentry culture was transformed into a standard available to many Americans, see Bushman, *Refinement of America*, 402–48.

23. Weems called it "a school book" and told Jefferson that Washington's life was one that "all our youth should know, that they may love and imitate his Virtues." Weems to TJ, 1 February 1809, in Skeel, *Mason Locke Weems*, II, 389. According to Fliegelman, the father-son relationship is the crux of the Weems book. See Fliegelman, *Prodigals and Pilgrims,* chapter 5. Readers read the book in that spirit. As one exuberant booster of Weems's work wrote, "Providence has opened to our children a volume so pure and instructive, as THE LIFE OF WASHINGTON! Ye American PARENTS, and TEACHERS of youth! Study this volume; become masters of its important contents; transcribe them into your own hearts and lives; and thus convey them with happiest effect to your children and pupils." David Tappan, *An Oration* (Charlestown, 1800), as cited in Fliegelman, *Prodigals and Pilgrims*, 203.

24. For the partisan use of Washington during the 1790s, see Newman, "Principles or Men?"

25. Waldstreicher notes that people were obsessed with Washington's face (replacing the focus on the king's body), because the face could be described in writing, satisfying the needs of print culture. Waldstreicher, *Perpetual Fetes*, 119–24.

26. Weems's *Life* is filled with familial imagery as a means of describing the nation.

27. Weems included, for example, lengthy excerpts from Washington's first inaugural (see 148 ff.) and from his Circular Letter to the States (see 179), as well as his Farewell Address. Weems rendered Washington as a father speaking to his country through his various national addresses. Onuf writes, "*The Life of Washington* succeeds brilliantly in memorializing the great rhetorical moments that marked, and to a large extent constituted, Washington's career." Onuf, "Introduction," in Weems, *Life*, xxi. For an exploration of the Farewell Address as a political testament to secure Washington's political ideas, see Felix Gilbert, *To the Farewell*

Address: Ideas of Early American Foreign Policy (Princeton, N.J.: Princeton University Press, 1961), 89–104, 127–34.

28. See, for example, 175 and 179. In his Farewell Address, Washington himself emphasized the importance of the Union as the foundation of all of America's blessings. He wrote, "The Unity of Government which constitutes you one people is also now dear to you. It is justly so; for it is a main Pillar in the Edifice of your real independence, the support of your tranquility at home; your peace abroad; of your safety; of your prosperity; of that very Liberty which you so highly prize." He called on Americans to remember that "you, should properly estimate the immense value of your national Union to your collective and individual happiness; that you should cherish a cordial, habitual and immoveable attachment to it; accustoming yourselves to think and speak of it as of the Palladium of your political safety and prosperity." GW, Farewell Address, 19 September 1796, WGW, XXXV, 218–19.

29. Weems knew how to trim his sails, though. As the years passed and the Federalists faded from power, he turned to Jefferson for an endorsement of his biography, arguing that he presented Washington not as "an Aristocrat . . . to mislead and enslave the nation, but a pure Republican." Weems to TJ, 1 February 1809, in Skeel, *Mason Locke Weems*, II, 389.

30. TJ to John Holmes, 22 April 1820, *Writings*, 1435.

31. TJ to Richard Rush, 20 October 1820, Lipscomb and Bergh, *Writings of Thomas Jefferson*, XV, 283.

32. TJ to John Holmes, 22 April 1820, *Writings*, 1434–35. For Jefferson's repeated thoughts of death and even suicide during the crisis, see Onuf, *Jefferson's Empire*, chapter 3.

33. AH to Gouverneur Morris, 29 February 1802, *PAH*, XXV, 544.

34. JA to TJ, 3 February 1812, *Adams-Jefferson Letters*, II, 295.

35. JA to Joseph Mulligan, 20 November 1818, Adams Papers, reel 123, as cited in Ellis, *Passionate Sage*, 134.

36. See Lyman H. Butterfield, "The Jubilee of Independence, July 4, 1826," *The Virginia Magazine of History and Biography* 61 (1953): 134–35, for a description of his final day.

37. South Carolina first raised the issue of nullification after the "Tariff of Abominations" in 1828, backing down with the election of Andrew Jackson. The nullifiers' position made constitutional interpretation the province of each individual state, which would return the country to the chaos of the Articles of Confederation—precisely the chaos that the Constitution was supposed to end. When the revised tariff of 1832 failed to lower tariffs enough, though, South Carolina quickly began nullification proceedings again. Although eventually mollified with the tariff of 1833, the nullifiers remained unrepentant. After rescinding their nullification of the 1832 tariff, they held firmly to their right to nullify by symbolically nullifying the Force Act, which authorized Jackson to use force to collect the tariff in South Carolina.

38. JM, "Advice to My Country, October [1834?], in *Mind of the Founder*, ed. Meyers, 443.

39. JM to Jared Sparks, 1 June 1831, *WJM*, IX, 460.

INDEX

Adams, Abigail, 31, 87–90, 135, 163 n. 78

Adams, Henry, 155 n. 6

Adams, John, 4, 9, 133, 135, 138, 140, 143, 145, 178 n. 110, 179 n. 116; on Alexander Hamilton, 45, 68, 177 nn. 98, 99, 183 n. 37; on Benjamin Franklin, 8, 83, 97; on the charge that he was corrupted, 104–5; on commerce and virtue, 87–88, 90; compared to Alexander Hamilton, 76–77, 100; compared to Thomas Jefferson, 76–77, 184 n. 45; on controlling the aristocracy, 99–100; on the Declaration of Independence, 184 n. 52. *See also* Declaration of Independence; and *A Defence of the Constitutions of Government of the United States of America*, 91–94, 100, 104; and his diary, 9, 77–80, 81, 94–95, 180 n. 7, 181, n. 9. *See also* genre; and *Discourses on Davila*, 98–102; and disinterestedness, 95–97; and his distinction between public and private life, 76, 78, 79–80, 86–87, 90, 93, 94, 101; and his distrust of popularity, 78, 80–81, 182 nn. 26, 27; and the furnace of affliction, 90–91; and gender, 87–88; on George Washington, xii, 97, 183 n. 38, 188 n. 103, 201 n. 20; historians on, 180 n. 6; influence of European thought on, 91, 98–99, 103, 186 n. 77, 188 n. 112; and the influence of Puritanism, 97–98, 180 n. 7; on national character, 86–94, 99–104; as Novanglus, 83; and paranoia, 8–9, 76; and the passion for distinction, 77, 99–104; on the Pennsylvania Constitution, 95–96, 186 n. 77; and his political character, 77–81; and the professionalization of politics, 95–98; on the proper form of government, 93–94; and his readers, 77, 92; and republicanism, 78, 90, 92,

95–97, 188 n. 105; on the Senate, U.S., 99–100; on Shays's Rebellion, 87; and his skepticism about the virtue of others, 8–9, 76, 79, 81–87, 94–95, 185 n. 58, 187 nn. 89, 90, 103, 189 n. 122; as spectator, 75; on Thomas Hutchinson, 183 n. 37; on Thomas Jefferson, 84–85, 184 n. 52; and *Thoughts on Government*, 92; and titles, 98, 102–4; vanity of, 80, 81, 182 n. 23, 184 n. 46; as vice president, 154–55 n. 2; on women, 88–90. *See also* Hamilton, Jefferson, Madison, and Weems

Adams, John Quincy, 145

Alien and Sedition Acts, 13–14, 26, 62, 135, 154–55 n. 2

American Revolution, xi, 1–5, 21, 23, 47, 85, 103, 137; and Alexander Hamilton, 6–8, 61, 65, 175–76 n. 24; and James Madison, 9–11, 113, 122, 124, 126, 129, 146; and John Adams, 8–9, 82–83, 87–88, 90–91, 99, 145, 153 n. 36, 188 n. 105; and Thomas Jefferson, 5–6, 15, 37, 144, 152–53 n. 25

Ames Fisher, 70, 179 n. 112

Antifederalists, 23, 110, 124, 126, 191 n. 10, 192 n. 17, 195 n. 50

Bacon, Francis, 133, 179 n. 113

Beckley, John, 50, 71, 178 n.112

Bingham, William, 65

Blair, Hugh, 16, 109, 111, 123, 138–39

Bland, Martha 111

Brackenridge, Hugh Henry, 198–99 n. 92

Burr, Aaron, 145, 170–71 n. 18. *See also* Hamilton

Burroughs, Stephen, 151 n. 16

Cabot, George, 69–70

Callender, James, 45, 47, 48, 66, 114